BLESSED SINGLENESS

A Biblical Guide to Joyous, Fruitful Singleness!

CODY BOTELLA

Author Photos by Mark Chaudhary
Edited by Christopher Edward Miller
Endnotes by Allyson Walker
Formatting by Rich Meyer

BLESSED SINGLENESS
A Biblical Guide to Joyous, Fruitful Singleness!
Copyright © 2014 by Cody Botella
All Rights Reserved. No part of this book may be used or reproduced in any manner — electronic, mechanical, digital, photocopy, recording, or any other — except for brief quotations in articles and reviews, without the prior permission of the publisher. This book is licensed for personal use only. Please do not resell this work with prior permission and proper remuneration.

ISBN-13: 978-0692317938 (Custom)
ISBN-10: 0692317937

Unless otherwise noted, Scripture excerpts are from the English Standard Version® of the Holy Bible, copyright © 2001 by Crossway Bibles, a publishing ministry of Good News Publishers. The ESV® Bible (The Holy Bible, English Standard Version®) is adapted from the Revised Standard Version of the Bible, copyright Division of Christian Education of the National Council of the Churches of Christ in the U.S.A. All rights reserved. ESV® Text Edition: 2011.

Other Scripture Excerpts From (As Noted):
Holy Bible, New International Version®, NIV® Copyright © 1973, 1978, 1984, 2011 by Biblica, Inc.®
Holy Bible, New Living Translation, Copyright © 1996, 2004, 2007. Tyndale House Publishers, Inc., Carol Stream, Illinois 60188.
New American Standard Bible Copyright © 1960, 1962, 1963, 1968, 1971, 1972, 1973, 1975, 1977, 1995 by The Lockman Foundation, La Habra, Calif.
King James Bible (Public Domain)
Young's Literal Translation of the Holy Bible
Holman Christian Standard Bible®, Copyright © 1999, 2000, 2002, 2003, 2009 by Holman Bible Publishers.
The Message (MSG) Copyright © 1993, 1994, 1995, 1996, 2000, 2001, 2002 by Eugene H. Peterson
The American King James Version is Produced by Stone Engelbrite. It is a simple word for word update from the King James English. Care was taken to change nothing doctrinally, but to simply update the spelling and vocabulary. Grammar has not been changed. Use in any manner you wish: copy it, sell it, modify it, etc. You may not copyright it or prevent others from using it. You may not claim that you created it, because you didn't.

Printed in the United States of America

Doxology:

Soli Deo Gloria

CONTENTS

Preface	1
Section A: The Truth Will Set You Free	
1. Identity – Section Intro	15
2. Who Said You Were Naked?	20
3. What is That to You?	60
Section B: Change Diapers or Lives?	
1. The Stewardship of Liberty – Section Intro	98
2. Be Fruitful and Multiply	109
3. Sobriety	155
Section C: Prepare Yourself…	
1. Your True Good – Section Intro	173
2. Strength	178
3. Discipline	202
4. Work	232
Section D: The Wait…	
1. Altar the Altar – Section Intro	259
2. Purity	271
3. Courtship	289
4. When?	311
Epilogue	334
About the Author	339
Endnotes	340

ACKNOWLEDGMENTS

I would like to first thank the amazing Christopher Edward Miller, my Editor. Your knowledgeable oversight, strict editing, and Scriptural erudition have been an invaluable blessing to this work and me. So thankful to God for you my dear brother!

To others who read and edited early versions/chapters of this book: especially Natalie Winter & Cory Marsh, thank you so much for your precious time and help. You're both such a blessing to the Body of Christ!

To my local church family at Compass Bible Church in Aliso Viejo, CA, thank you so much for the steadfast prayer and encouragement regarding this work over the past several years. I know God has answered and is answering your prayers. I love you all!

To my parents, Mary and Brian Torres. Never once during this process have you doubted its consummation. For that encouragement and for your prayers I wish to express my deepest thanks. God has blessed me beyond measure to be able to call you two Mom and Dad!

To my first pastor, Mr. Jon Benzinger, the first man of God to teach me about the blessings and callings of single Christians. Your ministry has impacted the lives of so many, and we all love you PJ!

To Allyson Walker, my beloved daughter in Christ, immense thanks for your help with the Endnotes for this book. Without your help, I wouldn't have known what APA and MLA even were, much less how I should use them to cite references!

To Rahul Jain, Kate Price, and Josh Ruiz. You all read

full chapters of this book before completion, and your encouraging feedback only fueled my desire to complete this work. I appreciate you all so much!

To my dear brothers Jim Dolan, Tracy Thackrah, Jason Parker, Jon Davies and Joel Ferraro, your steadfast encouragement and prayers have been such a blessing. I love you guys!

To the godly Pastors and Bible teachers who have influenced, edified, convicted, and encouraged me immensely: Dr. Mike Fabarez, Dr. John MacArthur, Mark Driscoll, Dr. Timothy Keller, Jerry Bridges, Dr. Harry Kraus, John Piper...thank you for your uncompromising commitment to preaching the unadulterated Word of God!

To the awesome brethren who run the web ministries of Biblehub.com and singleness.org, thank you so very much for all of the content and resources you produce and make freely available!

To everyone who has asked me when this book was going to be released so that you or someone you know could read it...your prayers and interest have heartened me more than you know, thank you all so very much!

PREFACE

"I wish everyone were single, just as I am.
So I say to those who aren't married and to widows—
it's better to stay unmarried, just as I am.
I want you to be free from the concerns of this life.
An unmarried man can spend his time
doing the Lord's work and thinking how to please him.
I am saying this for your benefit,
not to place restrictions on you.
I want you to do whatever will help you serve the Lord best,
with as few distractions as possible.
So the person who marries does well,
and the one who doesn't marry does even better."

- The Apostle Paul
(1 Corinthians 7:7a,8,28ac,32,35,38, NLT)

The first time I thoughtfully read those verses, and that entire chapter, God put a strong desire on my heart to dive deeper into the truths there. I wanted, or rather, I *needed* to know exactly what Paul was saying in that chapter. Was he really saying that singleness was a blessing and that it was actually even *better* than marriage in certain ways?

So I committed to an extensive, in depth study of that chapter. During this time, I came across another mind-blowing passage of Scripture in **Matthew 19**. There, our Lord Jesus was teaching His disciples about marriage and divorce, and this was a part of the exchange: **"The disciples said to him, 'If this is the situation between a husband and wife, it is better not to marry.' Jesus replied, 'Not everyone can accept this word, but only those to whom it has been given. For there are eunuchs who were born that way, and there are eunuchs who have been made eunuchs by others—and there are those who choose to live like eunuchs for the sake of the kingdom of heaven. The one who can accept this should accept it'"** (vv. 10-12, NIV).

After reading that, my passion to discover the truths of what God's word says about singleness was burning hotter than ever! So I decided to not only study this subject intensely, but to write about it as well. I drew upon a myriad of resources and produced a formal paper on this research, including my own thoughts. I then had some of the more Biblically strong, spiritually mature brothers from my home church read it and had them give me their thoughts and critiques. Using this feedback, I refined the document and after doing so, God gave me a very strong heart burden to expand those thoughts into a full book. And here we are.

The purpose of this book is not to espouse "Kingdom," that is, lifelong singleness. My studies on this subject have shown me that for most Christians, that should not be their life story! Rather, the purpose of this book is to encourage single Christians to maximize their temporal singleness for God's kingdom, while preparing themselves to be a Godly spouse. It is written for those children of God who are currently single, praying for marriage, and don't want their singleness to be unfruitful!

Just as Paul says in our text that opened this chapter, my goal is "not to place restrictions on you" concerning marriage, but only "to help you serve the Lord best." Your current singleness is a huge blessing from God in so many different ways.

The key is learning to see and use those blessings to glorify God and bless others, while growing in the grace and knowledge of our Lord Jesus Christ, and preparing yourself for godly marriage.

Before we jump into the study, let me give you a little background, just so you know a little about me and why you should care what I have to say.

Amazing Grace In The Life of Cody Botella...

"The saying is trustworthy
and deserving of full acceptance,
that Christ Jesus came into the world
to save sinners, of whom I am the foremost."

(1 Timothy 1:15)

I grew up in southeastern New Mexico, on the Mescalero Apache Indian reservation. The common religious life in that place was a strange amalgamation of Roman Catholicism and long-standing traditional Native American beliefs and rituals. Looking back at history, it's easy to see why such a seemingly paradoxical syncretism could exist there.

During the Spanish colonization of America, the conquistadors were committed to converting the Native American peoples to Roman Catholicism, due to Vatican decree. Thus, under Spanish government charter, in the late 1500s the Franciscan friars established missions all throughout western & southwest America. The result of those efforts however was not exactly what the Spanish had in mind. Rather than achieving a complete mass conversion to Roman Catholicism, the native peoples merely agglomerated Catholic beliefs with their own traditional practices, forming a very unique paradigm. As an aside, this "culture clash" is also the reason why, like many other Native Americans in the Southwest, I have a Spanish last name.

Fast forward 400 years to 1983, the year I'm born into the aftermath and fallout of the aforementioned coalescence of divergent beliefs. In this place, I was raised to be both a devout Roman Catholic and to "honor my ancestors" by also practicing the traditional Apache rituals. I was baptized in the Catholic church as an infant, went through the catechism, served at church, practiced the "sacraments," and even went to a Catholic school. All the while, I regularly practiced the tribal rituals and attended the tribal ceremonies traditionally celebrated on the reservation. At the time, the absurdity of observing both sets of those contradictory beliefs never occurred to me. It was how I was raised, so I just accepted it as normal. Besides, I wasn't truly devoted to either set of beliefs. They were all just things I did to appease my own conscience and to prevent becoming a complete social outcast.

So, even though I may have considered myself a Christian, I didn't truly know God. This was evidenced by both the sinfulness and unhappiness of my life. Sadly, it seemed that much of the reservation shared the same plight. Alcoholism and other harmful addictions, crime, and poverty were rampant throughout the land. It was perfect living proof that a place overflowing with "religion" & "spirituality," but without knowing the One True God, is bound for bedlam. My tribe corporately, and especially myself personally, desperately needed a Savior.

In high school, when I was about 16, I heard the Gospel of the Lord Jesus Christ for the first time. I heard about how I was a sinner because I had broken God's law **(cf. Romans 3:23)**. And I heard that the Lord Jesus Christ died to pay for all of my sins **(cf. Romans 5:8, 6:23)**. I had tons of conviction, gave mental ascent to the facts, and was ostensibly saved. I even went through a brief period of what some would call being "on fire" for God. But I wasn't really "born again" **(cf. John 3:3)**. There was no real repentance from sin and trust in The Lord Jesus Christ as my savior. So I just withered away.

Enter misanthropy. Then came college, at the University of New Mexico, a very liberal school. Professors there preached evolution as if it were fact, even in classes that had nothing to do with the subject. This led to my ostensible "agnostic" phase. I claimed I didn't believe in the Lord, but really I was just suppressing the truth in unrighteousness **(cf. Romans 1:18)**. I didn't submit to God, not because He wasn't there, but because my sinful heart didn't want Him, because I couldn't handle His grace. Sin started to reign in my life and so began my "misanthropic" phase, due to my terribly selfish heart. I treated other people horribly, including my parents. My soul grew blacker daily.

Enter golf. In the summer between high school and college, I needed a summer job and my tribe's golf course was hiring. I got hired instantly because I was a tribal member and I started playing the game often because it was now free for me. I grew more and more enamored with the game for two reasons. For one, though I would not admit the source of the gift at the time, I had a God-given talent for the game **(cf. James 1:17)**. Second, and most of all, it was a solitary game. My misanthropy loved it because I didn't have to deal with other people. And most of all, my selfish prideful heart loved it because all of the glory from playing it went to me and to no one else. I was a Godless wretch indeed.

As I attended the University of New Mexico, golf became an increasingly larger idol in my life. I worshipped at the throne of golf. I'd practice nearly every day, often until my fingers bled. This led to the desire to turn professional and make a living at the game. I heard of the Professional Golfers Career College in Temecula, CA. It seemed like heaven, a place where I could train at golf daily, get a degree in golf, and escape the cold New Mexico winters. I applied, got accepted, and packed up and left. I took only what I could fit in my Jeep. I cared about no one but myself. My only focus was pro golf.

Enter gambling. The golf college's campus was located very close to one of the largest poker rooms in Southern California. One day I was invited by a classmate to come along and watch, as I had never played the game before. I was instantly hooked by the ability to make large sums of money in a day with very little "work". I bought the whole "poker is all skill, not gambling" slogan hook, line, and sinker. I convinced myself of that, as I didn't want to think of myself as a "gambler," and started to "train" hard at the game. I read poker books, online poker forums, and played constantly. Soon I had some skill at the game, started making money, and now had a brand new idol in my life. My life was now ruled by two false gods, golf and poker. I'd practice golf until dark, change clothes, and head to the casino. I thought of nothing and no one else.

In August of 2007, I graduated from the golf college and got a job in Newport Beach, at one of the finest golf resorts in America. I was of course single because of my attitude and thus, I had no responsibilities. So suddenly, I was a heathen with money, living in Orange County, one of the most spiritually dark places in the world. A place that worships the idols of money, status, and beauty.

Enter fornication. While still being as misanthropic as ever, the lust of my flesh began to take over. Living in "the OC," I was surrounded by beautiful women and I wanted them all. And thus began a long period of lasciviousness. I began to fornicate with basically any and every physically attractive woman I could. I cared nothing about them; I only cared about serving my own insatiable lust. Why God didn't just destroy me violently is but one testament to His amazing grace and mercy, as I was "by nature a child of wrath" **(cf. Ephesians 2:1-3)**.

Even though my soul was blacker than Arabian horses, I was still human. Thus, in living this lifestyle, my heart became increasingly wounded. As this continued happening, I began noticing churches again. I would drive by them and read the messages on their billboards thinking that I should try to attend one of their services. But this thought was quickly quelled by my ever-growing lust. Rather than go to church that weekend, I would look for my next "romantic" interlude, and on and on the cycle went. Yet in all of this hedonism, I was never satisfied. I fought depression and anxiety, two pains that I sometimes attempted to drown in alcohol.

The Lord says that when two people have sex they become "one flesh" **(cf. Mark 10:6-9)**. This is why it was impossible to have sex without developing feelings for a girl, no matter how much I tried to suppress them. This is also one of the reasons why God commands monogamy and prohibits polygamy. Sex is a spiritual union of two souls, designed by God to happen only within the covenant of marriage. It is *not* merely a physical activity.

Finally, after my increasingly wounded heart sank lower and lower, I hit rock bottom. I was Godless, empty, and suicidal. I knew in my heart I needed God and I finally began admitting that to myself. I swore off women altogether, out of self-preservation, not yet as a matter of repentance.

Enter "the church". Soon thereafter, I was playing golf with one of the few friends I had at the time. After the round we took his clubs back to his car and I saw his license plate cover. It had the name of a large, local church emblazoned on the border. I was intrigued, so I asked him about it and He said "Ya, that's my pastor's church." Little did I know that "his pastor" would be a man whom God would soon use to change my life and eternity.

I asked my friend if I could attend a service with him and his wife sometime and he said "sure." They took me to my first service at the church one Sunday and the young adults pastor noticed that I was young and single, so he invited me to his ministry's weekly service. This was the twenty to thirty-something singles service at the church, a ministry that would soon become my home. Later that week, I bought my first Holy Bible in years and I started attending both the young adults meetings and the main weekend services at the church frequently.

I was getting closer to salvation, but I still didn't truly know the Lord, or his grace and love. I had "religion" once again, but not yet Jesus Christ.

Enter the Truth. One weekend, during one of the senior pastor's sermons, IT happened. He was preaching through Romans 5, a chapter that is all about justification by faith in the Lord Jesus Christ. Before this sermon, although I had thoughts to the contrary, I never really understood the Gospel of the Lord Jesus Christ in truth.

Previous to that day, I had thought that I could "gain" or "lose" my salvation by my works. As the pastor preached about salvation that day, one phrase he said changed me forever. He said to the congregation of Christians: "It's an insult to doubt your salvation, because then you're saying that what Christ did on the cross was not ¹enough!" BOOM! I finally "got it"; I finally understood the real truth. I became a Christian because of that phrase, which God used to once and for all bring me to Him and unite us forever. I was finally **"born again to a living hope through the resurrection of Jesus Christ from the dead"** (cf. 1 Peter 1:3).

I realized that being saved meant not trusting in yourself or your "works" at all, but trusting in Christ and His finished work on the Cross alone! There was nothing I could do to make up for my sins or "earn" my way back to God, as I could never be good enough on my own, but God didn't let that come between us. That's why he sent his holy Son, his only begotten Son, to earth to die for my sins **(cf. John 3:16)**. Jesus came to pay the penalty that I couldn't pay; to live the perfect life that I couldn't live; to unite God's perfect love and perfect justice on an old rugged cross in Israel. Praise The Lord!

I placed my trust in Christ and got saved, and God brought me to repentance. The Holy Spirit baptized me into the Body of Christ and sealed me into God's family forever **(cf. Ephesians 1:13)**. He began sanctifying me from the inside out. Gone was "religion," I was now a "new creation" **(cf. 2 Corinthians 5:17)**.

God began changing my thoughts and behavior. Gone were the fornication, the gambling, and the drinking. It was replaced by fellowship, Bible study, and prayer. Gone were the endless golf practice sessions, being replaced by endless theological discussions with my new brothers in Christ. Gone was the misanthropy, replaced by love for my new family in Christ, and people in general.

Not all of this sanctification was instantaneous of course. It has been progressively increasing, it still is, and it will be until the Lord calls me home.

I share all this background with you for two big reasons. First and foremost, it is to glorify God. This is all a testament to His amazing grace and mercy. A testament to His ability to save *anyone* who comes to Him through the Lord Jesus Christ...even those like myself who rival Paul as the chief of sinners. It's a testament to God's power to give "new life" to *whosoever* calls on Him **(cf. Romans 6:4, 10:9-13)**.

Second, I share this so you "understand that I understand"; so you know that I am not ignorant about this subject. I have experienced singleness both before and in Christ, including all of the temptations and spiritual battles that come with it. So I know about everything you're going through.

The existence of this book is a testament to how God has changed someone who used to loathe his singleness into someone who now loves it...someone who sees and gives thanks for Blessed Singleness.

You see, during the "infancy" stage of my new eternal life **(cf. John 17:3)**, for approximately the first six months or so, a major pain plagued my heart. I would see all of the married couples that filled the main services on the weekends and I would long for what they had. I would often feel incomplete, depressed, discouraged, and discontented. Those feelings were further exacerbated by the thought that I would never get married, because with my sexual past I didn't feel that God would or could ever bless me with a Christian wife. I also felt that no Christian woman would ever want to marry me because of the very same reason.

God has now changed all of those paradigms. Through the study for this book, God has shown me the real truth about all single Christians.

God removed the scales from my eyes and revealed to me the unfathomably awesome truth that we are totally and absolutely complete! This is the truth by which we can receive perfect peace and contentment in *all* life and marital states. This is the truth which empowers us to obey the commands to **"Rejoice *always*, pray without ceasing, give thanks in *all* circumstances; for this is the will of God in Christ Jesus for you"** (1 Thessalonians 5:16-18, italics mine). This is the truth that will fuel all of our prolific evangelism and tireless service for others. This is the truth that will give us ever-increasing victory over the sin in our lives.

To see this truth we must wear a special pair of "glasses," seeing everyone and everything through One viewpoint, as we'll study throughout the book.

At this point you might be thinking, "Okay, great testimony, praise the Lord! But how does that qualify you to write a Bible-based book? How can I trust your exegesis? Where's your seminary degree?"

I have studied the subjects discussed in this book extensively and I have written about them from a completely Biblical point of view. However, my official response must be a personalized paraphrase from our brother Amos when he was rebuked for preaching God's word in Bethel.

Amaziah, the "official" priest there, told him: **"Get out of here, you prophet! Go on back to the land of Judah, and earn your living by prophesying there! Don't bother us with your prophecies here in Bethel. This is the king's sanctuary and the national place of worship!"** But *Amos replied, "I'm not a* *professional prophet, and I was never trained to be one. I'm just a shepherd, and I take care of sycamore-fig trees. But the LORD called me away from my flock and told me, 'Go and prophesy to my people in Israel.'* **Now then, listen to this message from the LORD"** (Amos 7:12-16a, NLT, italics mine).

Accordingly, *my* only response is: I'm not a professional pastor, and I was never trained to be one. I'm just a golf pro. I hit little white balls around big green fields and teach others how to do the same. But the LORD my God sovereignly called me to write this book, as a ministry to His people, to serve and feed His single sheep **(cf. John 21:15-17)**.

I never intended to be an author, much less a *Bible-based* author, a person called to the terrifying task of being **"a good worker, one who does not need to be ashamed and who correctly explains the word of truth"** (cf. 2 Timothy 2:15b, NLT).

But our Savior uses crooked sticks to make straight arrows, that way H*e* gets all the glory. For **"God chose what is foolish in the world to shame the wise; God chose what is weak in the world to shame the strong; God chose what is low and despised in the world, even things that are not, to bring to nothing things that are, so that no human being might boast in the presence of God"** (1 Corinthians 1:27-29). So, if you're seeking the writings of a world-renowned theologian, I'm afraid I'm not him. If you're looking for an acronym like M. Div. or D. Min. after my name, it's not there.

Thus my only boast is this...that I know the Lord of Lords and King of Kings, and most of all, that he knows me **(cf. Revelation 19:16, John 10:14-15)**.

Yet...that is enough. **"Thus says the LORD: 'Let not the wise man boast in his wisdom, let not the mighty man boast in his might, let not the rich man boast in his riches, but let him who**

boasts boast in this, that he understands and knows me, that I am the LORD who practices steadfast love, justice, and righteousness in the earth. For in these things I delight, declares the LORD'" (Jeremiah 9:23-24). On that note, let's enter the study. Dear single brethren, I pray that by it you're immeasurably blessed, encouraged and edified.

Cody Botella
Laguna Beach, CA
November 2014

Section A:

The Truth Will Set You Free

IDENTITY – SECTION INTRO

"So if the Son sets you free, you will be free indeed."
(John 8:36)

Kayla is a single Christian woman who just turned 25. She has a strong desire to get married, but has not yet met a Christian man with whom she could see this happening. Her sister Shannon just turned 22 and recently had her first baby with her husband of two years. Shannon is constantly pestering Kayla about the "lack" in her single life, just like Peninnah did to Hannah **(cf. 1 Samuel 1:1-7)**. Kayla's mom, grandmother, and basically every other woman in her family, tell her that her "biological clock is ticking" and that she better "hurry up". Her dad is always trying to hook her up with every single Christian man he knows, including some who are 10 years Kayla's senior, with zero compatibility. At the doctor's office, Kayla flips through magazines and sees articles detailing the "disease of singleness" and how it can be "remedied." Even worse, seemingly every married couple and friend at church asks her why she is "still" single, and some even accuse her of being "too picky". Kayla despairs daily about her "situation" and she occasionally wonders if God really loves her as much as He loves her sister...

Brian is in love with the Lord, and as a young man closing in on 30, he is single and joyous. But his joy is attacked constantly by the proclivities of his coworkers, friends, and family about his singleness. His coworkers accuse him of being gay, behind his back but within earshot. His mother asks him what is "wrong" with him. His dad reminds him that there is still no one to carry on the family name and that his life is thus "incomplete". His uncle regularly remarks that when he was Brian's age, he already had a wife and 2 kids and that Brian is being selfish by remaining single. His grandma always asks when he is going to give her some great grandchildren to enjoy. His single friends tell him he should stay single for the rest of his life to avoid "all the issues" of marriage. Brian is discouraged about his "problem", sometimes wondering if he'll *ever* be able to get married...

What is the true root of Kayla and Brian's suffering? What is the real cause of Brian's discouragement and Kayla's despair? What really is Kayla's "situation" and Brian's "problem"?

It lies not in the reality of their lives. Rather, it lies in the fact that Kayla and Brian are listening to others, themselves, and the evil one about the direction of their lives, rather than the Lord Jesus Christ! Because of this, they are believing lies, and thus allowing their entire life paradigms to be tainted by this fallen world.

The only true remedy is God's holy & eternal word, which He has graciously given us! And the beautiful thing is that we not only have God's word, but as Christians we also have the *Author* of God's word living within us! Just as the Lord Jesus Christ promised: **"I will ask the Father, and he will give you another**

Helper, to be with you forever, even the Spirit of truth, whom the world cannot receive, because it neither sees him nor knows him. You know him, for he dwells with you and will be in you" (John 14:16-17). God the Holy Spirit wrote the Holy Bible so that, among many other things, we don't have to be "guessing" or "wondering" what views we're supposed to adopt. We're not left searching endlessly for truth. Not only did He write the word, the Holy Spirit also gives us the guidance, discernment, and wisdom we need to understand this truth. Remember what our Lord promised us: **"When the Spirit of truth comes, he will guide you into all the truth, for he will not speak on his own authority, but whatever he hears he will speak, and he will declare to you the things that are to come"** (John 16:13).

Accordingly, we must no longer neglect these unfathomable, immeasurable blessings. It's time for us to ignore all other voices and listen only to the Voice of Truth. As Jesus said: **"Everyone who is of the truth listens to my voice"** (John 18:37c).

Kayla, Brian, and every unmarried Christian need to base their views of themselves, others, and their relationships on God's word alone! They need to see themselves and others through God's eyes, trusting in the Lord who lived and died for them!

So what *is* this truth? What *does* God say about how we should see ourselves and our brethren, especially in our relationships? It's **"the word of truth, the gospel of your salvation"** (Ephesians 1:13a). It's the same truth the whole world needs to hear:

"For our sake he made him to be sin who knew no sin, so that in him we might become the righteousness of God."
(2 Corinthians 5:21)

"For you have died,
and your life is hidden with Christ in God."
(Colossians 3:3)

"For Christ died for sins once for all,
the righteous for the unrighteous,
to bring you to God."
(1 Peter 3:18a, NIV)

"It is because of him that you are in Christ Jesus,
who has become for us wisdom from God —
that is, our righteousness, holiness and redemption."
(1 Corinthians 1:30, NIV)

Gospel Glasses...

Right now you might be saying, "Yes, I know the gospel, that's how I got saved. So what do all of those verses have to do with practical living as a single Christian?" And the answer is...*everything!*

You see my brothers and sisters, the gospel of God's grace **(cf. Acts 20:24)** is the most radical and amazing truth in the history of the universe! **"This Good News tells us how God makes us right in his sight. This is accomplished from start to finish by faith. As the Scriptures say, 'It is through faith that a righteous person has life'"** (Romans 1:15-17, NLT). Thus, an increasingly stronger understanding of the gospel is the key to a truly victorious and free life, especially for us as single Christians.

Accordingly, though this book is filled with practical instruction, you'll see that it must all be fueled by and based in the gospel of our Lord Jesus Christ. The gospel that saved you is the same one that will sanctify, transform, and complete you.

Seeing yourself through this "God-view" is exactly what Paul was talking about when he wrote: **"I care very little if I am judged by you or by any human court; indeed, I do not even judge myself"** (1 Corinthians 4:3, NIV). There, he's effectively saying, "I don't care what you think of me, but I don't care what I think of myself either. All that matters is what God thinks of me, what I look like through His eyes."[2] Paul's identity was connected not to the lies of the world, the under-informed opinions of others, or his own reflection in the mirror. His identity was based in the absolute *truth* of the Gospel, so ours must be also.

Thus, let's begin our study by learning how the Lord says we should see and treat ourselves and our brethren. We'll learn what we all look like through "Gospel Glasses". In doing so, we will lay claim to our Lord's gracious and perfect promise:

> **"Then you will know the truth,
> and the truth will set you free."**
>
> (John 8:32)

WHO SAID YOU WERE NAKED?

> "Who told you that you were naked?" the LORD God asked.
> "Have you eaten from the tree whose fruit
> I commanded you not to eat?"
>
> (Genesis 3:11, NLT)

Everyone loves to tell us how we should feel about our singleness. From virtually every source flows conflicting information about how we should see ourselves. Thus, we are left with a choice. We can believe one of the myriad vain human philosophies we're presented with; one of the lies that comes to us from the evil one and the culture he controls; our own reflections in the mirror...or we can believe what God says about us.

The biggest key to embracing the blessing of your singleness, indeed of your entire life, is seeing yourself the way God sees you. Thus, you *must* put on your gospel glasses and keep them on always. Without them you're blind. Without them you're just stumbling around in the dark searching for light. But with your gospel glasses on, you have true "20/20" vision — you have complete clarity. With your gospel glasses on, no matter how the world, the evil one, or the mirror tries to make you view yourself...the only view you'll see is God's view.

So let's learn how to put on these gospel glasses and see ourselves and the world anew.

The Collapse of Identity...

> **"Adam and his wife were both naked,**
> **and they felt no shame."**
>
> (Genesis 2:25, NIV)

Before the Fall, Adam and Eve didn't have the "self-awareness" that every human being now lives with. This was an immense blessing. There was no such thing as insecurity, shame, guilt or self-esteem. Indeed, the concept of "self" as we now know it, did not yet exist.

Adam and Eve were perfect beings, created in God's image for His own glory and to do His will. Thus their security, and the rest of their identity, was all tied up in God and His perfection. They had direct communion and fellowship with the Lord who loved them fully, and they had perfect companionship with each other. They had it all. They were complete and perfectly content in God. They saw themselves through God's eyes.

But when the deceiver tempted them, being the "father of lies" **(cf. John 8:44)**, he spoke in his native tongue. He lied to them, saying, **"For God knows that when you eat of it your eyes will be opened, and you will be like God, knowing good and evil"** (Genesis 3:5). When they ate of the tree because they believed this lie, the lie that they were not complete and whole in their relationship with God, that perfect relationship was lost.

The effects were immediate:

> **"Then the eyes of both were opened,**
> **and they knew that they were naked.**
> **And they sewed fig leaves together**
> **and made themselves loincloths."**
>
> (Genesis 3:7)

For the first time in their lives, they felt that they "lacked" something. In that immediate case, it was clothing to cover their bodies; clothing that they had never before "needed"; clothing that they weren't created to need. Without this clothing, they now saw themselves as "naked" for the first time. For the very first time, they now saw themselves as incomplete.

They had eaten the fruit in the hopes of having their eyes opened. And indeed this happened, but not in the way they had envisioned. Instead of seeing things "like God," as they were told, they now saw things through their own eyes. And thus, the origin of "self".

Adam & Eve had sinned. They had disobeyed God by searching for fulfillment and knowledge outside of Him. Indeed, that's what all sin is — an attempt to find purpose and pleasure outside of God. No matter what activity or form it comes in, all sin stems from a heart that's unsatisfied or insecure in God.

Because of Adam & Eve's transgression, this is a heart that all humans are now spiritually born with. It's a heart that believes the lies of others, of the tempter, and of ourselves. In causing this fall of the human heart, the devil had succeeded, but only temporarily.

Check it out. Immediately after the fall, God made the promise declaring how He would remedy this situation! Right there in Eden, God told that old lying serpent, **"I'm declaring war between you and the Woman, between your offspring and hers. He'll wound your head, you'll wound his heel"** (Genesis 3:15, MSG). Theologians call this verse the *Protoeuangelion*, which is Greek for "The First Gospel". Let's keep rolling through that chapter because this whole event in the Garden only gets better.

Without delay, God subsequently **"made leather clothing for Adam and his wife and dressed them"** (Genesis 3:21, MSG). We must unpack this passage to understand its amazing eternal ramifications! Adam & Eve had just hastily entered into "nakedness" through their sin. And what did God do? Did he leave them nude? No, He quickly *clothed* them! And how did God do this? He killed an animal, no doubt a *spotless* animal being that they were in Eden, in order to make *clothing* for His children! This was all a perfect foreshadowing of the work the Lord would later complete. It was an amazing prophetic picture of the day when God would kill his own perfect & holy Son, **"the sinless, spotless Lamb of God"** (cf. 1 Peter 1:19b), the Lord Jesus Christ! This is an act that God would bring to fruition in order to eternally "clothe" His children in the perfect righteousness of their holy Savior!

For we know that **"The reason the Son of God appeared was to destroy the works of the devil"** (1 John 3:8). And our Lord has succeeded! Because of His eternal victory at Calvary, Jesus has restored the relationship lost in the garden! For **"it was the Lord's good plan to crush him and cause him grief. Yet when his life is made an offering for sin, he will have many descendants. He will enjoy a long life, and the Lord's good plan will prosper in his hands. When he sees all that is accomplished by his anguish, he will be satisfied. And because of his experience, my righteous servant will make it possible for many to be counted righteous, for he will bear all their sins"** (Isaiah 53:10-11, NLT).

Praise the Lord God forever!

So now, we no longer have to believe the lies that caused our human ancestors to fall. As Christians, our holy God, **"according to His great mercy has caused us to be born again to a living hope through the resurrection of Jesus Christ from the dead"** (1 Peter 1:3b, NASB). He has now fulfilled the promise He made when He said, **"I will give you a new heart and put a new spirit in you; I will remove from you your heart of stone and give you a heart of flesh"** (Ezekiel 36:26). We now have a heart that can receive and fully imbibe God's truths, including the truth of how He sees us.

The evil one still tries to tempt us with the same old lie he used in Eden, the lie that we are not complete in our relationship with God. Specifically for us as singles, he tries to feed us the lie that we are not complete without a spouse and kids. He tries to use this lie to tempt us to many other sins to fill this ostensible "hole" in our lives. Just as he told Adam & Eve that they were naked, he tries to tell us that we too are not whole, that we too are naked.

Because we now belong to the Truth, the Lord Jesus Christ **(cf. John 14:6)**, we can and must resist and overcome the evil one's lies. These are lies he proliferates through whispers in our ears, the media that he controls, and people who are still under his influence. So unlike Adam & Eve, when the deceiver tries to tell us that we are "naked" without a spouse, or without anything else outside of God, we can tell him to go away.

As a Christian you are commanded to **"be transformed by the renewal of your mind, that by testing you may discern what is the will of God, what is good and acceptable and perfect"** (Romans 12:2). In this transformation of your mind, of all of your paradigms, you must necessarily conform your "self-views" into

"God-views". Your identity must be replaced. In doing so, you will experience freedom you've never known before.

On that note, let's now dive into God's word to learn and adopt these views. It's time to get fitted for your gospel glasses.

You are a Loved Child...

> **"See what kind of love the Father has given to us,
> that we should be called children of God;
> and so we are."**
>
> (1 John 3:1a)

You are adopted. God the Father...the eternal, self-existent Creator of the universe...has adopted you as His own child through the Lord Jesus Christ **(cf. Ephesians 1:5)**! This is why Jesus instructed us: **"call no man your father on earth, for you have one Father, who is in heaven"** (Matthew 23:9).

Knowing this, think about the children in your life. They might be your nephews/nieces, friends' children, or maybe even your own. Then think about how much you love them. Think about how you, a sinner, would do anything for them. Then think about how little you can truly do for them in your finite nature.

In doing this, you can begin to realize just what being a child of the living God really means. If we lowly sinners can love our children so much, imagine just how much, on an infinitely grander scale...God loves you. If we lowly sinners, in our extremely limited bodies, can desire so much for our children...imagine God's desire for you. And of course, what he desires for you, He can and will bring to fruition. Indeed, God **"is able to do far more abundantly than all that we ask or think, according to the power at work within us"** (Ephesians 3:20).

Everything we've ever wanted to do for our children, God has *already* exceeded in what he's done for us!

"**For God so loved the world, that he gave his only Son, that whoever believes in him should not perish but have eternal life**" (John 3:16). God killed His own Son for you. You were separated from Him by your sin, and knowing that the only way he could justly reconcile you to himself was to kill Jesus, He did just that. All of our sin God imputed to Christ that day at Calvary, and He poured out all of His righteous anger on our perfect Savior.

Out of His love, "**For our sake he made him to be sin who knew no sin, so that in him we might become the righteousness of God**" (2 Corinthians 5:21). This "great exchange" is unfathomable. Knowing this, we can exclaim with Paul, "**He who did not spare his own Son but gave him up for us all, how will he not also with him graciously give us all things?**" (Romans 8:32).

Beloved, we are God's children now, and God is an infinitely greater parent than anyone you know or could possibly imagine. The greatest human parent is still wicked compared to God. Remember Jesus' words: "*If you then, who are evil,* **know how to give good gifts to your children, how much more will** *your Father* **who is in heaven give good things to those who ask him!**" (Matthew 7:11, italics mine).

Sadly, in this fallen world, many people have had their views of "fathers" tainted by the actions of human parents. Maybe your own father was absent, abusive, or unloving. But God is your Father now, and He's nothing like that. He loves you more than you could possibly know; indeed, his love transcends our knowledge. That's why when Paul prayed for Ephesus, he prayed that they would "**know the love of Christ that surpasses knowledge**" (Ephesians 3:19). Christ is transforming our minds (cf. **Romans 12:2**), and it's only with these increasingly transformed minds that we can even begin to fathom and understand God's love for us.

In this ever-increasing understanding of God's love for you as His child, and in your ever-growing relationship with Him as your Father, you realize just how much the love of a human spouse pales in comparison. God sees you as His child now, and espousing this view as you look in the mirror brings complete liberation from every competing view that's thrown at you.

Being a child of the living God also means that **"you are no longer a slave, but a son, and if a son, then an heir through God"** (Galatians 4:7). We are His children, **"and if children, then heirs—heirs of God and fellow heirs with Christ"** (Romans 8:17a), heirs to His eternal kingdom!

Just as you would love to give your own children everything you could, **"it is your Father's good pleasure to give you the kingdom"** (Luke 12:32). He loves to bless you with His eternal presence...because you are His child.

Because He is King, you are now royalty. We are **"a royal priesthood"** (cf. 1 Peter 2:9). We will be judging angels **(cf. 1 Corinthians 6:3)**. We will be reigning with Christ **(cf. Revelation 2:26, 3:21, 5:10; 2 Timothy 2:12)**. As unfathomable as this is, and as unworthy as we are, it's nonetheless true *because of the gospel.*

Please go read **Luke 15** carefully. Study the three parables there, and more importantly, *personalize* them. *You* are the sheep that Jesus has laid on His shoulders and rejoices over **(vv. 5-7)**. *You* are the one over whom the angels of God celebrate **(v. 10)**. *You* are the child who **"was dead, and is alive; he was lost, and is found"** (v. 32).

Personally imbibe those amazing truths and remember the Lord's words: **"What do you think? If a man has a hundred** sheep, and one of them has gone astray, does he not leave the ninety-nine on the mountains and go in search of the one that went astray? And if he finds it, truly, I say to you, he rejoices over it more than over the ninety-nine that never went astray" (Luke 18:12-13).

This means that *your* salvation is *very* personal. For even if you were the *only* fallen human being on the planet, the Lord Jesus Christ would *still* have come to earth to live, die, and rise again...for *you*.

It was for communal relationship with God that *you* were created. Having this relationship from your perfect holy God severed by your sin, the Lord repaired the relationship *Himself*. God is so perfectly holy and righteous that He couldn't even have you in His presence unless you were like Him.

So rather than just shunning you forever, He *remade* you like Him. For God is both **"just and the justifier of the one who has faith in Jesus"** (Romans 3:26). Isn't that beyond amazing? God loves *you* so much, that even though *you* were His enemy **(cf. Romans 5:10, Colossians 1:21)**, He still reconciled *you* to Himself **(cf. 2 Corinthians 5:18)**!

Sweet Freedom...

Jesus asked Peter, **'"what do you think, Simon? From whom do kings of the earth take toll or tax? From their sons or from others?"' And when he said, 'From others,' Jesus said to him, 'Then the sons are free'"** (Matthew 17:25b-26). The "sons of this world," the unbelievers, will be "taxed" for their sin; they will have to pay for themselves what is due to the Lord. Indeed, **"It is a fearful thing to fall into the hands of the living God"** (Hebrews 10:31). But that is something you will never have to fear, for as God's child your "tax" has already been paid. As God's child, you are free, *truly* free.

Among many other freedoms, you are completely free from God's wrath. As Paul wrote, **"There is therefore now no condemnation for those who are in Christ Jesus"** (Romans 8:1). Beloved, once again, please *personalize* this text. There is *no* condemnation for *you* in Christ the King! That truth alone can make even someone sitting in a maximum-security prison feel free as a jaybird. It can make their heart and mind soar like one too! Brethren, let this truth do the same for you.

The universe is a theocracy, regardless of the human institutions and political systems that God may currently have in place. It all exists under the Kingship of God and you live and move and breathe in this universe as a child of the Ruler of this Kingdom. Children of human kings don't live their lives in fear of anyone, as they walk in their father's power and authority, and we must adopt a similar attitude.

However, ours is not one of pride or arrogance in our position, but rather it is in the freedom and confidence of our position. All of humanity will stand before the throne of God to be judged for their deeds **(cf. Revelation 20:11-15)**. And the beautiful thing is that the Judge is our Father, so we have nothing to fear there. We're already free, Praise the Lord!

As Paul also wrote, **"Who shall bring any charge against God's elect? It is God who justifies. Who is to condemn? Christ Jesus is the one who died—more than that, who was raised—who is at the right hand of God, who indeed is interceding for us"** (Romans 8:33-34).

As the Lord Jesus Christ said, **"My sheep hear my voice, and I know them, and they follow me. I give them eternal life, and they will never perish, and no one will snatch them out of my hand. My Father, who has given them to me, is greater than all,** and no one is able to snatch them out of the Father's hand. I and the Father are one" (John 10:27:30).

God has entered into covenant love with you through the Lord Jesus Christ **(cf. Hebrews 9:15)** and God *never* breaks His covenants, so you are completely secure. Indeed, He has promised to **"never leave you nor forsake you"** (cf. Hebrews 13:5). As Paul wrote: **"For I am sure that neither death nor life, nor angels nor rulers, nor things present nor things to come, nor powers, nor height nor depth, nor anything else in all creation, will be able to separate us from the love of God in Christ Jesus our Lord"** (Romans 8:38-39).

God sees you as *His* child, whom He *personally* loves, and it's time for you to see yourself the same way. Will you put your gospel glasses on? Who said you weren't a child of the King? Who said you weren't loved? *Who* said you were naked?

You are Holy...

"Yet now he has reconciled you to himself
through the death of Christ in his physical body.
As a result, he has brought you into his own presence,
and *you are holy and blameless
as you stand before him without a single fault."*
(Colossians 1:22, NLT, italics mine)

The evil one loves to throw your past into your face, as do other people, and even your own mind. They love to remind you about the sins you've committed, the pain you've caused, and the evil you've done. When this happens, we are tempted to give in and believe the lie that this is still who we are, but that is wrong.

It's wrong because *you* are new! **"This means that anyone who belongs to Christ has become a new person. The old life is** gone; a new life has begun!" (2 Corinthians 5:17, NLT).

In Christ, **"as far as the east is from the west, so far does he remove our transgressions from us"** (Psalm 103:12). In Christ, God's promise has been fully realized that **"he will tread our iniquities underfoot. You will cast all our sins into the depths of the sea"** (Micah 7:19). God says: **"I, I am he who blots out your transgressions for my own sake, and I will not remember your sins"** (Isaiah 43:25). The Lord Jesus Christ has **"washed us from our sins in his own blood"** (Revelation 1:5, AKJV).

Paul opened the letter of **1 Corinthians** like this: **"To the church of God that is in Corinth, to those *sanctified* in Christ Jesus, called to be *saints* together with all those who in every place call upon the name of our Lord Jesus Christ, both their Lord and ours"** (v. 1:2, italics mine). The Greek word translated as "sanctified" there is *hēgiasmenois*, which means to be treated and *set apart* as holy, special, and different[3]. The use of this word in this context is very amazing when you consider the fact that 1 Corinthians was, for the most part, a *corrective* letter.

In much of his writing in this epistle, Paul is rebuking Corinth for how divisive and rebellious that church had become. There was sexual immorality **(cf. 5:1-13)**, one-upmanship among the elders **(cf. 1:10-17)**, disregard for the weaker & poorer members of the church **(cf. 11:17-22)**, selfish social ambition **(cf. 3, 4:6-7)**, and major theological confusion **(cf. 8)**. Yet, Paul still called them *saints*. And since this letter is God-breathed Scripture, that means *God* was calling them saints.

God called them saints for the same reason He now calls *us* saints. It's not because we are holy based on our own works, for we could never be perfectly holy on our own.

But that is why Christ lived and died for us! Always remember, **"Christ died for sins once for all, the righteous for** the unrighteous, to bring you to God" (1 Peter 3:18a, NIV). For that reason, and for that reason alone, God can and has forgotten your past. **"For you have died, and your life is hidden with Christ in God"** (Colossians 3:3). Christ's blood has made us holy, *positionally* holy, forever. Thus, when He looks at you, God doesn't see your sins, He sees Christ's perfection. *He* has made us holy. *He* has made us saints by *His* sovereign grace. God has made *you* a saint!

So memorize and build your life on this immutable truth: **"For our sake he made him to be sin who knew no sin, so that in him we might become the righteousness of God"** (2 Corinthians 5:21).

The Lord has given you a complete resume' replacement; not a resume' improvement. By faith in Christ, God the Father now sees you as He sees Christ, that is, *perfectly* holy in every way. Theologians call this positional, perfect holiness "definitive sanctification".

And because you possess that, God the Holy Spirit has now given you a strong desire for *practical* holiness, which theologians call "experiential sanctification". Beloved, **"When you came to Christ, you were 'circumcised,' but not by a physical procedure. Christ performed a spiritual circumcision--the cutting away of your sinful nature"** (Colossians 2:11, NLT).

So it's time to let go of your past completely. You're not who you were. You **"have put on the new self, which is being renewed in knowledge after the image of its creator"** (Colossians 3:10).

As Paul wrote to the Christians at Galatia who were holding on to their legalistic past, **"It doesn't matter whether we have been circumcised or not. What counts is whether we have been transformed into a new creation"** (Galatians 6:15, NLT).

As new creations, **"we all, with unveiled face, beholding the glory of the Lord, are being transformed into the same image from one degree of glory to another. For this comes from the Lord who is the Spirit"** (2 Corinthians 3:18). You are being made more and more like Christ every day, so whatever was done in the past doesn't matter now.

Like Paul, we can now say, **"I have been crucified with Christ. It is no longer I who live, but Christ who lives in me. And the life I now live in the flesh I live by faith in the Son of God, who loved me and gave himself for me"** (Galatians 2:20).

So forget your old life and as Paul wrote, **"Take hold of the eternal life to which you were called"** (1 Timothy 6:12). This is the *real* life in which you now live; a life that is *everlasting* **(cf. John 3:16)**!

Though the evil one may still try to accuse you of old sins day and night, you must remember exactly what happened at Calvary. There, God **"canceled the record of the charges against us and took it away by nailing it to the cross. In this way, he disarmed the spiritual rulers and authorities. He shamed them publicly by his victory over them on the cross"** (Colossians 2:14-15, NLT).

This means there are no longer any legal grounds for accusing you before God. So when the evil one tries to do that now, it's to his shame because the final verdict on your soul has already been rendered.

Yes, you've committed many sins, but the Lord Jesus Christ has already paid for them all! This forgiveness was eternally actuated the moment you placed your trust in Him. You're living "post-gavel". You're now a free person, so don't try to walk back into the courtroom. Instead, like Paul you must always be **"forgetting what lies behind and straining forward to what lies ahead"** (Philippians 3:13).

It's time to drop all the shame. It's time to see yourself completely through God's eyes. The One who says **"Behold, I am making all things new"** (cf. Revelation 21:5) is making you new too.

It's time to release all the regrets. As Paul said, **"I count everything as loss because of the surpassing worth of knowing Christ Jesus my Lord. For his sake I have suffered the loss of all things and count them as rubbish, in order that I may gain Christ"** (Philippians 3:8).

Whatever sins you've left behind; whatever relationships you've lost; whatever you feel guilty remorse over...count it all as loss! You know Jesus Christ as Lord and Savior now, so leave it all behind. Walk off the courtroom steps and don't look back.

God loves *you*. He has made you new and that's how He now sees you. Who do you see?

Will you put your gospel glasses on? Who said you were still that old person? Who said you were guilty? Who said you weren't new? Who said you weren't Holy? *Who* said you were naked?

You are Beautiful...

The mirror, the media, and the evil one — all three seem to attack us every day with the "lie of ugliness".

Every morning when we look in the mirror, we seem to be able to find a new physical flaw. This can tempt us to silly, self-disparaging comments like, "no wonder you're single".

Then we walk outside and get bombarded with messages from the media that we're physically "imperfect" in some way, that we're "lacking" something. Seemingly every piece of pop culture idolizes beauty in some way. Worldly magazines airbrush all of their photos, creating a false physical "perfection" that exists only within their pages.

Many TV shows cast the most "beautiful" people in their lead roles, and then hire professional make-up artists to "perfect" their beauty before putting them in front of the cameras. All of this creates the false reality of physical perfection and broadcasts it around the world.

The evil one uses these avenues to come at you with attacks like — "God loves those people more than you. That's why they're so beautiful and you're not."

It's no wonder that the personal fitness, beauty, and plastic surgery industries make billions of dollars a year. Millions of people spend their daily lives pursuing an idealistic physical "flawlessness" that they'll never attain.

Sadly, far too many single Christians fall for this nonsense. Beloved, this must not be so for you. You must distinguish lies from the truth!

The mirror lies and says, "look how flawed and ugly you are. You need to dress yourself in splendor and perfect your beauty".

The media lies and says, "Look how beautiful other people are compared to you. They are dressed in splendor and perfect beauty".

The evil one lies and says, "God has clothed others in splendor and perfect beauty, but not you".

But the God of Truth says:

"I wrapped my cloak around you to cover your nakedness and declared my marriage vows. I made a covenant with you, says the Sovereign LORD, and you became mine. I dressed you in my splendor and perfected your beauty, says the Sovereign LORD" (Ezekiel 16:12b,14b, NLT).

Those words were originally written to national Israel because they were God's chosen covenant people.

Since we are now God's chosen eternal covenant people through the Gospel of our Lord Jesus Christ, by extension we know that those truths now apply to us as well.

Those are the truths of who we are in God's eyes, the truths of who we *really* are.

It was said of our Savior on the cross, **"He had no beauty or majesty to attract us to him, nothing in his appearance that we should desire him. Like one from whom men hide their faces he was despised, and we esteemed him not"** (Isaiah 53:2b,3b, NIV). That was how men saw our Lord, how the world saw Him, as so ugly that they hid their faces from Him.

Jesus probably wouldn't have been on the cover of People magazine's "100 Most Beautiful People" issue. He probably wouldn't have been considered a "heartthrob" by this fallen world.

But God saw something different; He saw who Jesus really was. God saw the Lord's true beauty and He has given His people a glimpse of that magnificent, radiantly perfect beauty.

One day, the Lord Jesus Christ took Peter, James, and John up on a mountain and there, **"As the men watched, Jesus' appearance was transformed so that his face shone like the sun, and his clothes became as white as light"** (Matthew 17:2, NLT).

That's why John could write, **"we have seen his glory, glory as of the only Son from the Father, full of grace and truth"** (John 1:14).

That's why Peter could write, **"We saw his majestic splendor with our own eyes"** (2 Peter 1:16b, NLT).

Later in John's life, the Lord's glorious beauty was once again revealed to him. John described it like this: **"He was wearing a long robe with a gold sash across his chest. His head and his hair were white like wool, as white as snow. And his eyes were** like flames of fire. His feet were like polished bronze refined in a furnace, and his voice thundered like mighty ocean waves. And his face was like the sun in all its brilliance"** (Revelation 1:13b-15,16b, NLT).

Knowing this, the passage from Isaiah that we just read becomes an indictment of the world. It shows the world's false definition of beauty. It shows the world's inability to even see real beauty.

How many celebrities are there whose face "shines like the sun in all its brilliance"? How many of the world's heartthrobs on magazine covers have "eyes like flames of fire"? None. Yet the world worships those people. They have **"exchanged the glory of the immortal God for images resembling mortal man"** (Romans 1:23a).

The world exalts six-pack abs, flawless skin, perfect teeth, and fine clothes as beauty. But you must remember, **"what is exalted among men is an abomination in the sight of God"** (Luke 16:15b).

The world says beauty comes from adorning your body on the outside. The Lord says, **"let your adorning be the hidden person of the heart with the imperishable beauty of a gentle and quiet spirit, which in God's sight is very precious"** (1 Peter 3:4).

The world judges beauty by a person's physical appearance. But **"The LORD does not look at the things man looks at. Man looks at the outward appearance, but the LORD looks at the heart"** (1 Samuel 16:7, NIV).

The world says, "be charming and beautiful, and you will be praised". God says, **"Charm is deceitful, and beauty is vain, but a woman who fears the LORD is to be praised"** (Proverbs 31:30).

Single Christian, wholeheartedly imbibe these truths. Though the mirror, the world, and the evil one will try to call you ugly, their lying must now be obvious. The world called our Lord and Savior "ugly," when in reality He is beautiful beyond all compare!

Because you are in Christ, God has already "dressed you in splendor and perfected your beauty". You must see yourself this way. When that's hard, remember these words: **"Dear friends, we are already God's children, but he has not yet shown us what we will be like when Christ appears. But we do know that we will be like him, for we will see him as he really is"** (1 John 3:2, NLT).

Brethren, you're not single right now because you're ugly. You're single right now because the God who loves you has a purpose for your singleness.

So don't believe the lies, believe the truth. You are beautiful. You are perfect.

Beloved, will you put your gospel glasses on? Who said you were ugly? Who said you weren't beautiful? *Who* said you were naked?

You are Accomplished and Wealthy...

> "It is because of him that you are in Christ Jesus,
> who has become for us wisdom from God
> — that is, our righteousness, holiness and redemption."
>
> (1 Corinthians 1:30, NIV)

Once again, because you are in Christ, God sees Christ's perfection when He looks at you. Thus, you are completely and perfectly accomplished and wealthy in His eyes!

Do you see yourself that way? If not, it's time to adopt that view!

Unfortunately, so much of our self-image is tied up in what we've accomplished and what we own. We are constantly tempted to live our lives trying to please and appease God and others, but this is an exercise in futility, as no matter how much *you* do, it will *never* be enough. Never enough to please everyone else, and *definitely* never enough to appease God. Theologians have labeled this futile race "the performance trap". It's the lie that enslaves so many people, as it "traps" them into believing that their worth is based on their "performance". Beloved, this must not be so for us.

This applies not only to our holiness and righteousness, but also to every other area of accomplishment and "wealth" in life.

So much social, political, career, and sadly even church ambition arises from this search for "validation". Anytime you seek this type of personal affirmation outside of God and how he sees you, you're in bondage because of a lie.

The world doesn't know God **(cf. Romans 1:18-32, Galatians 4:8-9)**. Accordingly, it seeks validation from every source *but* God, in a vain attempt to garner attention and love.

This is one of the reasons pride is such a prevalent human sin. You see, pride is very often used as a defense mechanism, rather than being a person's true heart view of themselves. A person who does not know God has no way of knowing who they *truly* are, and rather than facing that fact and the resulting depression, they create an inflated mental image of themselves that pleases their ego.

Being that the ego is never fully satisfied, many people spend their whole lives trying to keep up with and exceed everyone else in accomplishment and wealth. This paradigm of course makes its way into the media, and thus just gets proliferated throughout the world.

It must be categorically stated again that those views are pure bondage. I know that bondage personally because that is exactly who I used to be before the Lord Jesus Christ saved me. But now that I am in Christ, my identity is no longer tied to *my* righteous heavenly merit, my selfish earthly accomplishments, or my wealth.

My gospel glasses are on now and the view through them is beautiful!

This is especially and exceedingly important for us as singles. Because we don't have spouses and most of us don't have kids, we can be tempted to try to accomplish, or "gain" as much as possible in our lives in a fruitless effort to rest in our own works, deeds, and possessions.

However, as we learn from Solomon, *all* of **"this too is vanity"** (cf. Ecclesiastes). It is vanity because none of our works are perfect and none of our works are eternal. It is vanity because, outside of Christ, even billionaires are pitiably poor.

Check out our Lord's strong rebuke of the Laodicean church, who fancied themselves rich and accomplished because of their earthly wealth and works: **"For you say, I am rich, I have prospered, and I need nothing, not realizing that you are wretched, pitiable, poor, blind, and naked. I counsel you to buy from me gold refined by fire, so that you may be rich, and white garments so that you may clothe yourself and the shame of your nakedness may not be seen, and salve to anoint your eyes, so that you may see"** (Revelation 3:17-18).

You see, looking at yourself through the window of *your* accomplishments and *your* possessions will always leave you empty and in sin.

You can try to clothe your "nakedness" yourself with your own accomplishments and riches, or you can "anoint your eyes" and see yourself through gospel glasses, having the "shame of your nakedness" covered by the Lord Jesus Christ's righteousness, wealth, and accomplishments. The choice is very clear.

Think about the biggest "accomplishments" of men throughout history. Men have ruled vast empires, procreated at prolific rates, and amassed colossal amounts of wealth. But here's the thing about all those "giants" of Human achievement: they all died and *stayed* dead.

Now look through your gospel glasses and see that regarding accomplishments, in Christ your works are *done*. Receive this truth: The greatest accomplishment in history, the only one that's truly eternal, has already happened. And it *wasn't* done *by* you **(cf. Ephesians 2:8-9)**, but it *was* done *for* you **(cf. 1 Timothy 1:15)**! The Lord Jesus Christ has already lived the perfect life God requires **(cf. Romans 5:10)**. That's why Jesus said on the cross, *"Tetelestai,"* which means **"It is finished"** (cf. John 19:30). The only One who could possibly please and appease God has already done so on your behalf. The 2 greatest problems facing humanity were sin and death, and our Lord Jesus Christ crushed them both! **"For sin is the sting that results in death, and the law gives sin its power. But thank God! He gives us victory over sin and death through our Lord Jesus Christ"** (1 Corinthians 15:57-58, NLT). The grave was absolutely no match for our Lord. After Christ died, **"God raised him up, loosing the pangs of death, because** *it was not possible for him to be held by it"* (Acts 2:24, italics mine).

With gospel glasses on, regarding wealth, you will see that it's time to stop seeking reasons to boast about yourself. Rather, you'll be able to heed Paul's admonition: **"So let no one boast in men. For all things are yours, whether Paul or Apollos or Cephas or the** *world or life or death or the present or the future—all are yours,* **and you are Christ's, and Christ is God's"** (1 Corinthians 3:21-23, italics mine).

Understand and walk in that truth, and regardless of any earthly circumstance, you'll be able to say with our brother, **"Our hearts ache, but we always have joy. We are poor, but we give spiritual riches to others. We own nothing, and yet we have everything. You know the generous grace of our Lord Jesus Christ. Though he was rich, yet for your sakes he became poor, so that by his poverty he could make you rich"** (2 Corinthians 6:10, 8:9 NLT).

The church at Smyrna didn't have a lot of money, but hear the Lord's word to them: "**I know about your suffering and your poverty--but you are rich!"** (Revelation 2:9).

You say you're poor? I think not! **"Listen, my dear brothers and sisters: Has not God chosen those who are poor in the eyes of the world to be rich in faith and to inherit the kingdom he promised those who love him?"** (James 2:5, NIV).

So it's time to give up. It's time to submit. It's time to stop trying to outdo the Lord with your achievements. It's time to stop trying to be richer than Him. It's time to stop trying to steal His fame. It's time to stop trying to grab His glory. It's time to abandon the utterly futile pursuit of achieving any real identity outside of Him. It's time to rest in Him! As the writer of **Hebrews** tells us, because we are united by faith in Christ: **"So then, there remains a Sabbath rest for the people of God, for whoever has entered God's rest has also rested from his works as God did from his"** (vv. 4:9-10).

This doesn't mean we shouldn't strive to glorify and serve God through ever-increasing experiential sanctification and service to others, as we most definitely should. What it means is that we mustn't tie our identity to these works, or to *any* of *our* accomplishments or possessions. Those things must not be the lenses through which we see ourselves.

Will you put your gospel glasses on? Who said you were unaccomplished and poor? *Who* said you were naked?

You Have a Huge Family...

> **"We are many parts of one body,
> and we all belong to each other."**
>
> (Romans 12:5b, NLT)

You are told that you are incomplete without a spouse and kids. You are told that you don't have a "family" without them. You are told that you are lacking...but not by God.

God says that you are now a member of the largest family in existence!

All throughout the New Testament we are called *adelphos*, the Greek word translated as "brothers and sisters," as we are all part of one family.

We are told: **"There is neither Jew nor Greek, there is neither bond nor free, there is neither male nor female: for you are all one in Christ Jesus"** (Galatians 3:28). We are all one **"brotherhood throughout the world"** (cf. 1 Peter 5:9).

In addition to Himself, God has given us each other. The fellowship we experience among each other, as believers, transcends every human familial relationship.

Just as God is triune, three Persons yet One...we are many, yet one.

Thus, no human family could ever compare to the beloved family to which you now belong. We are **"the assembly of the firstborn who are enrolled in heaven"** (Hebrews 12:23). This is why we are commanded: **"Let us not give up meeting together, as some are in the habit of doing, but let us encourage one another--and all the more as you see the Day approaching"** (Hebrews 10:25, NIV). Once again, this is especially important for us as Christian singles. *You* must never forsake gathering with *your* family.

I've personally experienced the love of my "global" family when traveling. On vacation across the sea, I've gone into a Bible church and been welcomed and loved on instantly, because I walked into a gathering of family. The fact that we had never met personally was irrelevant because we are *truly* brothers and sisters spiritually.

Remember, we are sheep among wolves **(cf. Matthew 10:16)**, and no sheep can survive outside the flock. You are most susceptible to the lies of the world when you are outside of fellowship.

The biggest wolf of all is the evil one and he **"prowls around like a roaring lion, seeking someone to devour"** (cf. 1 Peter 5:8). It's the lone sheep, away from the flock, which is easiest to devour with the lie of incompleteness in Christ, the "lie of lack".

You have a large, awesome family, so don't ever forsake them. We are commanded to be a blessing to each other, so let us both obey and receive those blessings. You gave up the right to "independent individualism" when you became a Christian, so you must accept and grow in your new family.

Christ died to make you a part of this family, so don't ever take it for granted. Referring to Jesus, the writer of **Hebrews** tells us, **"he who sanctifies and those who are sanctified all have one source. That is why he is not ashamed to call them brothers"** (v. 2:11).

Christ bought our family and He isn't ashamed of us, so you mustn't be either.

When the world tries to tell you to drop your head in shame over your ostensible lack, you must think of your true family.

Remember, Jesus didn't consider Joseph and Mary and their sons to be his true family. Rather, He said: **"Who are my mother** and my brothers? For whoever does the will of God, he is my brother and sister and mother" (Mark 3:33, 35).

You must think the same way. Your family consists of the children of God, regardless of the human family you may or may not have, and this family is huge and worldwide.

This family was promised to you. **"Jesus said, "Truly, I say to you, there is no one who has left house or brothers or sisters or mother or father or children or lands, for my sake and for the gospel, who will not receive a hundredfold now in this time, houses and *brothers and sisters and mothers and children* and lands, with persecutions, and in the age to come eternal life"** (Mark 10:29-30, italics mine). This is why Paul commanded us, **"Do not rebuke an older man but encourage him as you would a father, younger men as brothers, older women as mothers, younger women as sisters, in all purity"** (1 Timothy 5:1-2).

God sees you as having a huge family. He sees all of your brothers, sisters, and parents. He even sees your "children," which we'll study more deeply in a later chapter. To see them yourself...

Will you put your gospel glasses on? Who said you were an only child? Who said you don't have a family? *Who* said you were naked?

You are Engaged...

"Come, I will show you the Bride, the wife of the Lamb."
(Revelation 21:9b)

You're never going to get married...or at least that's what the voices around you love to say. They also love to tell you that, without a spouse, your life is lacking and empty. But God says something different because God sees something different.

Regardless of whether or not you will ever have a human spouse, you are engaged. You are engaged to Christ; engaged to be married; betrothed for a marriage that will *never* end!

Human marriage, like everything else in this world, is temporary.

When some Sadducees used the resurrection to try to test our Lord, using marriage as an example, Jesus said: **"The sons of this age marry and are given in marriage, but those who are considered worthy to attain to that age and to the resurrection from the dead** *neither marry nor are given in marriage, for they cannot die anymore, because they are equal to angels and are sons of God, being sons of the resurrection"* (Luke 20:34-36, italics mine).

There we see one thing that the common secular wedding vows have gotten right is the line, "until death do us part". Because that is true, for as soon as one spouse passes away, that marriage is over.

We go to heaven to worship and enjoy the direct presence of the Lord, not to continue living our earthly lives. The lion will lay with the lamb and the saints will praise and enjoy the Lord together as one. This entire current planet and its systems will be utterly abolished, including human marriage.

Remember the LORD'S promise: "**Look! I am creating new heavens and a new earth, and no one will even think about the old ones anymore**" (Isaiah 65:17, NLT).

God sees things eternally. He sees the beginning and the end of all things, and He knows that only what's eternal will truly last. God doesn't live in or concentrate on the temporal world like us. Remember, **"the things that are seen are transient, but the things that are unseen are eternal"** (2 Corinthians 4:18).

Thus, we must keep an eternal perspective on all things,

especially marriage. Why waste time fretting over something so temporal?

Remember, **"What is your life? For you are a mist that appears for a little time and then vanishes"** (James 4:14b). So while our mist is still visible, we must concentrate on the things that *truly* matter; the things that will last; the things of the Lord! As John wrote, **"The world is passing away, and also its lusts; but the one who does the will of God lives forever"** (1 John 2:17, NASB).

> "Only one life, 'twill soon be past,
> only what's done for Christ will last."
>
> - Anonymous

Thus, our major life emphasis must be on making ourselves and others ready for the only marriage that will last, the *true* eternal marriage in the life everlasting.

God promised our betrothal to Him when He said, **"I will betroth you to me forever. I will betroth you to me in righteousness and in justice, in steadfast love and in mercy. I will betroth you to me in faithfulness. And you shall know the LORD"** (Hosea 2:19-20). Through **Isaiah**, God said, **"your Maker is your husband, the LORD of hosts is his name; and the Holy One of Israel is your Redeemer, the God of the whole earth he is called. For the LORD has called you like a wife deserted and grieved in spirit, like a wife of youth when she is cast off, says your God"** (vv. 54:5-6).

As John the Baptist said, when speaking of Jesus: **"The one who has the bride is the bridegroom"** (John 3:29). Jesus referred to Himself as our bridegroom more than once, including when referring to His death and resurrection and ascension to heaven:

"**The days will come when the bridegroom is taken away from them**" (Mark 2:20).

We see an example of this betrothal to Christ as bridegroom come to fruition when Paul wrote to Corinth, "**I feel a divine jealousy for you, since I betrothed you to one husband, to present you as a pure virgin to Christ**" (2 Corinthians 11:2).

And Paul expanded on this truth even more! Check it: "**As the Scriptures say, 'A man leaves his father and mother and is joined to his wife, and the two are united into one.' This is a great mystery, but it is an illustration of the way Christ and the church are one**" (Ephesians 5:31-32, NLT). We'll jump deeper into that amazing truth in a later chapter, but for now, just understand that marriage is not what the world thinks.

So in the meantime, simply remember that we will one day exclaim what John prophesied we would: "**Let us rejoice and exult and give him the glory, for the marriage of the Lamb has come, and his Bride has made herself ready; it was granted her to clothe herself with fine linen, bright and pure**"— for the fine linen is the righteous deeds of the saints. And the angel said to me, "**Write this:** *Blessed are those who are invited to the marriage supper of the Lamb.*" **And he said to me, "These are the true words of God**" (Revelation 19:7-9, italics mine). *We* are those blessed people, those invited to the greatest marriage supper in history.

You *are* going to get married. You're already engaged! To see your bridegroom...

Will you put your gospel glasses on? Who said you weren't already engaged? Who said you are never going to get married? *Who* said you were naked?

You're Never Alone...

"And behold, I am with you always, to the end of the age."

(Matthew 28:20b)

Just before the Lord left the earth to ascend to His heavenly throne He made us that promise, a promise we *must* remember and *personally* accept.

Single Christians are often tempted to think they are alone, sometimes even in a room full of other believers, but this could not be further from the truth. As Christians we are *never* alone, not for one second of any day.

God has given us Himself, as well as His angelic host.

God eternally exists in three persons... Father, Son, and Holy Spirit. God is always joyous, from everlasting to everlasting, because He exists in this perfect triune fellowship.

He is not lacking anything, so He didn't create us out of any personal need. He created us out of love because He wanted us to share in this perfect fellowship, to share in this joy...for His glory.

Please re-read the last paragraph carefully and think deeply about its truths because therein lies the cure to loneliness.

God the Father isn't lacking anything because He has the Son and the Holy Spirit. God the Son isn't lacking anything because He has the Father and the Holy Spirit. God the Holy Spirit isn't lacking anything because He has the Father and the Son.

Because they are complete in each other, we become complete *in them*.

As Paul wrote of our Lord Jesus Christ:

"**all things were created through him and FOR him.**"

(Colossians 1:16b, emphasis mine)

This is why it is absolutely impossible to be truly joyous and complete apart from Christ, regardless of *any* abundance of human relationships!

We were created *for* Jesus...to love, serve, and be in relationship with Him. We weren't created to live for or by ourselves, or for our human families & friends. Remember, the Lord Jesus Christ came to restore the sin-broken relationship between us and God:

> **"he died for all,**
> **that those who live might no longer live for themselves**
> *but for him who for their sake died and was raised."*
> (2 Corinthians 5:15, italics mine)

For *our* sake He died and was raised, so that we would no longer wallow in the futility of vain selfish living, but instead live for the reason we were created...a *personal* relationship with God!

As the Lord Jesus Christ told the Samaritan woman at the well, a lady who had been through many human romantic relationships, "**If you only knew the gift God has for you and who you are speaking to, you would ask me, and I would give you living water**" (John 4:10, NLT). Therein lies yet another awesome truth we'll dive into more profoundly in a later chapter. In the interim, perceive that the Lord was speaking of a relationship with *Him*, the only fellowship that truly and completely satisfies.

So let us once again enjoy that perfect fellowship; let us once and for all be complete; let us learn to live and walk in this relationship *now*, while we're single.

In this way, any desires we harbor for spouses and kids will have the same motivation our God had in creating *us*. It won't be so that a human family will *complete* us, but rather, our motivation will be that because we *are* complete in God, we want to share that joy with others!

THE Comforter...

Beloved, please remember, our God *indwells* us! Check it: **"In him you also, when you heard the word of truth, the gospel of your salvation, and believed in him, were sealed with the promised Holy Spirit, who is the guarantee of our inheritance until we acquire possession of it, to the praise of his glory"** (Ephesians 1:13-14).

The Holy Spirit, who is God Himself, indwells us permanently. It is *He* who opened our hearts to see our need for Jesus and brought us to Him, and it is *He* who baptized us into the body of Christ. And now that we are Christians, He is with us *always*. He is the Spirit of Jesus, which means that while Christ reigns from His throne in heaven, He is always with us by proxy through the Holy Spirit.

Some of the most physically alone Christians in the world are those on long-term foreign missions. In discussing this, one of my brothers in Christ said: "The Holy Spirit needs to be your best friend."[4] In the context of that conversation, what he meant is that those who go on long-term foreign missions by themselves need to learn to rely on the Holy Spirit alone for their fellowship and joy, as they will be a lone sheep among many wolves.

But the truth espoused in that quote applies to all Christians in all situations, and especially to single Christians. The Holy Spirit *needs* to be our best friend.

Since God Himself indwells us, what greater relationship could we ever possibly desire? Yet, we often overlook and take this fact for granted, and of this we need to repent.

The Person who wrote the Bible, the Spirit who anointed Christ for His ministry, the God who is building the universal body of Christ...this same Person has sealed us and indwells us. So we must worship Him; confide in Him; pray to Him; solicit His guidance and counsel; ask Him for discernment and wisdom; and most importantly...submit to Him.

Stand boldly on this truth and live it out: **"The Spirit of God, who raised Jesus from the dead, lives in you. And just as God raised Christ Jesus from the dead, he will give life to your mortal bodies by this same Spirit living within you"** (Romans 8:11, NLT). It is *He* who sanctifies us from the inside out; it is *He* who continually makes us more like Christ; and it is *He* who must be our greatest comforter.

As our Lord Jesus said:

> "Nevertheless, I tell you the truth:
> it is to your advantage that I go away,
> for if I do not go away, the Helper will not come to you.
> But if I go, I will send him to you."
>
> (John 16:7)

Jesus said those words just before His crucifixion, just before He was to leave His disciples on earth and ascend back home to Heaven. He wanted them to know that they would not be left alone. He wanted them to know that God would always be with them. He wanted them to know that even though He wouldn't be with them physically, He would always indwell them spiritually.

God is one **(cf. Deuteronomy 6:4, Mark 12:29)**. Thus, I espouse the concept of the Holy Spirit as your best friend, not to separate Him or His work from the rest of the Holy Triune Godhead. Rather, it's to help you understand His specific ministry in your life; to help you understand that you are *never* alone, regardless of your singleness or any physical isolation.

In the verse quoted above from John 16, the Lord says it's *better* that He goes away, and it was better for two reasons.

One, because He knew he had to die, rise again, and ascend to His throne to secure our redemption. As He told His disciples on numerous occasions, "**The Son of Man must suffer many terrible things,**" he said. "**He will be rejected by the elders, the leading priests, and the teachers of religious law. He will be killed, but on the third day he will be raised from the dead**" (Luke 9:22, NLT). The Lord knew that this is why He had come to the earth. He was going to save us from the *condemnation* of sin.

And two, so that His relationship with His people could move from the physical to the spiritual, for the Lord was also going to give us real victory over the *power* of sin. Before He came to earth in a human body, the Lord's people knew Him and worshipped Him almost exclusively in a physical sense, by observing His laws and sacrificing animals for their sins against Him. But with the Lord's descent to earth, He was about to change everything, including how His people would know and worship Him. Check it: "**God went for the jugular when he sent his own Son. He didn't deal with the problem as something remote and unimportant. In his Son, Jesus, he personally took on the human condition, entered the disordered mess of struggling humanity in order to set it right once and for all. The law code, weakened as it always was by fractured human nature, could never have done that. The law always ended up being used as a Band-Aid on sin instead of a deep healing of it. And now what the law code asked for but we couldn't deliver is accomplished as we, instead of redoubling our own efforts, simply embrace what the Spirit is doing in us**" (Romans 8:3-4, MSG).

This relational shift from the physical to the spiritual was captured and illustrated perfectly in **John 4**. In the Lord's conversation with the Samaritan woman recorded there, she posited, **"Our fathers worshiped on this mountain, but you say that in Jerusalem is the place where people ought to worship"** (v. 20). She was looking for a definitive answer on where she should physically worship God. Our Lord's reply gave the answer to that question forevermore: **"Jesus said to her, 'Woman, believe me, the hour is coming when neither on this mountain nor in Jerusalem will you worship the Father. The hour is coming, and is now here, when the true worshipers will worship the Father in spirit and truth, for the Father is seeking such people to worship him. God is spirit, and those who worship him must worship in spirit and truth'"** (vv 4:21,23-24).

This is why during His earthly life, Jesus' relationship with His regular disciples was primarily physical. But during that earthly life, the Lord made another related promise at the Feast of Booths. **"On the last day of the feast, the great day, Jesus stood up and cried out, 'If anyone thirsts, let him come to me and drink. Whoever believes in me, as the Scripture has said, Out of his heart will flow rivers of living water.' Now this he said about the Spirit, whom those who believed in him were to receive, for as yet the Spirit had not been given, because Jesus was not yet glorified"** (John 7:37-39).

And very soon after His ascension, as recorded in **Acts 2**, The Lord's promises came to perfect fruition. **"On the day of Pentecost all the believers were meeting together in one place. Suddenly, there was a sound from heaven like the roaring of a mighty windstorm, and it filled the house where they were sitting. Then, what looked like flames or tongues of fire appeared and settled on each of them. And everyone present** was filled with the Holy Spirit and began speaking in other languages, as the Holy Spirit gave them this ability"** (vv. 2:1-4, NLT). Right after this happened, Peter stepped up and launched into one of the most epic sermons ever. He said: **"God raised Jesus from the dead, and we are all witnesses of this. Now he is exalted to the place of highest honor in heaven, at God's right hand. And the Father, as he had promised, gave him the Holy Spirit to pour out upon us, just as you see and hear today"** (vv. 32-33, NLT).

Now, because the Holy Spirit is here with us forever, we can echo our brother Paul's amazing sentiments: **"we are the circumcision, who worship by the Spirit of God and glory in Christ Jesus and put no confidence in the flesh"** (Philippians 3:3). Understanding and abounding in this worship, in this intimate Spiritual relationship with our Lord, is the key to a life free from loneliness. It's a major key to the truly "abundant" life the Lord has purposed for us **(cf. John 10:10b)**, regardless of earthly circumstance.

So once again, as a single Christian, this is *the most important relationship* for you to cultivate. As we'll discuss more deeply in a later chapter, this might be the exact reason why you are single right now, because you need to walk more closely with the LORD.

For now, think about this. How do you get closer to anyone? By spending time with them, communicating with them, and learning about them of course! We have an innate understanding of this in our relationships with other people; yet, we often overcomplicate and neglect this principle in our relationship with God.

Friendships are cultivated by getting to know a person more intimately. It's very simple. Accordingly, we get closer to God the Holy Spirit by spending time with Him. We do this by directing a part of our prayer lives directly to Him, and we learn more about Him and His will by spending time in the word He wrote.

If you didn't talk to your best friend, it would cause a slow deterioration of that relationship, and soon that person wouldn't be your best friend.

And so it is in our relationship with God the Holy Spirit. It must, with strong awe and deep reverence, be proactively cultivated; leading to ever-increasingly strong fellowship, which will result in progressively decreasing loneliness.

Surrounded by Love...

In addition to giving us Himself, the Lord also surrounds and protects us with His angelic host.

As David wrote, **"The angel of the LORD encamps around those who fear him, and delivers them"** (Psalm 34:7).

You may not see them, feel their presence, or even think about them very often...but they are there.

God has actually allowed me to personally see the angels protecting me once. When I was still a baby Christian, I and another young brother were going through some strong spiritual attacks. An elder in our men's Bible study group prayed for us one evening, asking the Lord to send His angelic host to surround and protect us.

We were grateful for the prayer, but I really didn't think very much about its ramifications that night before I went to bed.

In the middle of the night, I awoke and saw angels standing at the foot of my bed. It was surreal, but I was definitely awake and I still remember it pretty vividly. They were facing away from me, so I was only allowed to see their backs. They were huge, probably around 7-8 feet tall! They were literally lined up in front of my bed in a defensive formation.

When I saw them, I just remember feeling complete peace, and I leaned back and fell sound asleep for the rest of the night. I know this might sound unbelievable to you, but it really happened, and they really did look majestic. And honestly, the experience was epic and unforgettable.

I believe one of the reasons God allowed me to see their presence that night was for encouragement, as I was a very new Christian undergoing fiery spiritual attacks and this showed me that I was indeed being lovingly protected.

I haven't physically seen angels since then, but now that I've matured as a Christian, I know they're always around.

As the writer of **Hebrews** penned, **"Are not all angels ministering spirits sent to serve those who will inherit salvation?"** (v. 1:14, NIV). *We* are those blessed creatures who will inherit salvation, so we can stand on God's promise to protect and defend us through His angelic host!

Though we don't see them, they're everywhere around the people of God, especially when we are under attack.

We see this reality being described in **2 Kings 6**. There, Israel was at war with the Syrians. In the middle of the night, the enemy camp from Syria surrounded Israel's camp. When Elisha's servant arose early in the morning and walked outside, he saw the Syrian army all around them, poised and ready for attack. Panicked and fearful, he went to Elisha and asked how they were going to survive. Being the consummate man of God, Elisha calmly responded, **"'Do not be afraid, for those who are with us are more than those who are with them.'" Then Elisha prayed and said, 'O LORD, please open his eyes that he may see.' So the LORD opened the eyes of the young man, and he saw, and behold, the mountain was full of horses and chariots of fire all around Elisha"** (vv. 16-17).

I love the way Elisha answered, that those who are protecting us are *more* than those who would attack us. The area around them was *full* of angelic protection, filled with the unbeatable army of God. That's one of the main reasons our brother Elisha could be so chill during that time of war, because he knew the truth that he and the people of God were *never* alone. God was always with them, and so were His ministering servant spirits, so there was absolutely nothing to fear.

Single Christian, there is absolutely nothing for you to fear either. You are never alone, not for one second of your new and eternal life. God the Holy Spirit indwells you forever and the angelic armies of God surround you in protection.

So concentrate foremost on growing and deepening your relationship with our LORD God, of Whom David wrote, **"I look behind me and you're there, then up ahead and you're there, too—your reassuring presence, coming and going. This is too much, too wonderful—I can't take it all in!"** (Psalm 139:5-6, MSG).

Remind yourself everyday of the truth that your Father's angels guard and fight for you.

To see all of this...

Will you put your gospel glasses on? Who said you were alone? Who said you weren't protected? *Who* said you were naked?

CLARITY

You are the righteousness of God in Christ!

You are God's deeply, Personally loved child!

You are Holy!

You are Beautiful!

You are Accomplished & Wealthy!

You have a huge Family!
You are Engaged to be married!
You are Never Alone!
That is how God now sees you!

So when you look in the mirror that is how you *must* see yourself, through gospel glasses. If necessary, put Sticky notes on your mirror to remind yourself of these truths. Then memorize all of these scriptures and write them on your heart.

As the Lord has commanded us: **"My son, be attentive to my words; incline your ear to my sayings. Let them not escape from your sight; keep them within your heart. For they are life to those who find them, and healing to all their flesh"** (Proverbs 4:20-22).

In this way, when the world or the evil one or your own mind tries to attack you with lies about who you are, you can resolutely overcome them with God's eternal word.

By doing this, **"you will know the truth, and the truth will set you free"** (John 8:32).

So always wear your gospel glasses...and you will be able to look into any mirror, smile, and hear God gently whispering:

Who said you were naked?

WHAT IS THAT TO YOU?

> "Peter turned around and saw behind them
> the disciple Jesus loved. Peter asked Jesus,
> "*What about him*, Lord?" Jesus replied,
> "If I want him to remain alive until I return,
> *what is that to you? As for you, follow me.*"
> (John 21:20a-22, NLT, italics mine)

You can be having an otherwise great Sunday morning, rejoicing in the Lord and in His blessings, whistling while you walk into church that Sunday. You're ready to see your friends, ready to get your worship on, ready to jump into the Word of God...but then you see all those "perfect" families.

Suddenly, that "pep in your step" is gone. You feel incomplete, alone, and jealous. During worship, your lips move in vain quivers; your tongue emits nothing but empty words. As the sermon is preached, your heart is divided and your mind is sad. Walking out the door after service, your joy has left, your peace is gone, and your day was ruined...at church of all places! What happened?

This is exactly the type of thing the Lord knew would happen when he said: **"The thief comes only to steal and kill and destroy"** (John 10:10a).

Seeing you walking in the joy and peace of the Lord, headed to worship, ready to praise God and learn from His Word, the evil one went into attack mode. As you walked in the door, lies were whispered in your ear, lies like: "God loves all those people more than you. Why are you going to worship? What do you have to sing about? Everyone here is more blessed. You shouldn't even be here."

The second you believed those lies, the doors to the sins of envy and discontentment were opened. You just allowed the thief to steal your joy, to kill your peace, to destroy your day. You've just helped the thief to achieve his purpose for you, rather than helping the Lord to achieve His.

You see, envy and discontentment come not from reality, but from the evil one. He knows he can't steal your salvation or take you from God, so he tries to take God's other gifts, God's *fruit*, out of you. The evil one's purposes are against all Christians, regardless of marital status. For the married, he tries to incite acrimony, arguments, and adulterous thoughts. For us as singles, one of the main attacks is the type of scenario we just read.

Beloved, the Lord has very different purposes for you. As He said of us: **"I came that they may have life, and have it abundantly"** (John 10:10b, NASB). This life purpose applies for all Christians. Whether we're single, married, or widowed...all sharing the same abundant life.

It's the same for all of us because true abundance does not lie in marriage and children, *or* in the lack thereof. True abundance does not lie in riches or in poverty, in health or in sickness, in success or in failure. No, true abundance is this:

> **"love, joy, peace, patience, kindness, goodness, faithfulness, gentleness, and self-control"**
>
> (cf. Galatians 5:22b-23a, NLT)

This abundance comes from God the Holy Spirit. It's always available and given irrespective of circumstantial life differences. This fruit of the Spirit comes in spite of and above earthly plight. It gives us victory during trials and amplifies our blessings. *That* is abundant life!

Accordingly, victory over discontentment and envy lies not in changing *who and what* we see, but in changing *how* we see them. Just as we must see *ourselves* through gospel glasses, we must see *everyone else* through those same gospel glasses.

As we'll study more deeply in a later chapter, God's main purpose for your personal life is making you more like the Lord Jesus Christ. And the same applies for your brothers and sisters in Christ. God has placed your married brothers and sisters in marriage to sanctify them, just as He has placed you in singleness to do the same thing. *That* is how you must see your brethren in the body of Christ!

When you see the spouses and children of your brethren, you mustn't think "why them and not me?" You must instead imbibe the truth and think, "that's how God is sanctifying and growing them".

Therein lies true and lasting contentment.

If you're discontented, getting married and having a couple of babies won't be the cure. In fact, it will only exacerbate the sin. You see, if the attitude of your heart is one of envy, in marriage your heart will still be envious of those people with "cuter" babies and "more beautiful" spouses.

In our Lord Jesus Christ's perfect words:

"'There is nothing outside a person that by going into him can defile him, but the things that come out of a person are what defile him.' And he said, 'What comes out of a person is what defiles him. For from within, out of the heart of man, come evil thoughts, sexual immorality, theft, murder, adultery, *coveting*, wickedness, deceit, sensuality, *envy*, slander, pride, foolishness" (Mark 7:15,20-22, italics mine)

There we see that all sinful attitudes come not from input, but from output; not from without, but from within; not from what is seen, but from how it's seen. All evil thoughts come not from the light that passes through your cornea into your brain, but from the darkness pouring out of your heart.

As it is written: **"Everything is pure to those whose hearts are pure"** (Titus 1:15a, NLT). A pure and content single Christian can see a happy family, smile, and pray for them. A discontented, envious Christian can see that same family and only drop their head in self-imposed bitterness and shame.

Which do you want to be? What if it's God's will that you're years away from marriage? Are you going to spend those years as a jealous malcontent, or as a joyous, worshipful servant of our almighty God? Personally, I'll take the latter. And you?

Envy and discontentment come from believing the lie that someone is *more* blessed than you. Joy and contentment come from believing the truth that others just have *different* blessings than you.

We see this exemplified perfectly by how the Lord Jesus dealt with our apostolic brothers in the passage from John that opened this chapter.

There, Peter was concerned because the Lord was dealing differently with John than with him. When this happened, the Lord didn't say "you're right Peter, John is more blessed than you, I love him more". No, the Lord responded with a rebuke and basically said, "so what Peter? I love you both, but I have a different calling for John. What does that have to do with My calling and blessings for *your* life? You just follow *My* desire and *My* will, and don't worry about how I call or bless others".

And there is *our* command, *our* answer as well. As the Lord deals personally with His other children, what is that to us? We must follow *Him* and do what He commands *us* to do, regardless of His callings for others. If He calls our brothers and sisters to get married and have kids at this time, it doesn't change His current calling for us, and thus it mustn't change our answer to that call.

When we truly espouse this attitude, God's blessings on others will make us smile and we will **"Rejoice with those who rejoice"** (Romans 12:15a).

How then do we espouse this attitude? How do we live this truth out, specifically and practically?

First, we must Biblically define envy and discontentment. Then we can learn the specific ways that gospel glasses will free us from them.

Exposing Darkness...
"For this is the message that you have heard from the beginning, that we should love one another."

(1 John 3:11)

The sins of envy & discontentment are the attitude that everything the Lord has given you is not enough, unless those blessings equal or exceed those given to others. While this temptation has many entrances, the most common entrance for single Christians is through the door of marriage. But what heart issues cause these attitudes?

The Greek word most often translated as "envy" in the New Testament is *phthonos*. This word carries a very deep meaning in Greek, as it means to have a spiteful jealousy that embitters the mind. This word also carries with it a sense of displeasure at another's blessing and a sense of the mental state we now call "Schadenfreude," which means delighting in another's misfortune[5].

When envy is Biblically defined in this way, it gets exposed for what it really is...*hate*. There's no way around the truth. Envy is not some small, insignificant attitude. It is not only a lack of love for others, it is *hatred* for them. As our brother explained very clearly: **"We know that we have passed out of death into life, because we love the brothers. Whoever does not love abides in death. Everyone who hates his brother is a murderer, and you know that no murderer has eternal life abiding in him"** (1 John 3:14-15).

Notice how John directly contrasts love and hate. He presents us with only two choices, either love or hate. There's no true "indifference" toward others. Because we are commanded to love others, anything else is hatred, which is actually murder. That's why we're admonished thus: **"We should not be like Cain, who was of the evil one and murdered his brother. And why did he murder him? Because his own deeds were evil and his brother's righteous"** (1 John 3:12). Abel didn't do anything wrong, he only lived righteously before the LORD. Cain hated him without cause, simply out of envy.

The only difference between Cain and us, if we're not loving our brothers, is that Cain physically acted on his hate. But there's no real difference in God's eyes. As John said, whoever lacks love "abides in death". So even when hate is not expressed physically, it's still "heart murder".

Accordingly, if we're dressing up hatred as "impassivity," or excusing envy as a petty emotion, we're behaving just like Cain. If you're jealous of someone else, that's *your* sin, not theirs. Your married friends are not sinning against you by being married. So if their blessings are bothersome to you, it's time for *you* to repent, not them. Check out a few verses regarding the seriousness of the matter of how Christians treat other Christians:

Of a man and his wife —
> **"show her honor as a fellow heir of the grace of life,**
> **so that your prayers will not be hindered."**
>
> (1 Peter 3:7b)

Of one brother and another —
> **"that no man transgress and defraud his brother in the matter**
> **because the Lord is the avenger in all these things,**
> **just as we also told you before and solemnly warned you."**
>
> (1 Thessalonians 4:6)

There we see that our sin against each other really matters to God because we're His children.

To understand this a little better, just picture two sibling kids you know. Now imagine one of them walking up to the other and slapping them, completely unprovoked. What would happen? The offender would be disciplined of course, for two reasons. One, because of the sin itself, as no kid should do that to *anyone* at all. Second, the chastisement would be exacerbated by the fact that in this case the offended Party was a child of the parent administering the discipline. And so it is with us. As Peter said, when a Christian man is sinning against his Christian wife, God might not even be listening to the man's prayers until repentance is reached. As Paul said, a Christian man who commits adultery with another Christian man's wife awaits the fearful vengeance of God.

This is another reminder that The LORD loves *all* of His children, not only corporately, but individually as well. Accordingly, He takes sin against His people very seriously, even if the person committing the sin is another one of His children. This is simply our perfectly just God being perfectly just. It's perfectly loving and perfectly holy. So you must always see your treatment of your brethren with this truth in mind.

Beloved, as a Christian, *you* already have *all* of the love and blessings you'll ever need. If you're envious and discontent, you're walking totally blind to these truths. For **"whoever hates his brother is in the darkness and walks in the darkness, and does not know where he is going, because the darkness has blinded his eyes"** (1 John 2:11). So put your gospel glasses on and *see*!

Iconoclasm...

"Little children, keep yourselves from idols."

(1 John 5:21)

In the verses we've studied in this chapter, we can also see that discontentment is idolatry. It means that we are valuing temporal things and people above the Lord who has given us Himself. Remember, God has given us *all* of Himself. As we studied in the previous chapter, God indwells us permanently **(cf. Ephesians 1:13-14)**, and through the cross He has given us 24/7, unfettered access to the throne of grace **(cf. Hebrews 10:19-22)**.

What more could we ever ask for? Yet, the discontented heart just screams out to God, "You're not enough! I want more! I want what *they* have!"

It's the same sin of grumbling the Israelites committed when **"the whole congregation of the people of Israel grumbled against Moses and Aaron in the wilderness, and the people of Israel said to them, "Would that we had died by the hand of the LORD in the land of Egypt, when we sat by the meat pots and ate bread to the full, for you have brought us out into this wilderness to kill this whole assembly with hunger"** (Exodus 16:2-3).

The Lord had delivered the Israelites from slavery in the land of Egypt. He was about to send them into the Promised Land; yet, they were still discontent. By God's amazing grace, they had a terrible past behind them, an amazing future ahead of them, and they simply had to wait a little longer.

Brethren, we are in a similar, even more blessed situation. By God's unmerited grace, we have been delivered from a past of slavery that led to eternal death **(cf. Romans 6:16-23)**. We have an eternity in heaven with God ahead of us **(cf. 1 John 2:25, John 10:28)**, and now we just need to wait.

Just as Israel was in the wilderness for 40 years, we are currently in our own wilderness, in our own "time of exile" **(cf. 1 Peter 1:17)**. But Israel refused to be content and thus, **"with most of them God was not pleased, for they were overthrown in the wilderness"** (1 Corinthians 10:5). So let's learn what *not* to do from them:

> **"In the camp they grew envious of Moses and of Aaron,**
> **who was consecrated to the Lord.**
> **The earth opened up and swallowed Dathan;**

> it buried the company of Abiram.
> Fire blazed among their followers;
> a flame consumed the wicked."
> (Psalm 106:16-18, NIV)

> *"We must not put Christ to the test,*
> *as some of them did and were destroyed by serpents,*
> *nor grumble, as some of them did and were destroyed by the*
> *Destroyer. Now these things happened to them as an example,*
> *but they were written down for our instruction,*
> *on whom the end of the ages has come."*
> (1 Corinthians 10:9-11, italics mine)

We're so blessed to know what happened to *them*, so that *we* could learn what kind of attitude we all must espouse. So let's heed this warning and learn this lesson *right now*, while we are single.

The Greek word translated as "grumble" in that text, and in 6 other places in the New Testament, is *gogguzó*. It means to complain with muffled undertones out of smoldering discontent. The awesome thing about this Greek word, and a key to helping us understand its strength, is that it's an onomatopoeia, just like its English translation. That is, the word's etymology is based on how it sounds when pronounced[6]. Speak it out loud phonetically, looking in the mirror while you do so: "gong-good'-zo". Not a very attractive sight, is it?

You can really hear and see the complaining and grumbling undertones in your voice and on your face when you say this word. *This* is what God sees and hears whenever you are complaining about your plight.

Now let's keep cruising through God's word, to gain a

stronger comprehension of the seriousness of discontentment. The Lord Jesus Christ taught about this in the parable of the "Laborers in the Vineyard" found in **Matthew 20**.

In this parable, a vineyard owner hires several laborers at different times of the day. At the end of the day, all of those laborers received the same wage (one they had all agreed to upon hiring), regardless of how long they had worked.

Look at what happened afterward: **"Now when those hired first came, they thought they would receive more, but each of them also received a denarius. And on receiving it they** *grumbled* **at the master of the house, saying, 'These last worked only one hour, and you have made them equal to us who have borne the burden of the day and the scorching heat'"** (Matthew 20:12, italics mine). The English word translated as "grumble" there is once again *gogguzo*. So we see, when we are discontented and complaining about any *ostensible* inequity in God's dissemination of his blessings, we are thinking and acting just like those laborers.

It gets *worse* though. Check out the vineyard owner's response to the laborers: **"he replied to one of them, 'Friend, I am doing you no wrong'"** (Matthew 20:13a). There we see, when we are evincing this sinful attitude, we are actually accusing God of wrongdoing! That is the exact thing the Israelites did in the passage we just read above. Accordingly, Moses' response to them was a strong rebuke: **"Your grumbling is not against us but against the LORD"** (Exodus 16:8b). When we're complaining about our circumstances, we're really complaining against the God who controls them all.

Thus, if the attitude of our heart is "why do *they* have a spouse and kids [or anything else under the sun], and not *me*, it's so unfair!" we are saying that God is unjust and unrighteous in His dealings, even if that sentiment is not being expressed orally!

Knowing this, we can no longer deny the sinfulness of living in envious discontentment.

The vineyard owner then said to the laborer: **"Take what belongs to you and go"** (Matthew 20:14a). This means we must accept the blessings, callings, and ministries God gives *us*, making the most of them for His glory and the good of others **(cf. Matthew 25:14-30)**, and drop all the complaining.

The vineyard owner then said to the laborer: **"I choose to give to this last worker as I give to you. Am I not allowed to do what I choose with what belongs to me?"** (vv. 20:14b-15a). This is a further reiteration of God's *complete* sovereignty, which we must fully accept and to which we must completely acquiesce. This sovereignty absolutely includes how, where, and how much He blesses *His* creations. So let's heed this wisdom: **"What sorrow awaits those who argue with their Creator. Does a clay pot argue with its maker? Does the clay dispute with the one who shapes it, saying, 'Stop, you're doing it wrong!' Does the pot exclaim, 'How clumsy can you be?' How terrible it would be if a newborn baby said to its father, 'Why was I born?' or if it said to its mother, 'Why did you make me this way?'" This is what the Lord says—the Holy One of Israel and your Creator: "Do you question what I do for my children? Do you give me orders about the work of my hands?"** (Isaiah 45:9-11, NLT).

Will *we* command God to do *our* will? Of course not! That concept is utterly ridiculous. Yet, when we're complaining, that is exactly what we're attempting. It's sinful, useless, and totally futile.

Is God not allowed to give some the gift of marriage and some the equally large *gift* of singleness as He wills? Of course He is! So let's just be who He created *us* to be, do what He created *us* to do, and be completely content along the way.

The vineyard owner then said to the laborer: **"Or do you begrudge my generosity?"** (Matthew 20:15b.) There we see, discontentment is also the sin of ingratitude. Remember, we all deserve nothing but God's eternal, just wrath. We were all born with original sin and from the moment we were born, we all lived in our own autonomous rebellion against God. This means God could have justly killed and condemned every single one of us.

God could have simply written off our entire race and shut us out of His presence. Or as He did with the angels who fell, God could have provided us with no means of reconciliation **(cf. 2 Peter 2:4)**, thus letting us all just condemn ourselves, living lives with absolutely no hope for eternity.

But God *didn't*! Instead, He sent His own perfect Son to be born of sinful woman and walk this guilty sod. He then killed His own sinless Son, by laying on Him the full punishment for *our* sin!

And as described all throughout the New Testament, this reconciliation is *not* given to everyone! It's *only* given to God's elect! Before time began, God predestined *you* for salvation through His son, the Lord Jesus Christ **(cf. Ephesians 1:4-6)**. This was completely sovereign election. You did nothing to earn or deserve it; you only did your part by sinning. Check it: **"the gate is wide and the way is easy that leads to destruction, and those who enter by it are many. For the gate is narrow and the way is hard that leads to life, and those who find it are few"** (Matthew 7:13a-14). *You* are one of those chosen few! *We* are the people of God, His elect, His beloved **(cf. 1 Thessalonians 1:4-5)**!

As God's children, we have no excuse for living in discontentment. Instead, we should be praising and thanking God constantly and in all earthly circumstances **(cf. John 3:27, James 1:17, 1 Thessalonians 5:18, Ephesians 5:20, Colossians 3:17)**. This is yet another reason why you must see *everything* and *everyone* through gospel glasses.

As our brother C.J. Mahaney says, when someone asks him how he's doing, his reply is always: "better than I deserve". And that's true for all Christians. We are doing better than we deserve because we are forgiven and loved. Just by having food in our stomachs and roofs over our heads, we're doing better than we deserve. Simply by breathing in God's clean oxygen and converting it to carbon dioxide with our lungs, we're doing better than we deserve. Single, married, widowed...we're all doing better than we deserve. Praise God! Indeed, this *gospel humility* is one of the greatest keys to victory over discontentment.

As our brother Thomas Watson wrote: "The way for a man to be contented, is not by raising his estate higher, but by bringing his heart lower. By contentment a Christian gains a victory over himself. For a man to be able to rule his own spirit, this of all others is the most noble conquest.⁷"

As Paul penned: **"Now there is great gain in godliness with contentment, for we brought nothing into the world, and we cannot take anything out of the world. But if we have food and clothing, with these we will be content"** (1 Timothy 6:6-8). That Scripture doesn't say: "if we have food and clothing, *and spouse and kids and every blessing on earth*..." Rather, it says that as long as we have the *bare necessities* of life, we must be completely content. I love the CEV version of this text: **"And religion does make your life rich, by making you content with what you have"**.

You see, only for Christians is *complete* contentment truly possible. The worldly can never gain true and lasting contentment, as from nothing on earth can it be gained. We however, are freely given this contentment, not by receiving everything our flesh desires, but by *divorcing* those desires through the true freedom given to us in the gospel.

Beloved, the answer to discontentment does not lie in having more, it lies in being grateful for exactly what God has given you. True contentment lies in seeing not only yourself through God's eyes, but in seeing others through those same Eyes.

However, before we can discuss what everyone else looks like through gospel glasses, we need to first deal with someone else...us. You see, as single Christians, we're much more tempted to selfishness in general than our married brethren. Accordingly, we must first overcome two major sins before we can see others like God does.

Vanity

"For by the grace given to me I say to everyone among you not to think of himself more highly than he ought to think, but to think with sober judgment, each according to the measure of faith that God has assigned."

(Romans 12:3)

One of the dangerous paradigms that can arise from singleness is thinking that everyone else cares about you as much as you do. Or thinking that everyone else thinks as highly of you as you do. Since so much of our time is spent alone, pondering ourselves and our lives, we can be tempted to think that others share that same level of care.

With the modern day proliferation of social networking sites like Facebook, Twitter, YouTube, and personal blogs has come the temptation of self-promotion and "personal platform building." Most of us use at least one of these sites and their use brings with it many temptations to vanity.

We can start to think that everyone cares about our mundane status updates, boastful tweets, and effusive blog posts. We can become addicted to our number of "likes" on Facebook, twitter "followers," and blog "subscribers". Sadly, even our theology-based posts can be wrought with sinful pride, thinking we have some "knowledge" that others don't. But that's wrong. For the truth is: **"'all of us possess knowledge.' This 'knowledge' puffs up, but love builds up. If anyone imagines that he knows something, he does not yet know as he ought to know'"** (1 Corinthians 8:1a-2). So we must heed this admonition from the Lord: **"Who is wise and understanding among you?** *By his good conduct let him show his works in the meekness of wisdom"* (James 3:13, italics mine). True wisdom is *meek*! And meekness is power under control; a proactively ingrained lowliness of mind.

The Lord Jesus Christ is the greatest example of meekness in history. All the power in the universe rested in His hands, yet He had this power under complete control at all times. Thus, the only One we should be "liking," "following," and "subscribing to" is the Lord! We must be pointing others to Him, *not* to us! As John the Baptist said when people tried to venerate him: **"After me comes he who is mightier than I, the strap of whose sandals I am not worthy to stoop down and untie. He must increase, but I must decrease"** (Mark 1:7, John 3:30). John was single as well, and he spent his life glorifying and pointing others to the Lord, not to himself. Our online posts, and the message of our entire lives, must be about how great our God is, not about how great we think we are.

As with all sin, the key to overcoming this sin lies in the truth of God's eternal word, allowing us to view everything through gospel glasses. In seeing ourselves through God's eyes, we not only see how loved and blessed we are, but also how small we are. We **"are a mist that appears for a little time and then vanishes"** (James 4:14b). We are just dust from the ground that

God has breathed into life. We're merely clay the Potter has formed **(cf. Romans 9:20-21)**. We were all created to glorify, love, worship, and serve the Lord Jesus Christ, for **"all things were created through him and for him"** (cf. Colossians 1:16).

If we think that we are something more than anyone else, we must remember Paul's admonition: **"that none of you may be puffed up in favor of one against another. For who sees anything different in you? What do you have that you did not receive? If then you received it, why do you boast as if you did not receive it?"** (1 Corinthians 4:6b-7).

The temptation to vanity is nothing new; it's as old as the human race. Listen to Solomon's words, written over 3,000 years ago: **"vanity of vanities! All is vanity"** (Ecclesiastes 1:2b). The Hebrew word translated as "vanity" there, and in 72 other places in Holy Scripture, is *hebel*. Literally, it means "a breath, a vapor". But its actual usage transcends even those words, in that it describes something that is rendered meaningless by its evanescent and transitory nature[8]. As Solomon said of our earthly pursuits, they are all **"a striving after wind"** (cf. Ecclesiastes 1:14,17;2:11,17,26;4:4,6,16;6:9). Indeed, this book of wisdom is the greatest killer of vanity in the world. If you struggle with this sin, read Ecclesiastes regularly and you will see that **"What has been is what will be, and what has been done is what will be done, and there is nothing new under the sun"** (Ecclesiastes 1:9). Nothing you do, have done, or will do hasn't already been done before. Remember, nothing you do or are compares to what God has done and who He is. For only God's works are truly impressive and eternal. So imbibe the wisdom of Solomon, who also wrote: **"I have seen everything that is done under the sun, and behold, all is vanity"** (Ecclesiastes 1:14).

Killing Your Biggest Idol...

> "For if anyone thinks he is something,
> when he is nothing, he deceives himself."
>
> (Galatians 6:3)

Learning and fully imbibing these truths leads to one of the most liberating paradigm shifts in the life of a Christian: *getting over yourself.* By the physical nature into which we were born, we have trouble looking past the mirror and seeing things from a perspective outside of our own. But now that we're in Christ, through gospel glasses we see this fact: it's *not* about us! *All* of creation is about God, **"For everything comes from him and exists by his power and is intended for his glory. All glory to him forever! Amen"** (Romans 11:36, NLT).

Humility is not only a universal command for Christians, it's the only logical response to who God is and what He has revealed to us about who we are! I love this old saying: "God made the universe very big, and us very small, to show the difference between us and Him[9]." The LORD is eternal, self-existent, holy, and perfect in every way. We are sinful, mortal beings. We don't even get to decide whether or not we will wake up tomorrow morning **(cf. James 4:13-15)**. So how and why should we ever think pridefully of ourselves?

Another area where single Christians are tempted to vanity is, sadly, in service and ministry. As we've discussed, we absolutely should be serving as much as possible. But we cannot let vanity creep into our ministry, regardless of our level of service. The temptation tries to enter in like this: we're serving in multiple ministries, plus going on short term missions trips, etc., thus, we are being brought before the congregation regularly for prayer.

Vanity sees its entrance here and tries to gain a foothold. It says: "everyone is watching you, so do more and do better, to impress them." This motivation for service and ministry is wrong. Our level of ministry should not change regardless of whether or not we have a human audience. When we serve (or serve more) in this way, we are being no different from the Pharisees **(cf. Matthew 23:5-7)**. The Lord knew that we would be tempted to this and He has commanded us thus: **"Beware of practicing your righteousness before other people in order to be seen by them, for then you will have no reward from your Father who is in heaven"** (Matthew 6:1).

Once again, all these temptations to vanity stem from basing your identity in yourself and your works, rather than in God and His works. As we discussed in the last chapter, when your self-worth is based on who you are and what you do, you spend your life trying to build yourself up in your own and other's minds. But when your self-worth is based in who God is, and who you are in Him, you are free from this sin. You are free to spend your life venerating and serving the Lord, not yourself.

Indeed, this is one of the greatest keys to lifelong joy and peace, trusting in and glorifying the only One who is always good and perfect. You are a child of the King of Kings. You are deeply loved, blood-purchased, and eternally secure. When your identity is based on these indomitable truths, rather than lies, vanity has no foothold.

Overcoming Eritheia...

"For where jealousy and selfish ambition exist,
there will be disorder and every vile practice."

(James 3:16)

The Greek word above, eritheia, is the one translated as the phrase "selfish ambition". This word has a very deep and strong meaning. Its etymology is from the Greek words *erithos*, which means a "day laborer," and *eritheuō*, which means to "work for hire". Of course, there's nothing intrinsically sinful about either of those two things. But check this out, because this is where it gets interesting! Our word is a *derivative* of those two words because neither of them was strong or specific enough to convey the full meaning the Greeks wanted to convey. What our word truly means is *mercenary* work for hire. That is, work done *only* for selfish gain, with a detachment from how it affects the common good of others or the interests of the employer. The Greeks used it of those who were so self-seeking and engaged in rivalry that they placed their own interests ahead of what the Lord and other people said was right[10]. Knowing that *this* is what selfish ambition is, we can no longer treat it very lightly! The world calls this attitude "competitiveness". The Bible calls it sin. This sin stems from a selfish heart that says "I must be better than everyone else". It's a heart that's not satisfied in the goodness of God; a heart that doesn't rejoice in God's blessings on others. It's a heart that cries "anything you can do better, I can do better." Our brothers in "116 Clique" put it well regarding this sin when they wrote: "The fun in number 1 is the point that I'm up in front of 2[11]." Indeed, it is true that this sin stems from a heart that is bent on being ostensibly "better" than all.

Just as with everything else under the sun, this sin is not new. As Solomon wrote long ago: **"I have seen that every labor and every skill which is done is the result of rivalry between a man and his neighbor. This too is vanity and striving after wind"** (Ecclesiastes 4:4, NASB). The whole point of the word picture painted there is that you will *never* catch the wind! This means that if your life is based on outdoing your neighbor, you will *never* be satisfied! For there will always be someone new to compare yourself to, and thus more "competition"!

This being yet another timeless sin, it is no surprise that it happened directly in front of our Lord Jesus Christ, among His closest followers no less! As we read, when the apostles were eating the Passover meal in the Upper Room: **"A dispute also arose among them, as to which of them was to be regarded as the greatest"** (Luke 22:24). Remember, these were not mere disciples, these were *apostles* personally and physically appointed by King Jesus!

They had been traveling and living with the Lord for three years at this point, no doubt observing His perfect example of humility and selflessness the whole time. And yet, here they were, selfishly arguing about which one of them was the best, then compounding that sin by bringing the argument before the Lord to settle. For two of them, the selfish ambition was so strong that they even had their mom bring this request before the Lord: **"Then the mother of the sons of Zebedee came up to him with her sons, and kneeling before him she asked him for something. And he said to her, "What do you want?" She said to him, "Say that these two sons of mine are to sit, one at your right hand and one at your left, in your kingdom"** (Matthew 20:20-21). I write all of this not to condemn the apostles, but rather to show that if *they* were not immune to this temptation, how much more must *we* all be striving to overcome this sin?!

Sadly, as it was for them, a place where we especially encounter this temptation is in our service of the Lord. Just like them, we are tempted to seek the highest and most visible positions in the church, rather than espousing genuine humility like the psalmist who wrote: **"I would rather be a doorkeeper in** the house of my God" (Psalm 84:10c).

As the apostles were, we can be so influenced by the world's view of "rank" that we think higher "rankings" in the church are more important, and thus more desirable. In our worldly flesh, we can think that the "higher and more visible" parts of the body of Christ are the most honorable. But the world's view & the Lord's view of "rank & position" stand in diametric opposition: **"On the contrary, the parts of the body that seem to be weaker are indispensable, and on those parts of the body that we think less honorable we bestow the greater honor, and our unpresentable parts are treated with greater modesty, which our more presentable parts do not require. But God has so composed the body, giving greater honor to the part that lacked it, that there may be no division in the body, but that the members may have the same care for one another. If one member suffers, all suffer together; if one member is honored, all rejoice together"** (1 Corinthians 12:22-26). So now, most importantly, what was our Lord's response to His apostles' selfish ambition? Let's unpack that text, for within it lays the keys to killing this sin.

Jesus said: **"You know that the rulers of the Gentiles lord it over them, and their great ones exercise authority over them"** (Matthew 20:25b). The Greek word translated here as "lord it over" is *katakurieuo*. It means to subdue someone, to bring them under your control, to subject them to yourself. Peter used this Greek word when he exhorted church elders to shepherd by *"not **domineering** over those in your charge, but being examples to the flock"* (1 Peter 5:3, italics mine)[12]. Now, the Greek word translated in our text as "exercise authority over" is *katexousiazó*. It means to strongly and oppressively exert authority *downwards*. One awesome fact about this word is that it *wasn't* used by secular Greek authors! It was only used in this text and in the parallel text of **Mark 10:42**[13]. In our text above, the Lord indicts "the Gentiles" for this practice. Thus, He is calling selfish ambition a *worldly* practice. We see that the "rulers" & "great ones" of this world are those who selfishly use their power to command their subjugates. That's how they all define greatness.

Jesus then said: **"It shall not be so among you. But whoever would be great among you must be your servant, and whoever would be first among you must be your slave"** (Matthew 20:26-27). The Greek word translated as "servant" here, and in 22 other places in the New Testament, is *diakonos*. When used figuratively, it means a servant who seeks what's in the best interest of others, even if it means sacrificing their own[14]. As an aside, it's also the root of the English word "deacon". The Greek word translated as "slave" here, and in 57 other places in the New Testament, is once again *doulos*. It means literally a bondservant, someone owned by another, with no legal rights to themselves[15]. However, as we study its use in Scripture when referring to Christians, we see that it's not like the modern connotation of a "slave". For as blood-purchased "slaves" of Christ, we are deeply loved & cherished by our Master. And as His "slaves," we love our Master, so we don't treat Him like a human "owner". Our "slavery" is not a mere business transaction as the world refers to it, as it's an eternal relationship of love.

As an example of this, let's take a quick look at the "Parable of the Talents," where we learn more about the kingdom of heaven. Regarding the good servant, which refers to us, we read: **"His master said to him, 'Well done, good and faithful *slave*. You were faithful with a few things, I will put you in charge of many things; enter into the joy of your *master*'"** (Matthew 25:23, NASB, italics mine). "Slave" there is our *same* Greek word. So we see, our "slave" and "servant" relationship with the Lord vastly transcends the normal limitations of those words. And thus, we know that our "slave" and "servant" relationship with our brothers and sisters in Christ must be similar. We mustn't serve them out of rote obligation, but rather out of true love and care for their well-being. If we want to be "great" in God's kingdom, we must become "slaves" of all, just like Paul was **(cf. 1 Corinthians 9:19)**.

So we must replace our selfish, worldly ambition with Godly, selfless ambition. The world says "forget selfless love, outdo everyone in *receiving* honor". But our Lord Jesus Christ says: **"Love one another with brotherly affection. Outdo one another in *showing* honor"** (Romans 12:10, italics mine). The world says "motivate *yourself*, build *yourself* up". But God commands us thus: **"encourage *one another* and build *one another* up"** (1 Thessalonians 5:11, italics mine). That is how our Lord defines true greatness. So as His people, that is a definition we all must espouse.

Jesus then said: **"even as the Son of Man came not to be served but to serve, and to give his life as a ransom for many"** (Matthew 20:28). The phrases translated as "to be served" and "to serve" in this text are both the same Greek word, *diakoneó*. It's based in one of the Greek words we just studied, *diakonos*, but this one has a more specific meaning. It means a practical, *active* care for others' needs, as the Lord leads[16]. This is the same Greek word Paul dictated to Tertius when he wrote: **"At present, however, I am going to Jerusalem *bringing aid* to the saints"** (Romans 15:25, italics mine). The whole *purpose* of Paul's travel to that city was to serve the saints there, and thus we see the active nature of that word's use. Later in the same letter, Paul asked for prayers for this service to Jerusalem, using yet another word based in *"diakonos"*. He requested prayer **"that my service for Jerusalem may be** acceptable to the saints" (Romans 15:31b). There, he used the word *diakonia*, which also has a very specific meaning. It means ministry empowered by the Holy Spirit, done with a voluntary attitude, and thus guided by faith[17].

Through all of this, we learn about the type of service to which we are called. Our service should be led and empowered by the Holy Spirit, practical, active, done joyfully and voluntarily, guided by faith, and prayed over. Now, the Greek word translated to the phrase "as a ransom" in our Matthew text above is *lutron*. It means an expiatory sacrifice to purchase the freedom of slaves. It's based in the Greek word *luó*, which means to loose, untie, release, unbind something[18]. And thus, we can further understand our "slavery". Christ the King "purchased" us by His sacrifice on the cross at Calvary to be His "slaves," and in doing this He has "released" us from the "slavery" to sin and to self!

Now that we have a deeper understanding of some of the things the Lord *taught* us about service and killing selfish ambition, let's take a look at one of the many ways in which He *demonstrated* this. As we just studied, the Lord came to "serve" and "give His life". Of the multitudinous reasons He did this, one was to be a perfect example for us, to show us that *this* is how we must live. He did this in *innumerable* ways **(cf. John 21:25)**. Right after rebutting selfish ambition, The Lord Jesus Christ performed yet another of His *unfathomable* acts.

He **"rose from supper. He laid aside his outer garments, and taking a towel, tied it around his waist. Then he poured water into a basin and began to wash the disciples' feet and to wipe them with the towel that was wrapped around him"** (John 13:4-5). Picture this scene. The perfect King of Kings, the Lord of Glory, God Himself performing one of the greatest acts of divine condescension ever. The holy Lord of Lords served His sinful followers by humbling Himself to perform one of the most menial, lowly human tasks.

To understand just how low and menial this task was, we must remember something about first-century near-Eastern culture. In that time and place, many people didn't wear shoes, and those who did wear them only wore sandals. Also, people often traveled mostly by foot. Thus, when they arrived at a destination, in this case a dinner, their feet were usually filthy, much more so than any other part of their body. As Jesus said: **"The one who has bathed does not need to wash, except for his feet"** (John 13:10a). Because of this, one of the main tasks of a *common household slave* was to wash the feet of people as they arrived at a house.

And in that, we see our Lord Jesus Christ *perfectly* illustrating what He had just taught His disciples. Unlike us, He always *perfectly* "practiced what He preached". He was demonstrating *perfectly* what it means to truly humble yourself and serve.

The world says "do everything you can to go from rags to riches, to go from a slave to a king, to go from subjugate to subjugator". Whereas we see of our Savior: **"For you know the grace of our Lord Jesus Christ, that *though he was rich, yet for your sake he became poor*, so that you by his poverty might become rich"** (2 Corinthians 8:9, italics mine). The world says "make *something* of yourself". Whereas the Lord Jesus Christ *"made himself nothing,* **taking the form of a servant, being born in the likeness of men"** (Philippians 2:7, italics mine). And the Greek word translated as "servant" there is once again *doulos*, a bond-slave.

Thus, as the body of Christ, we are commanded to **"Rejoice with those who rejoice, weep with those who weep. Live in harmony with one another. Do not be haughty, but associate** with the lowly" (Romans 12:15-16). In the context of this book, this means we are commanded to rejoice when others are blessed, not to mourn and try to "outdo" them. Remember, selfish ambition **"is not the wisdom that comes down from above, but is earthly, unspiritual, demonic"** (James 3:15).

Thus we see, selfish ambition is not a merely "personal" sin. That is, it doesn't only affect the transgressor. It affects others in the body and causes divisions. Soon after condemning "rivalries" as a "work of the flesh" **(cf. Galatians 5:19-20)**, Paul wrote: **"Let us not become** *conceited*, **provoking one another,** *envying* **one another"** (Galatians 5:26). He used strong Greek words there.

The Greek word used for "conceited" there is *kenodoxos*. It appears *only once* in Scripture. It means baseless boasting and foolish delusions of grandeur[19]. This "conceit" is "foolish" and "baseless" because we have nothing to boast about in ourselves! This is by the Lord's design, **"so that no human being might boast in the presence of God"** (1 Corinthians 1:29). Instead, we're commanded to boast in the Lord alone **(cf. Romans 5:11, Isaiah 45:25, Psalm 20:7,34:2, Jeremiah 9:23-24, Galatians 6:14, 1 Corinthians 1:31, 2 Corinthians 10:17)**!

That's why Paul says that when we boast selfishly, we "provoke" others. The Greek word translated as "provoke" in our passage above is *prokaleómai*. It also appears *only once* in Scripture and means to call someone forth for a challenge, and thus to irritate them[20]. This is easy to understand practically. Our differences and uniqueness do not in themselves cause rivalries. It's only when those things are "flaunted" in a boastful, prideful way that provocation results.

As we know, God hates pride. This is why we're commanded: **"Clothe yourselves, all of you, with humility toward one another, for '*God opposes the proud* but gives grace to the** humble'"** (1 Peter 5:5b, italics mine). I believe this is why, as temples of God's Holy Spirit **(cf. 1 Corinthians 3:16, 6:19)**, being made continually more like Jesus **(cf. 2 Corinthians 3:18, Romans 8:29)**, we too hate pride. I remember that I strongly evinced pride before I was saved and I considered it an admirable trait in those I venerated. But now that I belong to the Lord Jesus Christ, I loathe and detest pride, both in others and in myself. It's abhorrent, irksome, and wholly unattractive. That's why we are "provoked" and "irritated" by those who evince this trait. It's why it stirs up "disorder and every vile practice," and why it incites a corporate temptation to envy.

The Greek word translated as "envying" in our passage is *phthoneó*. It has the same meaning as the contemporary English phrase "sour grapes," which means to be bitter about another's blessing[21].

Indeed, the vilest crime in history stemmed from selfish ambition, the Pharisaic condemnation of the Lord Jesus Christ! Even Pontius Pilate caught onto this: **"For he perceived that it was out of envy that the chief priests had delivered him up"** (Mark 15:10). The Lord had come to point them to the Father. But their evil, selfish hearts couldn't handle someone else being more "holy" than them (ha), so they condemned God Himself!

In what other ways can we kill this sin? Let's go to another place where the same Greek word for "selfish ambition" (*eritheia*) is used and learn how.

In his letter to the church at Philippi, Paul addresses this problem and gives us another cure! In that epistle, he exhorts us: **"Do nothing out of selfish ambition or vain conceit, but *in humility consider others better than yourselves*"** (Philippians 2:3, italics mine). *There* is another simple, yet profound, key to killing this attitude: *humility*. Just as this Godly character trait is a key to killing vanity, it's also a key to killing selfish ambition. Espousing true humility means considering others better than yourself, not in some faux self-deprecating way, but in true self-abnegation. It means abdicating our own self-appointed "throne," putting God there where he belongs, and then placing others before us there!

So how do we further put this into practice? Let's keep cruising through Philippians 2 to learn from Paul: **"Let each of you look not only to his own interests, but also to the interests of others"** (v. 4) We must proactively pray for, foster, and then evince an attitude of genuine care for the well-being of others. We are God's children. We cannot, and must not, espouse the "ironic detachment" philosophy of this fallen world. They can walk past someone in need without a second look, but as Christians we are admonished: **"if anyone has the world's goods and sees his brother in need, yet closes his heart against him, how does God's love abide in him?"** (1 John 3:17).

We don't live in a vacuum. No man, and especially no Christian, is an island[22]. This is an especially large battle for American Christians, as our culture is extremely individualistic. But we must remember once again, *we are not our own* **(cf. 1 Corinthians 6:19-20)**. We don't have the right to live a selfish life. We must care about the needs of the saints as much, if not more, than our own. As Barnes has written: "No one is at liberty to live for himself or to disregard the wants of others[23]."

The fallen world says: "live for yourself, do what makes *you* happy, forget everyone else". The Lord says: **"For none of us lives to himself, and none of us dies to himself"** (Romans 14:7). And the context of that verse is in *loving* our brothers.

Therein lies yet another cure for selfish ambition: *love*. As Paul writes to the church at Colossae, and thus us: **"Put on then, as God's chosen ones, holy and beloved, *compassionate hearts*,** *kindness, humility, meekness, and patience,* **bearing with one another**...*And above all these put on love,* **which binds everything together in perfect harmony"** (Colossians 3:12,14, italics mine). Thus, we have a choice to make. We can treat our brethren as competitors, thus making them foes to be vanquished; or, we can "put on love" for them, treating them as the *family* they all are. The former is sin, the latter is real obedience.

If you're locked up in selfish ambition, the peace of mind you seek will not be found by attempting to satiate your pride through the "outdoing" of your brethren. As our brother Matthew Henry said: "Christ came to humble us, let there not be among us a spirit of pride. Neither inward nor outward peace can be enjoyed, without lowliness of mind[24]."

Indeed, as we've learned, *that* is true peace of mind. Brothers and sisters, now that we have all of this *truth,* let us fully submit to the heart changes that will result. Let us forever forsake the empty well of sin that is selfish ambition and run to the overflowing wells of humility and love.

So Who are They?

"the brother for whom Christ died."

(1 Corinthians 8:11b)

Now that we better understand the sin of seeing our brothers and sisters through the lying eyes of envy and discontentment, let's see what they look like through the truth of gospel glasses.

Just like you, your brethren are deeply and personally loved children of God. Just like you, they are His elect. Just like you, they are people for whom the Lord Jesus Christ lived, died, and rose again. He didn't do this only for you, or only for them. He did it to build His body: **"For just as the body is one and has** many members, and all the members of the body, though many, are one body, so it is with Christ"** (1 Corinthians 12:12).

In our diversity, we see more of God's complexity. He could have easily made us all identical to each other. But He didn't, and that is beautiful, for even though we're all different, in the body of Christ we are **"one body and one Spirit—just as you were called to the one hope that belongs to your call— one Lord, one faith, one baptism, one God and Father of all, who is over all and through all and in all"** (Ephesians 4:4-6).

Just as the animals God created are incredibly diverse, we, as His image bearers, reflect that same ingenuity, except on a much higher level.

The world, in its apt cynicism, loves to say: "you're *not* a beautiful and unique snowflake, you're just like everyone else, nothing special". But the Lord says you are **"fearfully and wonderfully made"** (Psalm 139:14). Of all men, it is written that God **"made them a little lower than the angels and crowned them with glory and honor"** (Psalm 8:5, NIV). This knowledge must not puff you up with pride, but rather it must help you understand exactly who you and others truly are.

<u>Just like you, your brethren</u> are continually being made more like our Lord Jesus: **"all, with unveiled face, beholding the glory of the Lord, are being transformed into the same image from one degree of glory to another. For this comes from the Lord who is the Spirit"** (2 Corinthians 3:18).

One of the major ways the evil one tempts us to discontented envy of our brethren is by feeding us the lie that we are somehow more "deserving" of blessings than they are. Sadly, this temptation most often occurs when we are following hard after the Lord, seeking His face and doing His work.

When we are growing strong like this in our Biblical

knowledge, in our relationship with God, and in experiential sanctification, our flesh loves to give in to this temptation to prideful self-righteousness. When this happens, we can start behaving just like the elder brother did in "The Parable of the Prodigal Son" recorded in **Luke 15**.

There, when the "sinful" younger brother returns home in repentance, the Father showers love and blessings on him. Seeing this, the "holier than thou" elder brother angrily rebukes his own Father, saying: **"Look! All these years I've been slaving for you and never disobeyed your orders. Yet you never gave me even a young goat so I could celebrate with my friends"** (Luke 15:29, NIV). My dear brethren, we're not immune from this.

When we're using our singleness like we should be, by proactively & prolifically serving God's kingdom, we can be tempted to look down on our ostensibly "less sanctified" married brethren and grumble about their blessings. In our hearts, we can be tempted to say "God, I serve you so much, and yet you bless *them* with [insert blessing], why?"

When this happens, we've fallen headlong into what our brother Timothy Keller calls "elder brother syndrome"[25], and we actually "divorce" our own brothers and sisters in our hearts. We effectively end up referring to our brethren just like the elder brother did, as he said to his Father: **"when this *son of yours* came"** (Luke 15:30, italics mine). Catch that? He called his own brother "this son of yours," rather than "my brother". So deep was his self-righteousness that he wouldn't even accept his younger brother as a family member because of his own sinful envy and discontentment.

Indeed, as our brother Jerry Bridges penned: "We are all legalistic by nature; that is, we innately think so much performance by us earns so much blessing from God[26]." Beloved, let this not be so for us! Once again, the key to victory and freedom lies in seeing all through gospel glasses. Through them, we see that our "performance" earns nothing of God's favor because that is given solely by God's grace in the Lord Jesus Christ alone! No matter how much we "do" for the Lord and His kingdom, we don't "earn" anything more than anyone else. None of us "deserve" any of God's blessings. *Everything* we have is a gift of God's grace! As Bridges writes: "We are brought into God's kingdom by grace; we are sanctified by grace; we receive both temporal and spiritual blessings by grace; we are motivated to obedience by grace; we are called to serve and enabled to serve by grace; we receive strength to endure trials by grace; and finally, we are glorified by grace. The entire Christian life is lived under the reign of God's grace[27]."

Killing this toxic, "holier than thou elder brother syndrome" is one of the exact reasons why Paul exhorted us thus, **"that none of you may be puffed up in favor of one against another. For who sees anything different in you? What do you have that you did not receive? If then you received it, why do you boast as if you did not receive it?"** (1 Corinthians 4:6b-7). The blessings of your brethren, be they marriage, kids, or anything else, are all unmerited gifts of God's grace. The blessings of *your* life, be they high levels of service, sanctification, knowledge, and free time, are also all unmerited gifts of God's amazing grace.

So why boast or complain otherwise? Instead, as we proactively and prolifically serve our Lord, let's simply see our service as He directed us: **"So you also, when you have done all that you were commanded, say, 'We are unworthy servants; we have only done what was our duty'"** (Luke 17:10).

Rather than acting like the elder brother, let's instead personally imbibe the Father's loving response to his obedient child: **"Son, you are always with me, and all that is mine is yours"** (Luke 15:31). You see, regardless of His blessings on others, all that is God's is ours. Praise the Lord!

<u>Just like you, your brethren</u> experience trials and tribulations, regardless of their marital status.

One of the evil one's most prevalent lies to single Christians is that they're the only Christians who suffer. But our Lord Jesus Christ said: **"In the world you will have tribulation"** (John 16:33b), and we know logically that this truth applies to all Christians. However, we know experientially that our emotions often ignore logic, especially when under trial and temptation.

In the midst of your own personal tribulation, the sight of smiling faces can bring the temptation to think that you're alone in your suffering. This is especially prevalent if you don't live with other Christians. Christians in "co-habitation" see each other's problems. For example, married Christians experience firsthand the trials of the brother or sister to whom they're wed.

For a single Christian who only interacts with other Christians in an "official" church capacity, they may not see this reality. This ignorance is further exacerbated because most people put on their "shiny, happy face" when in public, so no one else sees their problems. Sunday services are filled with this "plastic perfection," which gives the illusory veneer of painless, smooth lives. Small talk is exchanged in church courtyards post-service. Shallow pleasantries are passed around and everyone hides all their flaws.

This brings the temptation for us to hop in our cars afterward and get lost in thought about the seeming "perfection" of others' lives in comparison to ours. What we don't see is that once those couples and their kids hop in their car, their lives are just like ours. They too face their own "conflagrations" and trials behind closed doors.

The evil one jumps on this opportunity to attack, whispering all sorts of lies in your ear. These lies are designed to make you fall into discontentment, envy, despair, and anger. Sadly, countless suicides have been caused by this exact spiritual attack. And believing this lie has caused multitudinous more cases of depression.

Brethren, achieving victory over these types of attacks is why we've received these commands:

> **"Resist the devil, and he will flee from you."**
> (James 4:7b)

> **"Resist him, firm in your faith,
> knowing that the same kinds of suffering are
> being experienced by your brotherhood throughout the world."**
> (1 Peter 5:9)

> **"Put on all of God's armor so
> that you will be able to stand
> firm against all strategies of the devil."**
> (Ephesians 6:11, NLT)

Phileo...

> **"In this is love, not that we have
> loved God but that he loved us and sent
> his Son to be the propitiation for our sins."**
> (1 John 4:10)

Here's our counter-attack: Brotherly Love.

Here's why and how that love is our greatest possible offensive weapon against evil schemes:

> **"We love each other because he loved us first."**
>
> (1 John 4:19)

It's the *gospel* that empowers our love!
It's the *gospel* that triumphs over the lies!

> **"This is the victory that has overcome the world—our faith."**
>
> (1 John 5:4b)

Through gospel glasses, we see just how much God loves us personally. Through gospel glasses, we see that God loves all of His other adopted children like that as well, regardless of any of the differences in their earthly lives.

Through gospel glasses, we walk into the assembly and see that **"The rich and the poor meet together; the LORD is the maker of them all"** (Proverbs 22:2). Through gospel glasses, we reason truthfully with ourselves: **"Did not he who made me in the womb make them? Did not the same one form us both within our mothers?"** (Job 31:15).

Through gospel glasses, we see that when people **"measure themselves by one another and compare themselves with one another, they are without understanding"** (2 Corinthians 10:12b); but when we're measured with the Lord, we all **"fall short of the glory of God"** (Romans 3:23b).

Through gospel glasses, we see that because our Lord Jesus Christ lived and died for us...God freely, completely, eternally, and unconditionally loves us all. Knowing this, our *only* acceptable response is to do the same, to *become* the same love.

Love is who we are now because our God is love **(cf. 1 John 3:14)**. When we look at ourselves and each other through gospel glasses, this love flows freely, and it delivers us from all forms of hatred, such as envy and discontentment. **"For the whole law is fulfilled in one word: 'You shall love your neighbor as yourself'"** (Galatians 5:14).

It's radical and amazing love...because the gospel is radical and amazing love...because God is radical and amazing love. Bless His name forever!

Beloved, will you stop looking at your brethren through lying eyes? Will you put your gospel glasses on? If you do, you'll be able to look at their blessings and hear the Lord lovingly say:

"What is that to you? I love you just as much. Follow me!"

Section B:

Change Diapers or Lives?

THE STEWARDSHIP OF LIBERTY - SECTION INTRO

"The seed that fell on good soil represents those who truly hear and understand God's word and produce a harvest of thirty, sixty, or even a hundred times as much as had been planted!"
(Matthew 13:23, NLT)

Get this: the average baby goes through 7,000 diapers[28] during their first three years of life...wow! Now there is absolutely no arguing the truth that **"children are a heritage from the LORD, the fruit of the womb a reward"** (Psalm 127:3). But for most of us, we don't yet have any children. Or more accurately, we don't yet have any *physical* children.

This means we all have a very big choice to make.

We can idly bide our time, just "waiting in the wings" until we have physical offspring. *Or,* we can maximize the *blessing* of singleness we've received and produce as many *spiritual* children as possible.

However, this "choice" is not really one of personal preference. Rather, in actuality, it's a choice between living obediently or disobediently to God.

Freedom...

> "And if you were free when the Lord called you,
> you are now a slave of Christ."
>
> (1 Corinthians 7:22b, NLT)

Single Christians are the freest people of all, for several reasons. First and foremost, because as we studied earlier, in Christ we are truly and completely free! The Lord has set us free from both the eternal penalty *and* the temporal power of sin. In Christ, we are free from condemnation **(cf. Romans 8:1)**, free from death **(cf. John 11:25)**, and free from sin's dominion **(cf. Romans 6:14)**. This gives us freedom from all legalistic "religion," and it gives us freedom from all guilt and shame.

Secondarily, on top of this awesome freedom given by amazing unmerited grace, most of us have large earthly freedom from the multitudinous responsibilities that come with having a spouse and kids. To be in this state is an unspeakable gift! Thus, my dear single brethren, please see it accordingly.

However, there are many temptations for single Christians to use their freedom in ungodly ways. Not having a spouse or kids, much of our time is spent by ourselves, and this can lead to the temptations of self-centeredness and unfruitful use of time. That is why the Lord has commanded us to not abuse our freedom by admonishing us thus:

> "For you were called to freedom, brothers.
> Only do not use your freedom as an opportunity

for the flesh, but through love serve one another."
>
> (Galatians 5:13)

> "Live as people who are free,
> not using your freedom as a cover-up for evil,
> but living as servants of God."
>
> (1 Peter 2:16)

We Are All Slaves...

The Greek word for slave is *"doulos,"* and this word is used many times in the New Testament to speak of us. And just how are we slaves? First of all, we're now slaves to God and His righteousness:

> "Just as you used to offer yourselves as slaves
> to impurity and to ever-increasing wickedness,
> so now offer yourselves as slaves
> to righteousness leading to holiness."
>
> (Romans 6:19b, NIV)

All of us were at one time slaves to sin and ourselves, but the Lord Jesus Christ has set us free from this slavery. In doing so, He has also made us slaves to righteousness. This slavery is not a works based soteriology, but rather the fact that we are *bought* slaves, purchased on the Cross at Calvary! It cost the Lord the highest price imaginable, His own precious blood, His perfect life and death, to deliver us from sin and sin's penalty.

Thus, we are now His. We no longer own the rights to ourselves or our lives. A common temptation for us as singles is to think that time is "ours" to do with as we will, but that is wrong. It's *His* time, not ours. It's *His* will be done, not ours. Through prayer and time in His word, we become able to discern exactly what His will is for us. And first and foremost, we must remember that His will for us is to continually grow in personal, practical holiness: **"For this is the will of God, your sanctification"** (1 Thessalonians 4:3a). The Lord both calls and empowers us to live this out. For even though we were all free people (meaning single and not imprisoned) before Christ, we now know this truth: **"Likewise he who was free when called is a slave of Christ"** (1 Corinthians 7:22).

Picture a slave auction with billions of slaves on a giant stage waiting to be purchased. Now imagine the Lord Jesus Christ walking up and handpicking a select few of these slaves...and you're one of them! This really happened. The Lord has elected you and me; He has ransomed us from death and the grave. He has saved us from the slavery block that leads to God's righteous, eternal wrath! And this was not of our own merit or worthiness, but by God's sovereign election of grace alone. This must be ever in our minds, to remember that we now belong to Him alone, not to ourselves. **"Or do you not know that your body is a temple of the Holy Spirit within you, whom you have from God? You are not your own, for you were bought with a price. So glorify God in your body"** (1 Corinthians 6:19-20).

Secondarily, we are now slaves to our brothers and sisters in Christ. Greatness in the kingdom of God isn't measured by how much we get; instead, it's measured by how much we *give* others:

> **"But whoever would be great among you must be your servant, and whoever would be first among you must be your slave, even as the Son of Man came not to be served but to serve, and to give his life as a ransom for many."**
>
> (The Lord Jesus Christ, Matthew 20:26b-28)

> "Love one another with brotherly affection.
> Outdo one another in *showing* honor."
>
> (Romans 12:10, italics mine)

Thus, we are to use our freedom to *serve, bless, love, and honor* God and others, not ourselves! As singles, we have relatively copious amounts of free time, even those of us with full time jobs. This time is a gift from the Lord, a gift He has given us for the benefit of both the unsaved through our evangelism and the body of Christ through discipleship.

Remember, as we studied in a previous chapter, it is God **"who comforts us in all our affliction, so that we may be able to comfort those who are in any affliction, with the comfort with which we ourselves are comforted by God"** (2 Corinthians 1:4). Thus, we must use the strength and wisdom we've gained, and continue to gain from our trials, to in-turn, comfort and strengthen our brethren.

In **1 Corinthians 12**, Paul tells us about the spiritual gifts that all Christians have. In verse 11 he instructs us: **"All these are empowered by one and the same Spirit, who apportions to each one individually as he wills."** And *why* does the Lord give us these gifts? In verse 7 Paul answers that question: **"To each is given the manifestation of the Spirit for the common good."** For the *common good*, that is, for the good of the Body of Christ, not for ourselves. We are all one body with many members. We are given blessings to *give* blessings.

What has the Lord given *you* to bless your brothers and sisters? I'm sure there are many gifts! For every gift, there is a practical way to use it for the benefit of the Body. In James 1:17 we learn that **"Every good gift and every perfect gift is from above,** coming down from the Father of lights with whom there is no variation or shadow due to change." Later in that same epistle, James tells us one of the reasons why we don't get certain things we ask for: **"You ask and do not receive, because you ask wrongly, to spend it on *your* passions"** (4:3, italics mine). What we learn from those two verses is that every good and perfect gift is from the Lord, given for the benefit of others, not for indulging our selfish passions...

Prayerfully study 1 Corinthians 12, asking God to show you the gifts He has given you and how He wants you to use them. Remember this: God has so composed the body **"that there may be no division in the body, but that the members may have the same care for one another"** (1 Corinthians 12:25).

Before I got saved, I was probably the biggest misanthrope on the planet. My past life was just as Paul described: **"For we ourselves were once foolish, disobedient, led astray, slaves to various passions and pleasures,** *passing our days in malice and envy, hated by others and hating one another"* (Titus 3:3, italics mine). I hated everyone and everything, including myself. In addition, I carried vast amounts of jealous envy of others in my heart.

That was my life until my salvation in Jesus Christ. Again, just as Paul described, I was lost: **"But when the goodness and loving kindness of God our Savior appeared, he saved us, not because of works done by us in righteousness, but according to his own mercy, by the washing of regeneration and renewal of the Holy Spirit, whom he poured out on us richly through Jesus Christ our Savior, so that being justified by his grace we might become heirs according to the hope of eternal life"** (Titus 3:4-7). And now, by that saving, sanctifying, transformative grace of God...I love my brothers and sisters so much! This is one of the ways that we know we're saved, that we're now God's kids: **"We know that we have passed out of death into life, because we love the brothers. Whoever does not love abides in death"** (1 John 3:14).

So now that we love our siblings, we must remember the plight of our family in this world. We are sheep among wolves. We are aliens and strangers in this world. Remember our Lord's exhortation: **"If the world hates you, know that it has hated me before it hated you. If you were of the world, the world would love you as its own; but because you are not of the world, but I chose you out of the world, therefore the world hates you"** (John 15:18-19). After experiencing this hatred firsthand, our brother says in his first epistle: **"Do not be surprised, brothers, that the world hates you"** (1 John 3:13). So it's important for us to understand that all we have in this fallen, evil world is God and each other. Thus, we must stick together and assist each other in every way we can. A stray, lone sheep has no chance of survival; a wolf will pick it off in no time. It's only when sheep travel and move in their flock that they can survive among wolves. And it is our great and perfect Shepherd who provides us this protection.

It is of paramount importance that we reiterate this truth: the Christian life is not meant to be a solitary life. For fellowship is both commanded & necessary: **"And let us consider how to stir up one another to love and good works, not neglecting to meet together, as is the habit of some, but encouraging one another, and all the more as you see the Day drawing near"** (Hebrews 10:24-25).

Efficacious Efficiency...

"Look carefully then how you walk, not as unwise but as wise, making the best use of the time, because the days are evil.

> **Therefore do not be foolish,
> but understand what the will of the Lord is."**
>
> (Ephesians 5:15-17)

That passage is an imperative command for us to redeem the time in godly ways and its implications are really quite extensive. You see, we are all going to be called to account for the "Return on Investment," or the "ROI," we have produced with the blessings, or "investments," God has given us.

We learn more about this in "The Parable of the Talents," recorded in **Matthew 25**. There, the Lord Jesus Christ tells an allegorical story about a wealthy man who, before heading away on a journey, **"called his servants and entrusted to them his property"** (Matthew 25:14b). He gave each one of them a different amount of money, though each one received a veritable *fortune*: **"To one he gave five talents, to another two, to another one, to each according to his ability"** (Matthew 25:15a). Now a "talent" was the equivalent of over *half a million dollars* in today's money! Thus, even though there were varying degrees of blessings distributed, each servant no doubt received a vast sum of blessings!

This parable is very easy to understand. For the wealthy man is King Jesus and we are His servants. **"Now after a long time the master of those servants came and settled accounts with them"** (Matthew 25:19). To the two servants who wisely produced a positive ROI, the Master said: **"Well done, good and faithful servant. You have been faithful over a little; I will set you over much. Enter into the joy of your master"** (Matthew 25:21,23).

But to the "servant" who passively sat on his blessings and produced no real ROI, the master said: **"You wicked and slothful servant! You knew that I reap where I have not sown and gather** where I scattered no seed? Then you ought to have invested my money with the bankers, and at my coming I should have received what was my own with interest. So take the talent from him and give it to him who has the ten talents. For to everyone who has will more be given, and he will have an abundance. But from the one who has not, even what he has will be taken away. For to everyone who has will more be given, and he will have an abundance. But from the one who has not, even what he has will be taken away. And cast the worthless servant into the outer darkness. In that place there will be weeping and gnashing of teeth"** (Matthew 25:26-30). There, we see something very serious. All *real* Christians *will* produce fruit! The only question is, *how much* fruit? You see, that "wicked and slothful servant" was cast into hell not because he was a Christian who didn't maximize his blessings. He was put in outer darkness because he wasn't a Christian at all. He never produced any fruit because he was never a believer. Whereas the two believers, because they were empowered by the Holy Spirit, both produced fruit (of varying amounts). As our brother said, **"For as the body apart from the spirit is dead, so also faith apart from works is dead"** (James 2:26).

This isn't legalism. This just means that those who truly belong to Christ will always be compelled to live that faith out in their works. Even the thief on the cross, who got saved on the day of his death, started bearing fruit immediately by becoming an instant evangelist **(cf. Luke 23:40-43)**.

All Christians, regardless of marital status, have received "talents," or gifts, from the Lord. As singles, two of the many gifts we've received are the *time* and *freedom* inherent in our singleness. And we *are* going to be called to account for how we've maximized these blessings for God's glorious Kingdom and the good of others. As Paul wrote about the faithfulness and fruitfulness of our service to the Lord: **"On the judgment day, fire will reveal what kind of work each builder has done. The fire will show if a person's work has any value. If the work survives, that builder will receive a reward. But if the work is burned up, the builder will suffer great loss. The builder will be saved, but like someone barely escaping through a wall of flames"** (1 Corinthians 3:13-15, NLT). Do you want your work to receive a reward, or be consumed by fire? This choice is really a very easy one to make! **"So you, too, must keep watch! For you don't know what day your Lord is coming"** (Matthew 24:42, NLT). Thus, once again the question comes down to this: when the Lord calls you home, which very well could be extremely soon, do you want to hear Him say "Well done"? But of course!

So how do we make sure we hear those sweet words when we enter the presence of our Lord? How do we fruitfully perform the faithful work and service that our Lord loves to reward us for?

By *maximizing* His ROI on the blessings He's given us! In our immediate context, it means we do this by using our singleness to both produce and nurture as many spiritual children as we possibly can!

We are the "seed that fell on good soil". So now, the only *real* question is: will we produce "30, 60, or 100 fold fruit" with our lives? No matter the size of each of our "harvests," what matters is that they're maximized by "each according to his ability".

How we can accomplish this, specifically and practically, is the subject of this section's study. So let's jump into God's word and learn how we can become "wise, making the best use of the time, not being foolish, but understanding what the will of the Lord is". Let's learn how to maximize the huge freedom we currently enjoy, our freedom for slavery to God and others. Let's learn how to prayerfully and proactively use this very special time in our lives, while we're not changing thousands of diapers...to change thousands of lives for eternity.

In this way, whether or not it is ever the Lord's will for us to raise physical progeny, our prolific and faithful Kingdom service will allow us to joyfully look forward to hearing the greatest words that could ever fall on the ears of any Christian:

> **"Well done, good and faithful servant.**
> **You have been faithful over a little;**
> **I will set you over much.**
> **Enter into the joy of your master."**
>
> (Matthew 25:21,23)

BE FRUITFUL AND MULTIPLY...

> "Jesus came and said to them,
> 'All authority in heaven and on earth has been given to me.
> Go therefore and make disciples of all nations, baptizing them
> in the name of the Father and of the Son and of the Holy Spirit,
> teaching them to observe all that I have commanded you.'"
>
> (Matthew 28:18-20a)

When you first read this chapter's title on the "Contents" page, you may have wondered what you'd find here. You may have thought to yourself, "how could a chapter with that title exist in a book on singleness?". Well, the reason is this: the word "multiply" has now been redefined for us! Thus, it's very important to know what *true* "fruitful multiplication" and "reproduction" now means for us.

In order to get there though, we need a little history lesson. So let's go back...*way* back...to the beginning...to the very creation of human beings.

In the very first book of His holy word, we see one of the Lord's first commands to Adam and Eve:

> **"God said to them, "Be fruitful and multiply and fill the earth"**
> (Genesis 1:28)

And then later, after God had destroyed earth and killed most of humanity by flood, He commanded Noah and his family once again in a similar manner:

> **"As for you, be fruitful and increase in number; multiply on the earth and increase upon it."**
> (Genesis 9:7, NIV)

And even later, the Lord God commanded Jacob:

> **"May God Almighty bless you and give you many children. And may your descendants multiply and become many nations!"**
> (Genesis 28:3, NLT)

Reading verses like these has caused many a single Christian to lament their lack of children.

But this lamentation must not exist any longer!

Exegesis...

> **"But their minds were made dull, for to this day the same veil remains when the old covenant is read. It has not been removed, because only in Christ is it taken away."**
> (2 Corinthians 3:14, NIV)

What's needed is a proper understanding of the context of those commands. They are, of course, all Old Testament commands given under the old covenant.

Through contextual study, we gain a stronger comprehension of the reasons why such physical reproduction was commanded for those people.

For Adam and Eve it's obvious; they were the only two human beings on the planet then.

For Noah and his sons, it's a very similar story. Their eight-person family represented the entirety of the human population on earth at that moment.

For Jacob, aka "Israel," though, the command had infinitely deeper implications, carrying with it an eternal, perfect promise. It was a reiteration of "the great promise" God had made to Jacob's grandpa, Abraham, when He said: **"I will make you extremely fruitful. Your descendants will become many nations, and kings will be among them! I will confirm my covenant with you and your descendants after you, from generation to generation. This is the everlasting covenant: I will always be your God and the God of your descendants after you. And I will give the entire land of Canaan, where you now live as a foreigner, to you and your descendants. It will be their possession forever, and I will be their God"** (Genesis 17:6-8, NLT).

And there we see *the* key reason that Israel was commanded to physically multiply prolifically: the Messiah was going to come through their lineage!

So, throughout those times, God's people were all looking forward to that single event: the coming of their Savior! All the prophets spoke of Him, all wanted Him to come, and of course, He wasn't going to come through their lineage unless people kept reproducing. Thus, all the peoples of Israel wanted to be an ancestor to the coming Lord. As such, to not have children was to remove the possibility of being a blessed ancestor of the promised Savior and thus, bear societal shame and reproach. So if you were a childless Israelite back then, you might have had cause to be woeful. But today you don't because all of that was about to change...

The arrival of The King...

"For unto you is born this day in the city of David a Savior, who is Christ the Lord."

(Luke 2:11)

At long last, the promised One had arrived! Our Lord and Savior Jesus Christ has already been born, lived His prophesied perfect life, died on a cross, and risen again to redeem us eternally! The focal point of the Abrahamic command to physically "be fruitful and multiply" has now been once-and-for-all fulfilled perfectly and completely! Through Paul, the LORD has perfectly explained this: **"God gave the promises to Abraham and his child. And notice that the Scripture doesn't say 'to his children,' as if it meant many descendants. Rather, it says 'to his child'** — **and that, of course, means Christ"** (Galatians 3:16, NLT, cf. Genesis 12:7).

The Shift...

"As it is written in Isaiah the prophet,
"Behold, I send my messenger before your face,
who will prepare your way,
the voice of one crying in the wilderness:
'Prepare the way of the Lord, make his paths straight,'"

(Mark 1:2-3)

That verse is about John the Baptist, *the* herald who would announce the coming arrival of King Jesus, the Savior who was going to change *everything* in the whole world. John shouted those words during the inter-testamental period, the time of "the great shift" from the Old Covenant to the New. As John told the "most Jewish of Jews," the members of the "elite" Sanhedrin, **"Don't just say to each other, 'We're safe, for we are descendants of Abraham.' That means nothing, for I tell you, God can create children of Abraham from these very stones. I baptize with water those who repent of their sins and turn to God. But someone is coming soon who is greater than I am—so much greater that I'm not worthy even to be his slave and carry his sandals. He will baptize you with the Holy Spirit and with fire"** (Matthew 3:9,11, NLT). Indeed, the One who is far mightier than all was about to usher in a whole new covenant!

And so today, **"This means that Abraham's physical descendants are not necessarily children of God. Only the children of the promise are considered to be Abraham's children"** (Romans 9:8, NLT).

No Baby, No Cry...

"The next day John saw Jesus coming toward him and said, "Look, the Lamb of God, who takes away the sin of the world!"

(John 1:29, NIV)

John's statement there marked the official start of the public ministry of the King of Kings and Lord of Lords, the God-Man who would forever change the world! As we just studied and now see, the original Abrahamic promise was a prophetic foreshadowing of the gospel! As Paul has written: **"The real** children of Abraham, then, are those who put their faith in God. What's more, the Scriptures looked forward to this time when God would declare the Gentiles to be righteous because of their faith. God proclaimed this good news to Abraham long ago when he said, 'All nations will be blessed through you.' So all who put their faith in Christ share the same blessing Abraham received because of his faith" (Galatians 3:7-9, NLT).

That is why physical reproduction is no longer a command for God's people. It's why the blood of goats and bulls is no longer required for sins, as that was never truly sufficient in the first place! **"That is why, when Christ came into the world, he said to God, 'You did not want animal sacrifices or sin offerings. But you have given me a body to offer'"** (Hebrews 10:5). Our Lord Jesus Christ has now, once and for all, fulfilled God's physical demands!

Same Command, New Obedience...

"If you love me, you will keep my commandments."
(The Lord Jesus Christ, John 14:15)

Now before our Lord Jesus left the earth, He gave us the command from Matthew 28 that opened this chapter. We are no longer commanded to go and reproduce physically, but we *are* commanded to "fruitfully multiply" via spiritual reproduction!

Accordingly, that should be the foremost overarching concentration of our lives — *making* disciples, birthing spiritual "babies"; not worrying about whether or not we're making physical babies.

We are reminded of this paradigm shift in the New Covenant when Jesus said: **"If anyone comes to me and does not hate his own father and mother and wife and CHILDREN and brothers** and sisters, yes, and even his own life, he cannot be my disciple" (Luke 14:26, emphasis mine). There, our Lord shows that no longer must our life emphasis be on building and growing our human families, but on building and growing our spiritual families. And that means our brothers and sisters in the Lord!

This point is further illustrated by the fact that the Lord said: **"Who is my mother, and who are my brothers?" And stretching out his hand toward his disciples, he said, "Here are my mother and my brothers! For whoever does the will of my Father in heaven is my brother and sister and mother"** (Matthew 12:48b-50). The Lord's family, and thus ours, were His *spiritual* family...not His physical.

Brethren, as we see, we *must* love God and His people more than anyone else, including our physical families if they're unbelievers! This is a truth shown even in the Old Testament, where we learn from the godly example of the Levites. When Moses told them to kill all their families and friends who were not on God's side, they obeyed. Moses told them: **"Today you have ordained yourselves for the service of the LORD, for you obeyed him even though it meant killing your own sons and brothers. Today you have earned a blessing"** (cf. Exodus 32:25-29, NLT). That's why Moses again praised them thus: **"The Levites obeyed your word and guarded your covenant. They were more loyal to you than to their own parents. They ignored their relatives and did not acknowledge their own children"** (Deuteronomy 33:9, NLT).

Contemporaneously, we're obviously not called to physically "kill" our families or friends who are in rebellion against God. However we *are* sometimes called to "kill" our relationships with them if they refuse to come to Christ. As Paul exhorted, **"Do not be unequally yoked with unbelievers. For what partnership has** righteousness with lawlessness? Or what fellowship has light with darkness?"** (2 Corinthians 6:14). Now, God commands us to honor our parents whether or not they're believers, and to raise any physical children given to us in the Lord, regardless of their spiritual state. So, practically for us as single Christians, this means that outside of our parents and physical children, our spiritual family takes precedence over our physical families.

None of this is to say that Jesus forbade marriage and the commensurate physical reproduction in any way; in fact, He did the opposite by reiterating and upholding the standards **(cf. Matthew 19:3-9)**! Thus, we now better understand the context of New Testament verses like these: **"So I advise these younger widows to marry again, have children, and take care of their own homes. Then the enemy will not be able to say anything against them"** (1 Timothy 5:14,NLT); **"An elder must live a blameless life. He must be faithful to his wife, and his children must be believers who don't have a reputation for being wild or rebellious"** (Titus 1:6, NLT). Those are not universal commands for all Christians to make physical kids. They are commands that pertain to specific groups of believers' living witness.

As the Lord Jesus said, **"Humans can reproduce only human life, but the Holy Spirit gives birth to spiritual life"** (John 3:6, NLT). Thus, in the post-resurrection New Testament, we do not see commands to physically repopulate earth, nor do we see any physically barren women lamenting over that fact.

What we *do* see is that our Lord has shifted the reproductive concentration of His people from the physical to the spiritual. That's why it is written of us Christians, **"They are reborn—not with a physical birth resulting from human passion or plan, but a birth that comes from God"** (John 1:13, NLT). Thus, let's learn how to live accordingly, as the spiritual children of God.

Mustard Trees...

> "Here is another illustration Jesus used:
> 'The Kingdom of Heaven is like a mustard seed planted in a field. It is the smallest of all seeds, but it becomes the largest of garden plants; it grows into a tree, and birds come and make nests in its branches.'"
>
> (Matthew 13:31-32, NLT)

As a single Christian, you can be tempted to think, "how can I, just one person, possibly make an impact for God's Kingdom?". But never forget this: the worldwide body of Christ started with a small group of people in an upper room in Jerusalem! They were obedient to the Lord's command to go and preach the Gospel to all the world. And now, 2,000 years later, *you* are a part of that very same body of believers, living in a place that's most likely very far geographically from the nation of Israel.

Beloved, it's the Lord of Lords who builds His church, by the power of God the Holy Spirit! Hence, it's not the amount of believers or size of churches that determines a ministry's fruitfulness, for it is *God* who bears that fruit through His people. So, when even one believer like *you*, in obedience to your Lord, plants a "small mustard seed" of truth, God can grow that ministry into a giant "mustard tree" of saints! Thus, don't ever give in to the lie that your service to God as a single person will be fruitless, for God has both commanded and promised: **"Always work enthusiastically for the Lord, for you know that *nothing* you do for the Lord is *ever* useless"** (1 Corinthians 15:58b, italics mine). *Ever.*

So, it's time to go from mustard seed to mustard tree. It's time to fulfill *your* great commission and start reproducing!

Fertility...

> "I planted, Apollos watered, but *God gave the growth.*"
>
> (1 Corinthians 3:6, italics mine)

Accordingly, brethren, please prayerfully consider this. The desire to have physical children is noble and there's nothing wrong with it, if it's for Godly reasons. But consider this huge blessing you currently enjoy: virtually unlimited ministry size!

Let me explain. If you have a spouse and 2 kids, you have a household ministry of 3 people. While serving them is awesome, they are going to take up most of your ministry time. Thus, your ministry size is limited by both practicality and responsibility.

But since you're single, your scope, size and breadth of ministry can be much larger and wider!

Anytime you're not working you can be serving! You can actively participate in *multiple* ministries! You have the freedom to go on an overseas mission at the drop of a hat. In a ministry like that, your ministry reach can be enormously broad and wide!

We need to truly and completely examine our capacities to serve the Lord and be a blessing to others. For singles, these opportunities are huge!

Beloved, as a single, your "womb" is not at all "barren". In fact, it's incredibly fertile! So, it's time to start using it. It's time to start "giving birth" to as many spiritual children as the Lord will allow! It's time for us all to "Be Fruitful and Multiply"!

So how do we do this?

> "**They preached the gospel** in that city and won a large number of **disciples.** *Then they returned* **to Lystra, Iconium and Antioch,** *strengthening the disciples and encouraging*

them to remain true to the faith."
(Acts 14:21-22a, NIV, Italics Mine)

That passage illustrates this fact: our Lord's great commission is a command that has two parts. First and foremost, it is a call to evangelism; a call to proselytize the lost in this fallen world. Second, it is a call to discipleship; a call to proactively teach, grow, and mature our brethren. Accordingly, let's study the parts in that order.

Scream the Gospel from the Rooftops...

"O Zion, messenger of good news, shout from the mountaintops! Shout it louder, O Jerusalem. Shout, and do not be afraid. Tell the towns of Judah, "Your God is coming!"
(Isaiah 40:9, NLT)

The Greek word that is translated as "Gospel" is *euaggelion*, which means "the good news"[29]. And that perfectly defines the message we are both commanded and empowered to share through our evangelism. It's the greatest news the human race could ever hear — the reconciliation of sinful man to his holy God, given freely by God's Divine grace!

Thus, it's very important to fully understand exactly what it is we're called to disseminate. The gospel must truly be "good news" to you before it will really be that same "good news" to others. **"For God, who said, 'Let there be light in the darkness,' has made this light shine in our hearts so we could know the glory of God that is seen in the face of Jesus Christ"** (2 Corinthians 4:6, NLT).

I *love* the way Paul described the good news there. It's *"the gospel of the glory of God in the face of Jesus Christ"*! Unfortunately, the world doesn't see this when they read the Holy Bible or hear it quoted. The unbelieving masses see and hear nothing but a set of moral rules and laws they're supposed to follow, thereby ostensibly "limiting their freedom". The legalistic religions see a set of commandments they're supposed to obey perfectly in order to be accepted by God and thus saved. The prideful "intellectuals" see nothing more than a set of small-minded, antiquated, archaic beliefs. Indeed, this is true of every kind and every form of unbeliever: **"Their minds are full of darkness; they wander far from the life God gives because they have closed their minds and hardened their hearts against him"** (Ephesians 4:18, NLT).

But praise God this is not true for us! As our Lord Jesus Christ said of His elect family, **"blessed are your eyes, for they see, and your ears, for they hear. For truly, I say to you, many prophets and righteous people longed to see what you see, and did not see it, and to hear what you hear, and did not hear it"** (Matthew 13:16-17).

Therefore, our promulgation of the gospel must not be out of rote, legalistic obligation like the Mormons or Jehovah's Witnesses. We're not earning God's love by doing this, so evangelism mustn't be treated like some religious "check box" on a form.

Rather, just like everything else in life, our evangelism must be seen through gospel glasses. Then it will be fueled by truly joyous and grateful obedience to our Savior and a genuine, love-filled compassion for the lost souls seen all around us.

As Paul wrote, God **"gave us this wonderful message of reconciliation. So we are Christ's ambassadors; God is making his appeal through us. We speak for Christ when we plead, "Come back to God!"** (2 Corinthians 5:19b-20, NLT). That's *us* He is talking about, *we* are the ambassadors of Christ in this fallen land! Thus, we should all be sharing the gospel as much as possible. The unsaved perish because they don't hear the message in time. They all *need* to hear the Truth so they can be saved!

As we've been exhorted, **"How then will they call on him in whom they have not believed? And how are they to believe in him of whom they have never heard?** *And how are they to hear without someone preaching?"* (Romans 10:14, italics mine.) So, how are those in *your* sphere of contact going to hear the gospel unless you open your mouth?

All Christians have a myriad of opportunities to share the gospel daily, and for us as singles, this is especially true on a relatively bigger scale. Given our larger amount of free time, and also our smaller amount of earthly familial responsibility, we have no excuse for not proclaiming God's good news fervently, prolifically, and very frequently.

This means engaging in both individualized one-on-one evangelism with those we know and the broader "corner coffee shop" types of evangelistic conversations we should be having with strangers.

And thanks to the blessing of the Internet, our immediate mission field has now expanded worldwide, in addition to our own neighborhoods! We can, and should, use the Internet to share the gospel through the many forms of communication and broadcasting available to us there, in addition to sharing via our spoken words where we live.

As our Lord Jesus Christ said, **"The harvest is plentiful, but the laborers are few"** (Luke 10:2a). So let's hasten the return of our Lord by *becoming* the laborers who harvest those bountiful fields!

Verisimilitude...

> "Always be prepared to give an answer to everyone who asks you to give the reason for the hope that you have. But do this with gentleness and respect."
>
> (1 Peter 3:15b, NIV)

Before we can maximize our vast multitude of evangelistic opportunities, it's important that we understand how to explain the *Biblical* gospel in its entirety and with love. This means being able to accurately present the authentic gospel, not one of the many false gospels that exist out there.

This is the true gospel: God is perfectly holy, men are not. God is just, so he has to punish sin. That's the bad news. The *good news* is that God sent His own perfect Son to live a perfect life for us, die a tortuous death for our sins, and rise from the grave to forever conquer sin and death on our behalf! A person responding to the gospel message in genuine repentance and faith in our Lord Jesus Christ freely receives this eternal grace.

As long as you can simply articulate those facts, the *core* of the gospel, you know everything you need to know to evangelize. As Paul wrote of his evangelism to Corinth: **"For I decided to know nothing among you except Jesus Christ and him crucified"** (1 Corinthians 2:2). In his original preaching there, Paul kept it simple and presented the true gospel in its basic form. That was all that was needed for God to save many Corinthians!

So don't be apprehensive about receiving varied apologetic questions concerning evolution, human suffering, manuscript evidence, dinosaurs, etc. Though it's great to study those subjects, as there are Biblically-based scientific answers for every one of them, that knowledge is not necessarily what saves men's souls. As we learn from Paul: **"So where does this leave the** philosophers, the scholars, and the world's brilliant debaters? God has made the wisdom of this world look foolish" (1 Corinthians 1:20, NLT).

Accordingly, here's the truth about anyone who espouses those ostensibly "unanswered questions" as valid reasoning for not accepting the gospel: **"When outsiders who have never heard of God's law follow it more or less by instinct, they confirm its truth by their obedience. They show that God's law is not something alien, imposed on us from without, but woven into the very fabric of our creation. There is something deep within them that echoes God's yes and no, right and wrong. Their response to God's yes and no will become public knowledge on the day God makes his final decision about every man and woman. The Message from God that I proclaim through Jesus Christ takes into account all these differences"** (Romans 2:14-16, MSG). And the message *we* proclaim 2,000 years later is exactly the same as back then!

As we see, in actuality, all unbelieving people merely **"suppress the truth in unrighteousness, because that which is known about God is evident within them; for God made it evident to them. For since the creation of the world His invisible attributes, His eternal power and divine nature, have been clearly seen, being understood through what has been made, so that they are without excuse"** (Romans 1:18b-20, NASB).

And just as Paul preached to the Athenian assembly of the Areopagus, **"In the past God overlooked such ignorance, but now he commands all people everywhere to repent. For he has set a day when he will judge the world with justice by the man he has appointed. He has given proof of this to everyone by raising him from the dead"** (Acts 17:30-31, NIV). The resurrection of the Lord Jesus Christ was a public event! There exists no memorial tomb for His body in Jerusalem because His body isn't there! **"And if our hope in Christ is only for this life, we are more to be pitied than anyone in the world. But in fact, Christ has been raised from the dead"** (1 Corinthians 15:19-20a, NLT). Never forget that this is an absolute *fact* we are sharing! With perfect veracity, we proclaim the truth of our crucified and eternally risen Savior!

Therefore, we fulfill the evangelistic aspect of our great commission by prayerfully sharing the unadulterated Biblical gospel. It really is that simple. **"Consequently, faith comes from hearing the message, and the message is heard through the word about Christ"** (Romans 10:17, NIV).

Tongues of fire...

> "The fear of man lays a snare,
> but whoever trusts in the LORD is safe."
>
> (Proverbs 29:25)

If you have a fear that you won't know what to say or how to say it, arm and strengthen yourself with this truth: Moses was just like you at first! Check it out. When the Lord told Moses to go to Egypt and be His mouthpiece: **"Moses pleaded with the LORD, 'O Lord, I'm not very good with words. I never have been, and I'm not now, even though you have spoken to me. I get tongue-tied, and my words get tangled.' Then the LORD asked Moses, 'Who makes a person's mouth? Who decides whether people speak or do not speak, hear or do not hear, see or do not see? Is it not I, the LORD? Now go! I will be with you as you speak, and I will instruct you in what to say'"** (Exodus 4:10-12, NLT).

This truth is precisely as our Lord Jesus Christ admonished us: **"When you are brought before synagogues, rulers and** authorities, do not worry about how you will defend yourselves or what you will say, for the Holy Spirit will teach you at that time what you should say" (Luke 12:11-12).

So fear not beloved, for it's not *your* eloquence or loquaciousness that matters when preaching the gospel. As Paul wrote to the church at Corinth, **"I didn't use lofty words and impressive wisdom to tell you God's secret plan. And my message and my preaching were very plain. Rather than using clever and persuasive speeches, I relied only on the power of the Holy Spirit. I did this so you would trust not in human wisdom but in the power of God"** (1 Corinthians 2:1b,4-5, NLT). Therefore, it doesn't matter if you got a "C" in English class, if you never participated in a debate club, or even if you're a naturally shy person. God has promised to empower your evangelistic tongue. Thus, it's time to stand on that promise and boldly start *speaking up!*

Beloved, please remember our Lord Jesus Christ has *commanded* us thus, **"Go into all the world and proclaim the gospel to the whole creation"** (Mark 16:15). Hence, we must drop every trepidation about our oratory abilities. Rather, we must simply pray for open evangelistic doors and the boldness to walk through them, fully trusting that the Lord will give us the words we need to correctly share His truth with others. Then, as one shoe company would say, we all need to "Just Do It!" (Nike® 1:1)

Intrepidity...

> **"Do not be afraid of those who kill the body but cannot kill the soul."**
>
> (Matthew 10:28a, NIV)

If you have a fear of negative life consequences or persecution because of your evangelism, it's time to leave those phobias behind as well. Opposition to your evangelistic efforts is promised. Indeed, a mere cursory reading of the New Testament shows the fulfillment of that promise, beginning with the very first followers of Christ. As our Lord has already said: **"all nations will hate you because you are my followers"** (Matthew 10:22a, NLT).

We must remember the way Paul exhorted Timothy, which extends to us: **"Don't be afraid of suffering for the Lord. Work at telling others the Good News, and fully carry out the ministry God has given you. For God has not given us a spirit of fear and timidity, but of power, love, and self-discipline. So never be ashamed to tell others about our Lord"** (2 Timothy 4:5bc,1:7-8a, NLT).

As our Lord Jesus Christ said, **"Behold, I am sending you out as sheep in the midst of wolves, so be wise as serpents and innocent as doves"** (Matthew 10:16). So, you must fully expect to be antagonized and you will be unshaken when it comes. **"For we do not wrestle against flesh and blood, but against the rulers, against the authorities, against the cosmic powers over this present darkness, against the spiritual forces of evil in the heavenly places"** (Ephesians 6:12).

Accordingly, we must step forward boldly, walking fearlessly in the fear of God. Because as David wrote of our Lord, **"You go before me and follow me. You place your hand of blessing on my head"** (Psalm 139:5, NLT). Indeed, this truth always stands: **"As the mountains surround Jerusalem, so the LORD surrounds his people, from this time forth and forevermore"** (Psalm 125:2). Amen.

Knowing all of this, let us evermore be those with no need for a podiatrist, those described thus:

> "How beautiful on the mountains are the feet of the messenger who brings good news, the good news of peace and salvation, the news that the God of Israel reigns! The watchmen shout and sing with joy, for before their very eyes they see the LORD returning to Jerusalem."
>
> (Isaiah 52:7-8, NLT)

Mathéteuó...

> "A disciple is not above his teacher, but everyone when he is fully trained will be like his teacher."
>
> (The Lord Jesus Christ, Luke 6:40)

The Greek word above is the word translated into the English *verb* meaning "to disciple". And that is the second aspect of fulfilling our Great Commission, our active obedience in discipleship.

Accordingly, the Greek word translated into the English *noun* "disciple" is *Mathétés*. This word is etymologically rooted in the Greek word *math*, which means "the *mental effort* needed to think something through". Accordingly, this word means someone who not only learns certain truths, but also *applies* those truths to transform their life[30].

Thus, our command to "make disciples" means far more than just inviting someone to church, or even just teaching others theology from the Holy Bible.

Real discipleship means to proactively instruct, mature, and develop our brethren in the body of Christ. It means instructing them to obey Christ's commands, edifying them through the word of God, praying for them, taking care of them, and at times, even rebuking them when necessary, all in love. It means truly becoming their spiritual "parent" and "raising" them as your spiritual kids accordingly.

Christian, this is not an obedience we can simply shirk or a command that can be passed off as our pastor's job. No, this is the duty of *every* believer.

Check it out: As Paul wrote of our pastors and leaders, **"Their responsibility is to equip God's people to do his work and build up the church, the body of Christ"** (Ephesians 4:12, NLT). Please read that verse again carefully. Our pastoral leaders' job is to endow *us* with everything *we* need to go out and do the same. It's not their duty to disciple every member of their congregation, but rather it's to "make disciples who make disciples". That means *us* my dear brethren...discipleship is *our* calling.

As an aside, your growth and maturation in this area will strongly prepare you to be a godly parent to your own physical children in the future, if that be God's will. You will already know how to both evangelize them *and* disciple them afterward. But I digress as that is not the point or subject of this chapter. So now, let's jump into God's word and learn w*hat it* really means to "disciple" our brothers and sisters as God commands and empowers.

Agape...

> **"Greater love hath no man than this,**
> **that a man lay down his life for his friends."**
> (The Lord Jesus Christ, John 15:13, KJB)

There are four Greek words for "love". There's *storge*, which means a "natural" affection, as a mother has for her children because they are her offspring. There's *phileo*, which is the affection close friends and "physically familial" brothers have for each other. There's *eros*, which describes a sensually physical desire and affection toward someone else. And then there's *agape*, which is *true* love, the love that is selfless and unconditional!

It's the latter Greek word that is used in our passage above. It's *gospel* love. It's the love our Lord perfectly exemplified when He laid down *His* life for us all! *That* is the type of love of which our Lord says there is none greater. It's the love He referred to when, during that same recorded discourse with His disciples, He said, **"This is my command: Love each other"** (John 15:17, NIV).

Thus, we can now understand the type of love we need to espouse and evince in this ministry. It's the love that will empower our service from the inside out. It is *selfless, self-forgetful* discipleship!

This is yet another area where we can learn from the great example of our brother Paul. He wanted to go home and be with Christ, just as all Christians should. However, Paul tempered this desire with the knowledge that he was still here on earth in order to serve and disciple his brethren, which is a paradigm we must likewise adopt. As he wrote: **"My desire is to depart and be with Christ, for that is far better.** *But to remain in the flesh is more necessary on your account.* **Convinced of this, I know that** *I will remain and continue with you all, for your progress and joy in the faith, so that in me you may have ample cause to glory in Christ Jesus"* (Philippians 1:23-26a, italics mine).

One of the ways we "lay down our lives" is by using our lives in this way, by focusing a big part of our attention and time on the spiritual growth and maturation of our brethren. This is one of the ways by which "we die, so that they may have life".

We must ask God for the empowerment and *agape* we need to live this out. Just as with every other action in our lives, we cannot do this on our own! Paul always acknowledged that fact. As he wrote of his ministry, **"So we tell others about Christ, warning everyone and teaching everyone** *with all the wisdom God has given us.* **We want to present them to God, perfect in their relationship to Christ. That's why I work and struggle so hard, depending on Christ's mighty power that works within me"** (Colossians 1:28-29, NLT, Italics Mine).

And we should all endeavor for that passage to be reflected in our lives as well. Though we won't all make disciples as prolifically as Paul, it should nonetheless be a goal we strive to achieve by "Christ's mighty power". For we are exhorted thus: **"Be devoted to one another in brotherly love; give preference to one another in honor"** (Romans 12:10). When our discipleship is done in this way, not only will our brethren be edified and mature, they will also be encouraged to go and do the same!

My dearly beloved, please remember: **"So now faith, hope, and love abide, these three; but the greatest of these is love"** (1 Corinthians 13:13).

Edification...

> "Yet among the mature we do impart wisdom,
> although it is not a wisdom of this age or of
> the rulers of this age, who are doomed to pass away.
> **But we impart a secret and hidden wisdom of God,
> which God decreed before the ages for our glory."**
>
> (1 Corinthians 2:6-7)

For us as singles, there is no reason why we shouldn't be discipling multiple individuals on a private, personally accountable basis regularly. This is yet another reason why we must study the word of God constantly! For we know that **"All Scripture is breathed out by God and profitable for teaching, for reproof, for correction, and for training in righteousness, that the man of God may be competent, equipped for every good work"** (2 Timothy 3:16-17). "Every good work" absolutely includes discipleship, and thus we need knowledge of God's word to be very competent in this ministry!

If you've been a Christian for any significant amount of time, you must understand your calling to the ever-increasing spiritual maturity that is achieved through gaining this knowledge.

As the writer of **Hebrews** admonished those early Christians: *"For though by this time you ought to be teachers,* **you need someone to teach you again the basic principles of the oracles of God. You need milk, not solid food, for everyone who lives on milk is unskilled in the word of righteousness, since he is a child. But solid food is for the mature, for those who have their powers of discernment trained by constant practice to distinguish good from evil"** (vv. 5:12-14, italics mine). When the writer says "you ought to be teachers", he doesn't mean that all Christians must be public teachers or pulpit preachers. Rather, it means that we should all be able to teach *at least* the basic truths of the gospel and the main tenets of the Christian faith to everyone, especially to our younger siblings in Christ. When that letter was written in the 60's AD, its readers didn't yet have the entire New Testament available to them.

Unlike them, we have the fully complete canon of Holy Scripture at our disposal. Thus, if *they* were commanded to understand and be able to teach the truths of Christ, how much more accountable are *we* for our response to this very same charge?

So let's wisely use the time God has given us in our singleness by studying His holy word with the scholarship to which we are called. In this way, we will be equipped to most effectively make disciples. And as our cognition of the Lord and His word increases, let us never forget how we are to use it: **"we know that 'all of us possess knowledge.' This 'knowledge' puffs up, but love builds up. If anyone imagines that he knows something, he does not yet know as he ought to know. But if anyone loves God, he is known by God"** (1 Corinthians 8:1b-3).

Epitomization...

> **"What you have learned and received and heard and seen in me— practice these things, and the God of peace will be with you."**
>
> (Philippians 4:9)

Our ability to disciple other people doesn't lie only in our knowledge of the word of God, but also in how much we ourselves have been changed by it through our own experiential sanctification. Just as Paul wrote to the Corinthians, **"But I, brothers, could not address you as spiritual people, but as people of the flesh, as infants in Christ. I fed you with milk, not solid food, for you were not ready for it. And even now you are not yet ready, for you are still of the flesh"** (1 Corinthians 3:1-3a).

Whether or not you realize it, newer believers are looking at you and your life for guidance. This is yet another reason why simply *knowing* the word of God is not enough. We have been commanded to **"be doers of the word, and not hearers only, deceiving yourselves"** (James 1:22).

You see, if we have not yet achieved victory over the most basic and besetting of human sins, how can we help others achieve that victory? As Solomon so wisely wrote, **"Iron sharpens iron, and one man sharpens another"** (Proverbs 27:17). Using a dull blade as a sharpener only makes other dull blades. So let us all become sharper than Ginsu® knives!

Thus, we must fully imbibe the fact that our personal growth in experiential sanctification is not only for our own benefit, but for the benefit of others as well. Just as a parent works hard to improve themselves for the benefit of their physical children, we must understand that our work to improve spiritually is also for the benefit of the spiritual children God graciously grants to us.

In order to raise Godly spiritual children, we must *live* as Godly spiritual children! The only way to set a Godly example is to *be* a Godly example! Teaching, but failing, to practice what we preach is often useless and can easily be disregarded. But when our teaching is followed by commensurate actions, it becomes even more powerful and life-changing! Our brother Paul lived what he taught and that's why he could write to one of his disciples thus: **"You, however, have followed my teaching, my conduct, my aim in life, my faith, my patience, my love, my steadfastness"** (2 Timothy 3:10).

Accordingly, all of our knowledge has to grow into action. We must move from hearers into doers! When that happens, regardless of our age, we can **"set the believers an example in speech, in conduct, in love, in faith, in purity"** (1 Timothy 4:12).

As we're continually made more like Christ in our discipleship, may we one day be able to honestly echo Paul's exhortation to his disciples: **"Be imitators of me, as I am of Christ"** (1 Corinthians 11:1).

Middle Child Syndrome: redefined...

"You have heard me teach things

that have been confirmed by many reliable witnesses. Now teach these truths to other trustworthy people who will be able to pass them on to others."

(2 Timothy 2:2, NLT)

Paul wrote those words to Timothy, the man many would call Paul's "little brother". In that verse, we see the New Testament pattern for discipleship. In order to most effectively disciple the "little brothers" below us, we all need "big brothers" above us. Thus, we all must now become "middle children". We all need "Pauls in order to be Pauls," and we all need "Timothys who will make more Timothys". We must all submit to the authority and knowledge of the Christians God has set over us, and in turn, use our own God-given authority and knowledge to help others grow to maturity in God.

One of the best ways we can truly live out this Biblical model of discipleship is by becoming devoted participants of a small group fellowship. As a member of such a ministry, you will disciple and be discipled, teach and be taught, rebuke and be rebuked, edify and be edified, love and be loved, bless and be a blessing. You will be building into each other's lives and holding each other accountable. The practical implications of this type of ministry are numerous. In the relationships cultivated in these groups, people's veneers are removed and you will be able to see their true needs, thus being able to tend to them. For The Lord has exhorted us: **"By this we know love, that he laid down his life for us, and we ought to lay down our lives for the brothers. Little children, let us not love in word or talk but in deed and in truth"** (1 John 3:16,18).

We love in deed and in truth by doing as much as we can to meet each other's practical day-to-day needs, as the Lord has equipped and lead us. These verses don't mean only financial assistance or "goods," the implications are more far-reaching than that. We are to be their advocate, their helper, and their friend...just as The Lord Jesus is, perfectly, to us.

In doing this, we'll all be following our Lord's perfect example of discipleship. Remember: **"One of those days Jesus went out to a mountainside to pray, and spent the night praying to God. When morning came, he called his disciples to him and chose twelve of them, whom he also designated apostles"** (Luke 6:12-13, NIV). Jesus chose a "small group" of twelve amazingly blessed men, then spent three years *personally* discipling them. During that time, the Lord was teaching them through His words, His living example, and God the Holy Spirit. The Lord taught His small group of apostles how to be like Him, in His communicable attributes, and how to do His will accordingly. In turn, those twelve men were able to go out and disciple others in the same way, starting of course with the first-century church.

As is recorded regarding the history of that early church: **"And they devoted themselves to the apostles' teaching and the fellowship, to the breaking of bread and the prayers. And all who believed were together and had all things in common. And they were selling their possessions and belongings and distributing the proceeds to all, as any had need. And day by day, attending the temple together and breaking bread in their homes, they received their food with glad and generous hearts, praising God and having favor with all the people. And the Lord added to their number day by day those who were being saved"** (Acts 2:42,44-47). Did you catch all of that? They *devoted* themselves to fellowship. It was a conscious, proactive decision to gather together. They had all things in common, that is, there was no "yours" and "mine," it was all "ours". Those who owned expensive things, like land, sold these possessions and distributed to those in need. And what was the result of all this obedient, selfless fellowship? The Lord saved many through them! And they were joyous and glad because they had God and each other, so they had *everything*. This example is really the ideal for us, and thus it is what we should be aspiring to as Christ's universal body.

A modern church that mirrors the early church will be "a church *of* small groups, not a church *with* small groups[31]". And though the entire congregation may gather every Sunday to hear the word of God being preached by the senior pastor, the *real-life* application of that preaching happens best in the intimate small group fellowships and one-on-one discipleships that follow thereafter.

If you're already blessed to be a member of such a small group, please pray and ask God to make you an ever-larger blessing there. If you're not yet in a small group, please pray and ask God for a group.

Remonstrance...

"An open rebuke is better than hidden love!"

(Proverbs 27:5, NLT)

Today, the world considers it "unloving" to discipline your children. Corporal punishment has now been banned in many public schools. Spankings, even for gross disobedience, are now called "child abuse". Nowadays, when children rebel, most simply get placed "in the corner," where they are free to seethe in anger and plot their next disobedient act.

Beloved, regardless of how you were raised or what your own personal beliefs are regarding effective discipline, our God has written: **"Whoever spares the rod hates his son, but he who** loves him is diligent to discipline him" (Proverbs 13:24). You can't argue with the truth. True *agape* includes real discipline, **"Think about it: Just as a parent disciplines a child, the LORD your God disciplines you for your own good"** (Deuteronomy 8:5, NLT).

Accordingly, in your discipleship, which is your "raising" of spiritual children, you are called to give disciplinary rebukes when necessary. Indeed, this even happened among the *apostles*! As Paul recorded, **"But when Peter came to Antioch, I had to oppose him to his face, for what he did was very wrong"** (Galatians 2:11, NLT). Remember, Peter was not a mere disciple like we are. He was Petros (**cf. Matthew 16:18**), "the rock", on which Christ would build His church! So if *he* was subjected to rebuke by a brother, we know that we, and those we disciple, are undoubtedly subject to that same correction!

Whether or not you've ever done this before with your own children or someone else's, this is a part of your calling in making disciples. One large aspect of parenthood is ingraining obedience into your children. Just as Solomon wrote, **"Discipline your son, and he will give you rest; he will give delight to your heart"** (Proverbs 29:17). Thus, this act of disciplining a sibling in Christ is a place where you must grow and mature. Now obviously, the type of loving rebukes described here are not *physical* in nature, for it's self-evident that we aren't called to go around "spanking" our grown brethren. No, we're called to **"reprove, rebuke, and exhort, with complete patience and teaching"** (2 Timothy 4:2c). The whole point of reproof is to make one another more like Christ, so it must be done in tender love.

After Paul wrote and sent his corrective first epistle to the church in Corinth, his second letter included this remark: **"Now I am glad I sent it, not because it hurt you, but because the pain** caused you to repent and change your ways" (2 Corinthians 7:9a). Indeed, rebukes are arduous at first, both for the administrator and the recipient. But it's true: **"No discipline is enjoyable while it is happening--it's painful! But afterward there will be a peaceful harvest of right living for those who are trained in this way"** (Hebrews 12:11, NLT).

Hence, if and when you ever have to administer this type of discipline to your brethren, at first you may receive a response of resentful anger. Don't be discouraged by this, for they will soon be led to thank the Lord, and you, for that rebuke. For it is written: **"Whoever rebukes a man will afterward find more favor than he who flatters with his tongue"** (Proverbs 28:23). So if we truly love each other, this will sometimes be necessary. As we are told: **"if anyone is caught in any transgression, you who are spiritual should restore him in a spirit of gentleness"** (Galatians 6:1a). This should not be done publicly, at least not at first, because the goal is not embarrassment, but contrition and repentance. In the Christian maturation process, a growing believer will learn to espouse the truth that **"Wounds from a sincere friend are better than many kisses from an enemy"** (Proverbs 27:6).

In summation of this point, any disciplinary action toward our brethren must be truly rooted in loving care for their obedience and experiential sanctification, rather than spiritual pride of any kind. That is the type of selfless concern espoused by Paul in his rebuke of the Galatians. This was evinced in his words to them when he wrote, **"Oh, my dear children! I feel as if I'm going through labor pains for you again, and they will continue until Christ is fully developed in your lives"** (Galatians 4:19, NLT). Brothers and sisters, may *that* agape be the type of love fueling any rebuke we ever give.

A Quick Reality Check...

> "A friend loves at all times,
> and a brother is born for adversity."
>
> (Proverbs 17:17)

We'd be daydreaming if we didn't touch on this in our discipleship discussion. We must never idealize this ministry when we're praying about it or living it out. This is a fallen world and though we have been saved from it, we still live here. Accordingly, *real* ministry on this planet is not always easy, fun, or convenient. *True* discipleship is sometimes messy, difficult, and not at all convenient or fun-filled. Adopting, raising, and dealing with the issues of spiritual children is sometimes just like doing the same with physical children. At times, like those, the only difference between the two lies in the details. Rather than dealing with crying babies at 3 am, we sometimes get that 3 am phone call from a brother who needs prayer and counsel badly. Rather than paying for diapers and baby food, we are sometimes called to bail a brother out of their financial bind. Rather than leaving the house extra early to get a child to preschool, we're sometimes called to leave the house early to get a car-less brother to work.

However, none of this should dissuade us in any way from engaging in prolific discipleship. In fact, when looking at everything through our gospel glasses, these things will actually *empower* us to disciple our brethren! That's because, through gospel glasses, we see that this is what Jesus has done (and does) in serving us! **"For even the Son of Man came not to be served but to serve"** (Mark 10:45a). Therefore, every ostensibly "hard" act of service must be emboldened by that truth. Then, though our ministries may at times be inconvenient, they will still be done joyously! As our Lord has admonished us, **"If I then, your Lord** and Teacher, have washed your feet, you also ought to wash one another's feet" (John 13:14). So we mustn't run from the hard jobs. Let's wash some proverbial "feet"!

Just as you would never say "no" to any need of your physical child, we should never deny a brother or sister in need. As our Lord told us, **"Give to those who ask, and don't turn away from those who want to borrow"** (Matthew 5:42, NLT). When we obey that command, we become God's hand of blessing to our brethren, and this is a *beautiful* thing!

Thus, we must see all sacrificial service of God's people as being unto the Lord himself. When looked at that way, our ministries will become empowered to the point that we hold nothing back from those in need! Then we will joyfully anticipate hearing these words from our Savior at the end of the age, **"I was hungry and you gave me food, I was thirsty and you gave me drink, I was a stranger and you welcomed me, I was naked and you clothed me, I was sick and you visited me, I was in prison and you came to me. Truly, I say to you, as you did it to one of the least of these my brothers, you did it to me"** (Matthew 25:35-36,40). So let's do it for *Him*!

The worldly can look at someone in need and turn away. Unbelievers can avoid hanging out with a friend when they know that friend will be requesting their help. But we are *not* of this world! That's why we are admonished thus, **"Let each of you look not only to his own interests, but also to the interests of others. Have this mind among yourselves, which is yours in Christ Jesus, who, though he was in the form of God, did not count equality with God a thing to be grasped, but made himself nothing, taking the form of a servant, being born in the likeness of men"** (Philippians 2:4-7).

So let's be willing to give the shirts off our backs if they are needed. Let's be *truly* godly parents to our spiritual children. Let's look through gospel glasses, see that King Jesus bore the burden of our sins, and thus **"Bear one another's burdens, and so fulfill the law of Christ"** (Galatians 6:2).

No matter how inconvenient, difficult, or self-sacrificial our discipleship may sometimes be, let's always remember this truth: **"Love is patient and kind; love does not envy or boast; it is not arrogant or rude. It does not insist on its own way; it is not irritable or resentful; it does not rejoice at wrongdoing, but rejoices with the truth. Love bears all things, believes all things, hopes all things, endures all things"** (1 Corinthians 13:4-7).

Discipleship: A Final Note...

"When he found him, *he brought him back to Antioch.*
Both of them stayed there with the church
for a full year, *teaching large crowds of people.*
(*It was at Antioch that the believers were first called Christians)"*
(Acts 11:26, NLT, italics mine)

Before that time in Antioch, Christians were called by different names. We called ourselves "brethren", "the church", "believers", "saints", etc. The Jews and some believers called us "the way". Many of the ostensibly "impartial" non-believers called us "Nazarenes" or "Galileans". The antagonistic unbelievers, however, called us "Christ*e*ans".

That little difference in spelling has huge historical significance. You see, we didn't invent the word "Christian" originally. Rather, those who hated us because of the Lord we follow originally coined the word "Christ*e*an" as a *derisive* term. It's why the word is only used three times in the New Testament **(cf. Acts 11:26; 1 Peter 4:14,16)**, each one referring to the word's use as a reproach.

Christos, which is the Greek word for "Christ," means "The Messiah, The Anointed One[32]". And thus, the Greek word translated as "Christians," *Christianos*, means "followers of The Anointed One". The first-century unbelievers refused to acknowledge Jesus as "The Anointed One," or they didn't understand or care about what that title meant. So they refused to call His followers something based on that title. Instead, they adopted a pun based on that name, *Chrestos*, which means "good, moral, virtuous". Accordingly, their appointed moniker for us, *Chrestianos*, colloquially meant "the goody two-shoes bunch". It was based on our evangelistic efforts to them, the good works they saw in our lives, and the holy lifestyles we evinced before them. For all of that, our brethren back then often received the same kind of backlash we often still receive from unbelievers today: **"They are surprised that you do not join them in their reckless, wild living, and they heap abuse on you"** (1 Peter 4:4, NIV). Our Lord Jesus promised this: **"They will treat you this way because of my name, for they do not know the one who sent me"** (John 5:21, NIV).

Eventually, we responded to this abuse by changing the "e" to an "i" and adopting that name as a self-descriptive. In doing so, we were able to redeem the name from its maligning use to one that brings glory to God. This change basically said to the hostile unsaved, "you call us 'followers of a do-gooder' because of how we live, but we are followers of The Anointed One, The Messiah, The Lord Jesus Christ! Our good, moral, and virtuous lives come from Him! So we'll gladly bear the name you use mockingly as a Name of honor, to God's glory!".

They didn't care about what the world called them, just like our brother Moses, for **"He considered the reproach of Christ** greater wealth than the treasures of Egypt, for he was looking to the reward"** (Hebrews 11:26). Among the heathen masses, they disregarded the reviling, knowing this truth: **"If you are insulted for the name of Christ, you are blessed, because the Spirit of glory and of God rests upon you"** (1 Peter 4:14). Among the Jews, they exemplified the obedience to which we're called: **"Therefore let us go to him outside the camp and bear the reproach he endured. For here we have no lasting city, but we seek the city that is to come"** (Hebrews 13:13-14).

And now, 2,000 years later, *we* are the bearers of the majestic name of Christ! Knowing all of this history, we must understand the fact that in our discipleship, we will be up against both evil spiritual forces and the world influenced by them. So, just as we must expect opposition against our evangelism, we must be prepared for the same antagonistic efforts against our discipleship. **"But it is no shame to suffer for being a Christian. Praise God for the privilege of being called by his name!"** (1 Peter 4:16, NLT). Walking in expectancy of this, you won't be surprised when it comes and it will only strengthen your discipleship. For our Lord Jesus Christ has promised us: **"Blessed are you when others revile you and persecute you and utter all kinds of evil against you falsely on my account. Rejoice and be glad, for your reward is great in heaven, for so they persecuted the prophets who were before you"** (Matthew 5:11-12). So let's all fight on accordingly, fully maximizing the blessing of our singleness and *make disciples*!

In doing this, we will all have the awesome blessing of being a part of the fulfillment of our Lord's perfect, precious promise about discipleship:

"This *will* continue until we *all* come

> to such unity in our faith and knowledge of
> God's Son that *we will be mature in the Lord*,
> measuring up to the full and complete standard of Christ."
>
> (Ephesians 4:13, NLT, italics mine)

Little People, Big God...

> "All those gathered here will know
> that it is not by sword or spear that the
> Lord saves; for the battle is the Lord's,
> and he will give all of you into our hands."
>
> (1 Samuel 17:47, NIV)

David said those words to Goliath just before he killed that Philistine by God's power! Picture that scene for a moment. A small young man boldly facing down a gigantic older man. A mere sheepherder, confidently defeating a veteran warrior *easily*.

David won that victory not because of *his* might or strength, but because of his unwavering trust in the Lord his God! When all the older warriors of Israel looked at Goliath, **"they began to run away in fright"** (1 Samuel 17:24b). They ran away because their focus and vision were wrong; they were concentrating on the size of their enemy rather than the size of their God! But David, being "a man after God's own heart" **(cf. 1 Samuel 13:14)**, saw things differently. When David looked at that gargantuan man across the valley, he wasn't at all impressed, much less scared. All David saw was this godless heathen, so his only question was, **"Who is this uncircumcised Philistine that he should defy the armies of the living God?"** (1 Samuel 17:26b).

That isn't the only time something similar has happened. Let's look back at one more story, that of Gideon, as recorded in **Judges 7-8**. There, Gideon was getting ready to lead the Israelite army into a battle with the formidable army of the Midianites.

The Israelites had quite the fight waiting for them, as the Midianite troops they were up against totaled 135,000 warriors! Israel's total number of troops didn't compare, at a relatively small 32,000.

Any human general would have had only one of two responses to this asymmetry: he'd go and recruit more troops to even out the battlefield, or surrender.

But check it out, this is awesome. God, *our* General, did neither! Unlike any human army commander, **"The LORD said to Gideon, 'You have too many warriors with you. If I let all of you fight the Midianites, the Israelites will boast to me that they saved themselves by their own strength'"** (Judges 7:2, NLT). Our Lord purposefully reduced the number of human troops on His side, all the way down to only 300! God then gave His ostensibly "outnumbered" people the victory. The Lord did this so that *He* would get the glory, not His people!

Beloved, perfectly illustrated in those stories are these facts: God plus one is a majority, and no servant is too small for Him to use mightily! For it's not the size of the servant, or even the number of servants that matters. What determines an outcome is the Master to whom those servants belong!

Please be edified and encouraged by the real, practical implications of all these truths. Your singleness is in no way a hindrance to God's ability to work mightily through you! In fact, it very well could turn out to be exactly the opposite result.

Do you realize how much God is glorified when just one of his children goes out and changes the world around them? Others see that it must be God at work, so all of the glory goes to Him, where it belongs! Beloved, please remember this: **"*You* are the light of the world. A city set on a hill cannot be hidden. Nor do** people light a lamp and put it under a basket, but on a stand, and it gives light to all in the house. In the same way, let *your* light shine before others, so that they may see *your* good works and give glory to *your* Father who is in heaven" (Matthew 5:14-16, italics mine).

Properly utilizing the huge plethora of service opportunities we've been given, our ministries as single Christians can add up to gigantic footprints for Christ in the world! A single, fully submitted servant of Christ can yield vast amounts of fruit!

Brethren, once again, please fully imbibe these words from our Lord Jesus Christ: **"I am the vine; you are the branches.** *If a man remains in me and I in him, he will bear much fruit; apart from me you can do nothing.* **This is to my Father's glory, that you bear much fruit, showing yourselves to be my disciples. You did not choose me, but I chose you and appointed you to go and bear fruit** — *fruit that will last"* (John 15:5,8,16a, italics mine).

This is one of the foremost ways we can maximize our current singleness, by bearing much fruit and, thus, bringing massive glory to God. So get moving!

Great Examples...

"I urge you, then, be imitators of me."
(The unmarried Apostle Paul, 1 Corinthians 4:16)

Do a little bit of Internet research about the many single Christians and lone missionaries who all throughout the last 2,000 years have served the Lord while unmarried, and in doing so they have reaped a giant harvest of souls for God's Kingdom!

We must learn from these Godly men and women, those saints who have exemplified what it means to maximize one's time and freedom as a single Christian, all by spiritually reproducing at highly prolific rates. And of course, we must start by looking at the awesome example set by our apostolic brothers.

Paul didn't raise physical children, at least not once he became a Christian, but he did spawn giant multitudes of spiritual children! That is why Paul could write to the saints at Corinth like this, **"I became your father in Christ Jesus through the gospel. That is why I sent you Timothy, my beloved and faithful child in the Lord, to remind you of my ways in Christ"** (1 Corinthians 4:15b,17a). It is why Paul was even able to make spiritual children while locked up in jail. And he didn't need any "conjugal" visits to do this! As Paul wrote to **Philemon: "I appeal to you for my child, Onesimus, whose father I became in my imprisonment"** (v. 1:10).

John, in his three epistles, quite often referred to his younger brethren as his "children" in this same way: **"My little children, I am writing these things to you so that you may not sin. I have no greater joy than to hear that my children are walking in the truth"** (1 John 2:1a, 3 John 1:4).

Peter called John Mark, the physical child of Barnabas' sister, **"Mark, my son"** (1 Peter 5:13b).

All three of these godly men "begat" multitudes of spiritual children! Each one "reproduced" at a prolific rate, through evangelism and discipleship. In fact, many people in the worldwide church today are spiritual descendants of these three godly men. As our Lord Jesus Christ said to His original disciples, **"I sent you to reap that for which you did not labor. Others have labored, and you have entered into their labor"** (John 4:38). We have now been called to the very same ministry field of our apostolic brothers, to engage in the same "labor". It is the same ministry field in which our brethren have been "sowing and reaping" for 2,000 years.

Beloved, if you desire to have children, then you desire the privilege of parenthood. You desire the responsibilities of raising, protecting, loving, disciplining, guiding, and edifying another person. If you desire to have children, then check this out: The Lord Jesus Christ says we've *already* been given a hundredfold **"brothers and sisters and mothers and *children*"** (cf. Mark 10:30, italics mine)! This means our brethren in the body of Christ! Our "children" are already here. This is a truth I've also learned experientially. I know much more about the true meaning of "fatherhood," the challenges & joys, by discipling my brothers in Christ.

Never forget this truth my brothers & sisters. You have the privilege and blessings of parenthood *right now*, and you're commanded to use this privilege! This means using all your gifts proactively for "making and raising" many children in the Lord!

Indeed, just as Solomon wrote: **"Children are a gift from the LORD; they are a reward from him"** (Psalm 127:3, NLT). Beloved, you don't have to wait until you're married to start living out this truth!

Our *Greatest* Example...

"Here am I, and the children God has given me."
(The Lord Jesus Christ, cf. Hebrews 2:13, NIV)

Beloved, please don't overlook this fact: our Lord Jesus Christ was unmarried in His humanity. And He is our perfect model in *everything*, which of course includes our evangelism and discipleship. Our Lord was here for one perfectly understood purpose, to do the will of His heavenly Father. As Jesus said, **"My food is to do the will of Him who sent Me and to accomplish**

His work" (John 4:34).

Our Lord Jesus Christ lived, died, and rose from the grave, **"in order that he might be the firstborn among many brothers"** (Romans 8:29b, NIV). Today, countless multitudes of human souls are now sons and daughters of God because of *the* Son of God!

The LORD has sovereignly, graciously included *us* in this salvific plan He authored to build up *His* family. That is the reason we have been saved. That is the reason we are still here on this planet, to do our Father's will by making more children for Him, as our Lord Jesus Christ has commanded. So let us never stray from that. We have received a calling to spiritually reproduce, a charge our God also empowers us to live out. Our Lord and Savior set us truly free to obey our callings to both evangelism and discipleship. The Lord has freed us both spiritually and physically to live as He lived, which means walking in complete acquiescence to our holy God's will, fruitfully multiplying along the way.

Birth Rate...

> **"Other seeds fell on good soil and produced grain,**
> *some a hundredfold, some sixty, some thirty."*
>
> (Matthew 13:8, italics mine)

A word of caution here. All the writing in this chapter is not to say that *every* unmarried believer will necessarily make exceedingly large quantities of spiritual children. Some will make one child, some will make ten children, and some will make thousands...

Thus, in responding to our call to go and make disciples, we must always acknowledge God's full sovereignty. We are commanded to share the gospel with as many people as possible and disciple them, but the fruit always belongs to God and God alone.

We must remember this: no matter how much we evangelize, people's salvation always **"depends not on human will or exertion, but on God, who has mercy. He has mercy on whomever he wills, and he hardens whomever he wills"** (Romans 9:16,18).

The obedience to share the gospel is where our responsibility lies; the response of other people is all up to God. This, therefore, is exactly *why* we all must preach the gospel to *all* peoples! As for some, **"God may perhaps grant them repentance leading to a knowledge of the truth"** (2 Timothy 2:25).

Just as God determines the amount of physical offspring anyone has, He, and He alone, determines the amount of spiritual offspring anyone will be able to make through evangelism and discipleship. **"So neither he who plants nor he who waters is anything, but** *only God who gives the growth.* **He who plants and he who waters are one, and each will receive his wages according to his labor. For we are God's fellow workers. You are God's field, God's building"** (1 Corinthians 3:7-9, italics mine).

In our evangelism and discipleship, some of us plant, some of us water, but God alone gives and determines the amount of growth. But how will a seed ever grow unless it's planted and watered?

Remember, as Christians, **"we all, with unveiled face, beholding the glory of the Lord,** *are being transformed into the same image from one degree of glory to another.* **For this comes from the Lord who is the Spirit"** (2 Corinthians 3:18, italics mine). That's yet another reason why we must proactively disciple our brothers and sisters, so that we may help God to grow them in His likeness and image! As we live this out, we see the fulfillment of

God's will for His adopted children: **"For those whom he foreknew** *he also predestined to be conformed to the image of his Son"* (Romans 8:29a, italics mine).

It is self-evident that sharing the Gospel and discipling God's children are "good works". And we know that we've been **"created in Christ Jesus for good works, which God prepared beforehand, that we should walk in them"** (Ephesians 2:10). For our Lord Jesus Christ came to this world in order **"to purify for himself a people for his own possession who are zealous for good works"** (Titus 2:14b).

Since we know that these are the primary works that were prepared for us before we were even born, let us *zealously walk* in them, evangelizing and discipling *many* souls in the love and grace of God. Seeing through gospel glasses, let us fully heed this admonition from our Lord Jesus Christ: **"I tell you, open your eyes and look at the fields! They are ripe for harvest"** (John 4:35b, NIV). Amen.

The Ultimate Imperative...

"Jesus said to them again, 'Peace be with you.
As the Father has sent me, even so I am sending you.'"

(John 20:21)

I'd be remiss if I didn't reiterate this truth one last time: the "Great Commission" we've been given is a *command*, not an optional activity in our lives! So it's of the utmost importance to understand this.

The Scripture doesn't say "once you get married, go therefore and make disciples...". It's irrespective of life status, unconditional in its admonition, and universal in its application. All Christians, single, married, or widowed have received this commission.

For us specifically, this means that *right now* we must be making disciples, by sharing the gospel with the unsaved and by teaching our brethren to obey the commandments of our Lord Jesus Christ. Just as you've been made a disciple through the evangelism and teaching of others, **"you must remain faithful to the things you have been taught. You know they are true, for you know you can trust those who taught you"** (2 Timothy 3:14, NLT).

Thus, Paul's self-description of his life should be one echoed by ours: **"For to me to live is Christ, and to die is gain. If I am to live in the flesh, that means fruitful labor for me"** (Philippians 1:21-22).

Apologies for the repetition, but this indeed bears repeating one last time: fulfilling our Lord's great commission is *why* we're still here on the earth, so we can engage in the same "fruitful labor" for God.

Our Heavenly Father is the gardener, our Lord Jesus Christ is the true grapevine, and our God the Holy Spirit gives the growth. We are the branches and God **"prunes the branches that do bear fruit so they will produce even more"** (John 15:2b, NLT). That is an amazing promise, so let's stand on it and seek to yield massive amounts of fruit accordingly!

The ministry opportunities and examples that I've presented in this chapter are a mere sampling of the multitudinous ways we can obey our command to make disciples. This must by no means be seen as a comprehensive list. In the modern church age we live in, there are now more areas to serve than ever before. We have graciously been given so many new technological avenues of communication. These all bring with them new service opportunities that our brethren of just 100 years ago didn't enjoy, as all of our new ministry tools require someone to use them. If you're not sure how you can serve, or how you can serve *more*, please pray for the Lord to reveal to you the many ministry opportunities in your life, then prayerfully walk through those doors.

The world needs to hear the gospel of the Lord Jesus Christ and His followers need discipleship. Meeting these needs must now be correctly seen as the reason we live; and God has given us the tools, freedom, and time we need to do this prolifically! Thus, as singles, we have no excuse for not serving in small *and* large group ministries, of many kinds.

Hence, let's all step forth obediently, "fruitfully multiplying" exponentially, for the glory of God and the eternal good of many souls! As Jesus said: **"Already the one who reaps is receiving wages and gathering fruit for eternal life, so that sower and reaper may rejoice together"** (John 4:36). So let's all be able to share in that joy! Let's all **"press on toward the goal for the prize of the upward call of God in Christ Jesus. Let those of us who are mature think this way, and if in anything you think otherwise, God will reveal that also to you. Only let us hold true to what we have attained"** (Philippians 3:14-16). Let's all play a part in the prophetic fulfillment of one of God's great promises:

> **"Then I will gather the remnant of my flock out of all the countries where I have driven them,**
> **and I will bring them back to their fold,**
> *and they shall be fruitful and multiply."*
>
> (Jeremiah 23:3, italics mine)

SOBRIETY

"Therefore, with minds that are alert and fully sober, set your hope on the grace to be brought to you when Jesus Christ is revealed at his coming."

(1 Peter 1:13, NIV)

Throughout this book we've discussed seeing yourself and everyone else through God's eyes. Now, we're going to discuss seeing the entire world around us through those same gospel glasses.

As single Christians, we have a special ability to see things that most others don't, and with this great clarity comes a commensurate responsibility. To begin understanding this concept, let's start by taking a little ride.

A Sunday Drive...

"So then let us not sleep, as others do, but let us keep awake and be sober."

(1 Thessalonians 5:6)

It's a typical Sunday morning. Katrina and Michael Thompson, along with their two kids, get in their car to head to church. Samantha Pott, their single next door neighbor who is a member of their same congregation, gets in her car to follow them.

Cleft Assiduities...

> "the married man is anxious about worldly things,
> how to please his wife, and his interests are divided.
> The married woman is anxious about worldly things,
> how to please her husband."
>
> (1 Corinthians 7:33-34a,c)

Along the way, Katrina and Michael discuss the weekend, their post-service plans, and the week ahead...as worship music plays in the background. Throughout the drive, Katrina has to lean back and break up scuffles between the kids, or clean up spilled juice bottles. To prevent further scuffles, she turns the worship music up and has the family sing along. Michael is constantly monitoring the digital clock on his dashboard, mentally preparing for the time-consuming weekly ritual of shuffling his kids to their respective Sunday School classes, then finding seats for he and his wife in the main sanctuary. As the Thompsons pull into the parking lot, they remark about the sunny, beautiful day...

Consecrated Concentration...

> "I want you to be free from anxieties. The unmarried man is
> anxious about the things of the Lord, how to please the Lord.
> And the unmarried or betrothed woman is anxious about the
> things of the Lord, how to be holy in body and spirit."
>
> (1 Corinthians 7:32,34B)

Samantha makes the same drive, right behind the Thompsons. Along the way, she notices the city's burgeoning homeless problem, evidenced by the growing number of transients camped out under freeway overpasses. This grieves her and she immediately lifts those people up in prayer. As she passes through the heart of the city, she notices several people standing outside a liquor store drinking from brown bottle bags. She immediately prays for them and makes a mental note to do some street evangelism there soon. She also notices two very near car collisions. One is caused by a careless driver who blatantly runs a red light, and the other by an impatient driver who rapidly changes lanes and cuts off another car. She immediately thanks God for protecting those drivers and prays for their hearts. As she gets closer to the church, she prays for the pastor's preaching, as well as open, focused hearts and minds for all who will be in attendance that day. As Samantha pulls into the parking lot, she thanks the Lord for a safe drive...

Idealism, Without The Ignorance...

**"I wish that all were as I myself am.
But each has his own gift from God,
one of one kind and one of another."**
(The Unmarried Apostle Paul, 1 Corinthians 7:7)

The Thompsons just made the same drive as Samantha, but the two experiences were worlds apart. Both parties just drove through the same city, on the same route, at the same time. But one party was actually engaging in "distracted driving," while the other truly noticed the fallen world around them.

Now obviously, this narrative we just read describes an *ideal* paradigm for a single Christian. Also, it is *not* written to in any way vilify married Christians, or to make a blanket claim of spiritual ignorance on their part. It's simply a parable, using extreme cases regarding two parties of God's children, and thus it's not a veneration of singles, nor an indictment of families. Rather, the narrative of this "Sunday Drive" merely describes a microcosm of the large and holistic experiential difference that *can* exist between the lives of the typical family and the typical single. I call this *potential* life paradigm the "Sobriety of Singleness," and it is a blessing! This is a (relatively) objective clarity that all single Christians should embrace, as it is yet another way we can glorify God and bless others!

Sanctified Single-Mindedness...

> **"Be dressed for service and keep your lamps burning, as though you were waiting for your master to return from the wedding feast. Then you will be ready to open the door and let him in the moment he arrives and knocks."**
>
> (The Lord Jesus Christ, Luke 12:35-36, NLT)

The worldly walk around with blinders on, completely oblivious to the spiritual warfare abounding all around and inside them. Remember, **"the god of this world has blinded the minds of the unbelievers, to keep them from seeing the light of the gospel of the glory of Christ, who is the image of God"** (2 Corinthians 4:4). Thus, the unbeliever sees things through lying eyes. They see others and the world around them through their own (ostensibly) "self-defined" lenses. **"For although they knew God, they did not honor him as God or give thanks to him, but they became futile in their thinking, and their foolish hearts**

were darkened" (Romans 1:21). Accordingly, they can live their lives ignorantly oblivious to the will of God and the true needs of themselves and others. They are amaurotic.

Married Christians, while indubitably recipients of godly sight themselves, have the responsibilities and distractions of raising a family, as well as the full-time ministry a godly marriage requires. These "divided interests" of the married person *can* lead to a relative lack of clarity, especially with regard to espousing a Biblical worldview by noticing the myriad details of life going on all around them.

We however, my dear brothers and sisters, cannot live the sightless lives of the unbeliever. Nor can we live the distracted lives of the married Christian. For we have been given not only real vision and knowledge of the truth, but also the gift of singleness, both of which are unfathomable blessings. Knowing that, we must remember this truth: **"Everyone to whom much was given, of him much will be required, and from him to whom they entrusted much, they will demand the more"** (Luke 12:48b).

In the context of this chapter, this means that with our apperception comes the requirement to use it for God's glory and to bless others in His name. Hence, we are left with an unmitigated call to action now. So it's time to truly focus our attentions. As singles, we have no excuse for having "divided interests," and thus we should repent of any existence of this in our lives. The "heart distractions" of singles can show up in a myriad of ways — our careers, education, social activities, money, and hobbies. Any one of those things *can* divide our interests and challenge our "sobriety," just as a family *can* do for the married person.

The Decree...

> "Be sober-minded; be watchful."
>
> (1 Peter 5:8a)

All throughout the New Testament we are commanded to be "sober," "alert," and "awake". I count approximately 15 occurrences of this universal Christian command therein. However, before we can learn how to obey this command, we must first take a look at what this Biblical "sobriety" really means. So let's go on a quick linguistic adventure...

As often happens in translations from the original Greek and Hebrew texts of the Holy Scriptures to English, the true meaning of every word is not always fully conveyed. That is very true here of the English words "sober-minded" and "watchful," as the contemporary English connotations for those words conjure up thoughts merely of "clear thinking" and "attentiveness". But neither of those definitions truly do justice to the words used here.

As an aside, this is also one of the reasons why the best way to truly *study* God's Word, rather than simply *reading* it, is by delving into the original language of the words used. But I'll digress, as that is a didactic lecture for another time, so onward let us move...

The Greek word translated as "sober-minded" in our passage, and in five other places in the New Testament, is *nēphō*[33]. It means to be free from all illusions, to be free from sin's intoxicating influences. It refers to a person having a clear, sound mind that is self-controlled and practices good judgment[34]. It's a *verb* and it appears in Scripture accordingly. In every Biblical occurrence, it's used as an *imperative* call to action, not as an *indicative* used for description. And thus we know that when we read this word in those texts, we are being *commanded* to do something, *not* merely being edified about something that we all *should* be practicing.

The Greek word translated in our passage as "watchful," and in twenty-two other places in the New Testament, is *grégoreó*[35]. It means to give strict and careful attention to something in a very proactive way. It carries a sense of urgency and warning, in that if it's not heeded, the result will be disaster[36]. It's also an *imperative verb*, and thus a given command...

Deference...

> **"I am saying this for your own good, not to restrict you, but that you may live in a right way in undivided devotion to the Lord."**
>
> (The Apostle Paul, 1 Corinthians 7:35, NIV)

This commanded sobriety is a charge that *can* be obeyed easier and *can* happen more organically for a single Christian, as opposed to the married believer for the reasons we've already discussed. This knowledge that we are commanded to be sober-minded, and that we have no excuse for not living in this sobriety, must serve as further "fuel for the fire" in the godly maximization of our singleness.

So how exactly does this happen? How do we practically obey this command in our everyday lives? What can we learn from our single sister Samantha? How can we as singles heed this command in a deeper way than most? There are several ways, and once again, they all involve seeing everything in the world through gospel glasses. So let's now jump deep into God's word in order to learn the truths that will give us this true clarity, in order to learn those truths that will make us ever more sober in a Biblical way.

Wholly Focalized Holiness...

> "I am the LORD your God; consecrate yourselves and be holy, because I am holy."
>
> (Leviticus 11:44a, NIV)

The first way we must all become "sober" is in our own personal walks with the Lord, in our own experiential sanctification. And as usual, this is something we can't do by ourselves. For **"who can discern their own errors?"** (Psalm 19:12a, NIV.) That's why we need a very Biblically clear view of *our own* sin in order to most effectively overcome it day by day. As our Lord Jesus Christ said, **"why worry about a speck in your friend's eye when you have a log in your own? Hypocrite! First get rid of the log in your own eye"** (Matthew 7:3,5a, NLT). You see, we're often tempted to easily notice the sins of others, while being blind to our own. That is yet another reason why we must always see ourselves through God's eyes! As Paul wrote, **"My conscience is clear, but that does not make me innocent. It is the Lord who judges me"** (1 Corinthians 4:4, NIV).

Thus, in order to gain this sobriety, we must pray like our brother David, **"Search me, O God, and know my heart! Try me and know my thoughts! And see if there be any grievous way in me, and lead me in the way everlasting! Create in me a clean heart, O God, and renew a right spirit within me"** (Psalm 139:23-24,51:10). This is also another reason why we must proactively study and memorize the word of God regularly. As the Psalmist wrote, **"The commandments of the LORD are right, bringing joy to the heart. The commands of the LORD are clear, giving insight for living. How can a young person stay pure? By obeying your word. I have hidden your word in my heart, that I might not sin against you"** (Psalm 19:8,119:9,11, NLT).

Remember, we are far too easily distracted by the cares of this world and by our own personal interests. These things can quite easily produce a state of "drunkenness" in this life, which destroys our true sobriety. Just like being drunk on alcohol, this prevents us from having the open eyes we need to see everyone and everything as God does. Our Lord Jesus Christ has admonished us against this! He exhorted us: **"Watch out! Don't let your hearts be dulled by carousing and drunkenness, and by the worries of this life"** (Luke 21:34a, NLT).

Do not be like those about whom the Lord warned us when He described them thus. They receive the word of God, **"but the cares of the world and the deceitfulness of riches and the desires for other things enter in and choke the word, and it proves unfruitful"** (Mark 4:19).

So continue to kill your sin. **"Wake up from your drunken stupor, as is right, and do not go on sinning"** (1 Corinthians 15:34a).

Keep it holy...because you are holy. For it is written of Christ our King and us, **"by a single offering he has perfected for all time those who are being sanctified"** (Hebrews 10:14).

Clean Your Gospel Glasses...

"I tell you, open your eyes and look at the fields!
They are ripe for harvest."
(The Lord Jesus Christ, John 4:35b, NIV)

Far too often, we pray for open evangelistic doors, yet completely fail to see the plethora of opportunities around us every day. And of this we need to repent because our failure to evangelize is almost always due to, not lack of opportunity, but our own spiritual blindness. It's due to our lack of *true* love for the lost souls all around us. For if we truly espoused the loving care for the unsaved we so often claim, we would not only see the open doors abounding in our lives, we'd *run* through them.

The Lord has commanded us to take our blinders off and see the "ripe fields" in which we all live. God has you where He does for very specific reasons, not the least of which is to be His mouthpiece there. So if The Lord were to call us home tomorrow, the whole "but I didn't have enough evangelistic opportunities" excuse simply wouldn't fly, and in our heart of hearts we know this to be true. Yet, we much too frequently tell ourselves shallow lies to the contrary in an attempt to exempt ourselves from this highest calling.

Single Christian, let this no longer be so for us. Not only do we have the same amount of, if not more, open doors than the married Christian, we have far more time and earthly freedom to obediently maximize those opportunities.

Think about the sheer amount of people you interact with on your average day. From the barista at your morning coffee stop, to your coworkers all morning, to the lady behind the counter at lunch, to your afternoon clients, to all the people at your gym in the evening. If we would plain and simply "open our eyes," as we're commanded, we'd see that the vast majority of these people desperately need Jesus! Yet with the barista we only see a caramel macchiato, with coworkers we only see projects that need to get done, with the counter lady we only see clam chowder, with our clients we only see dollar signs, and with those working out around us we only see the machines we want to use.

We see what we want to see, what's most "convenient" and "beneficial" for *us*, rather than seeing those people as God does. Remember, there's only *one* issue that truly bifurcates all of humanity and that is whether or not a human soul knows the

Lord Jesus Christ as their personal Savior. Thus, through gospel glasses, that is how we must see all people as well. Among the unsaved, we mustn't see black or white, female or male, old or young. We must only see a soul that urgently needs to be reconciled to God.

Once we see people this way, we will necessarily be burdened and emboldened to prayerfully point them to Christ. No longer will we cowardly avoid presenting the gospel, nor will we avoid evangelism because it may be "inconvenient" at the time. Instead, we will seek to save those walking on that narrow tightrope from which a fall will separate them from God forever. We'll proactively snatch them off that tightrope in obedience to our Lord and Savior Jesus Christ.

This will not happen unless we walk in sobriety daily. As Paul exhorted Timothy: **"As for you, *always* be sober-minded, endure suffering, do the work of an evangelist, fulfill your ministry"** (2 Timothy 4:5, italics mine). You see, if your interests in social interactions with unbelievers are merely focused on earthly concerns, you are not being wise. That's why we're admonished to **"Walk in wisdom toward outsiders, making the best use of the time. Let your speech always be gracious, seasoned with salt, so that you may know how you ought to answer each person"** (Colossians 4:5-6).

Secular society has coined the phrase "social intelligence," and praises those with a high level of this attribute. Basically what this means is the aptitude a person has in efficaciously communicating and interacting with other people. It means having both a strong level of self-control over one's tongue, discernment of others' needs and desires, and high situational awareness. Persons who evince this trait are the type sought for management positions in every vocational area. Though this may be a relatively new concept to the unbelieving world, for Christians this is something we've been commanded to espouse for 2,000 years. Check it: **"But in your hearts revere Christ as Lord.** *Always be prepared* **to give an answer to everyone who asks you to give the reason for the hope that you have.** *But do this with gentleness and respect"* (1 Peter 3:15, NIV, italics mine). *That* is real and true "social intelligence". Not merely knowing *how* to interact effectively, but knowing *what* information must be shared in every interaction.

Christians who possess an abundance of this characteristic will be the most highly effective in God's Kingdom. For those saints understand what Paul was saying when he wrote: **"I have become all things to all people, that by all means I might save some"** (1 Corinthians 9:22b). You see, in every social interaction, Paul wasn't merely interested in being a gentleman. Rather, he *custom-tailored* his exchanges with nonbelievers to ensure that he communicated the Gospel in the best way possible. To do this, he had to be *sober* enough to understand the other person and what they needed to hear to receive God's saving message.

As you grow in this biblical social intelligence, in this area of sobriety, remember to be fearless. For we have nothing to truly fear. Indeed, **"the righteous are bold as a lion"** (Proverbs 28:1b).

The "One Anothers"...

**"Therefore encourage one another and
build one another up, just as you are doing."**

(1 Thessalonians 5:11)

Another major area that demands our attentive sobriety is that of seeing and meeting the needs of our brethren. For we are commanded thus: **"So then, let us aim for harmony in the church** and try to build each other up" (Romans 14:19, NLT). Obedience to this command requires a *proactive* effort. We don't just naturally "build each other up," but rather this must be something that we consciously seek to accomplish. As our verse says, we must "aim" and "try" to make this happen.

The first place this must happen is in the sober control and choice of our words. As we've been commanded, **"Do not let any unwholesome talk come out of your mouths, but only what is helpful for building others up according to their needs, that it may benefit those who listen"** (Ephesians 4:29, NIV). This means that in all our conversations with other believers, we must proactively choose themes and words that make for the edification of our brethren. We mustn't engage in the coarse jesting, the childish crude joking, the inane blabber, or the baseless conjecture of this fallen world. Rather, we must see our intra-church interactions as they truly are...ministry fields. Every single time we meet or speak with each other is another opportunity to bless each other to God's glory.

And a beautiful truth about obeying this command is that it also comes with a promise. Check this out: **"And the Lord replied, 'A faithful, sensible servant is one to whom the master can give** *the responsibility of managing his other household servants and feeding them.* **If the master returns and finds that the servant has done a good job, there will be a reward. I tell you the truth, the master will put that servant in charge of all he owns'"** (Luke 12:42-44, NLT, italics mine). There we see, when we dutifully and lovingly "manage and feed" our Lord's servants, who are our brethren in Christ, this is pleasing to God and thus rewarded. So let's all be sober among each other and **"May the Lord make your love increase and overflow for each other and for everyone else, just as ours does for you"** (1 Thessalonians 3:12, NIV).

Beneficence...

> "Let each of you *look* not only to his own interests,
> but also to the interests of others."
>
> (Philippians 2:4, italics mine)

As we "open our eyes" to the truth of reality all around us, we see the vast and multitudinous needs of people everywhere. Once we see these, we can then proactively endeavor to meet those needs. As Solomon wrote, **"Do not withhold good from those who deserve it when it's in your power to help them. If you can help your neighbor now, don't say, "Come back tomorrow, and then I'll help you"** (Proverbs 3:27-28, NLT). This applies both to the believer and non-believer alike. As we've been exhorted, **"See that no one pays back evil for evil, but always try to do good *to each other and to all people*"** (1 Thessalonians 5:15, NLT, italics mine). Once again, we see this is something we must proactively "try" to achieve. It's not something that happens automatically or without effort.

Now, here's the most challenging area of "sober love" yet, that of consciously loving and serving our *enemies*. Our Lord Jesus Christ laid down this command: **"But I say, love your enemies! Pray for those who persecute you! In that way, you will be acting as true children of your Father in heaven. For he gives his sunlight to both the evil and the good, and he sends rain on the just and the unjust alike"** (Matthew 5:44-45, NLT). You see, our enemies, no matter who they are, are *human souls* in need of a savior. Remember, there are only two types of people, *saved* and *unsaved*. Through gospel glasses, we must see all people as such. Accordingly, when this happens, we'll see that our enemies need prayer and service too. Being sober enough to know this, we'll be much more enabled to obey the Lord's command to lovingly serve and minister to them all.

Thus, we must ceaselessly *look* for the abundance of opportunities we have to be a blessing. We then must continually and joyfully pursue those avenues of magnanimity. **"So let's not get tired of doing what is good. At just the right time we will reap a harvest of blessing if we don't give up. Therefore, whenever we have the opportunity, we should do good to everyone—especially to those in the family of faith"** (Galatians 6:9-10, NLT).

Imminence...

"**The end of all things is near. Therefore be alert and of sober mind so that you may pray.**"

(1 Peter 4:7, NIV)

In sports, the closer a game, match, or season gets to completion, the harder the athletes competing strive to excel. As the time in each competition moves forward, the pressure mounts accordingly. The competitors do not become more lackadaisical as this happens; instead, they become increasingly more alert, aware, and proactive. And beloved, remember this truth, **"Every athlete exercises self-control in all things. They do it to receive a perishable wreath,** *but we an imperishable*" (1 Corinthians 9:25, italics mine).

Since we pursue an indestructible crown of life, as our walks progress, we must become perpetually more sober, alert, and awake. For indeed, **"The night is far gone; the day is at hand. So then let us cast off the works of darkness and put on the armor of light"** (Romans 13:12).

We are in the final seconds of the final game of the "season," which is this life, the short side of eternity. So we must be sober-minded before that final "buzzer" sounds, or as Solomon put it, **"before the silver cord is snapped, or the golden bowl is broken, or the pitcher is shattered at the fountain, or the wheel broken at the cistern, and the dust returns to the earth as it was, and the spirit returns to God who gave it"** (Ecclesiastes 12:6-7).

It doesn't matter if you're 22 or 72, because God has not promised you a tomorrow on this earth. Thus, we must heed our Lord's admonition. He said: **"Look, I come like a thief! Blessed is the one who stays awake and remains clothed, so as not to go naked and be shamefully exposed"** (Revelation 16:15, NIV).

The world will tempt you all the time to pursue or acquiesce to its complacency, to its "sleepiness". But always remember, **"those who sleep, sleep at night, and those who get drunk, are drunk at night. But since we belong to the day, let us be sober, having put on the breastplate of faith and love, and for a helmet the hope of salvation"** (1 Thessalonians 5:7-8).

Though The Lord Jesus Christ has not told us *when* He will return, He has promised that He *will* do so at a time when many will not be ready. Therefore, my fellow servants of God, fully imbibe this truth: **"The servants who are ready and waiting for his return will be rewarded. I tell you the truth, he himself will seat them, put on an apron, and serve them as they sit and eat! He may come in the middle of the night or just before dawn. But whenever he comes, he will reward the servants who are ready. Understand this: If a homeowner knew exactly when a burglar was coming, he would not permit his house to be broken into. You also must be ready all the time, for the Son of Man will come when least expected"** (Luke 12:37-40, NLT).

Indeed, it's not only we who wait with bated breath for our Savior's glorious return, but **"all creation is waiting eagerly for** that future day when God will reveal who his children really are" (Romans 8:19, NLT).

So **"as for you, brothers and sisters, never tire of doing what is good"** (2 Thessalonians 3:13, NIV). I beseech you, saints of the most high God, to stay *sober* in your singleness and use it fully to the glory of our Lord. For **"When Christ who is your life appears, then you also will appear with him in glory"** (Colossians 3:4).

Beloved...stay focused on the Lord. Consecrate yourselves to Him. Sanctify your minds. Kill the worldly distractions. Be holy. Evangelize the lost all around you. Serve your brethren and everyone else. Sober up and open your eyes.

> **"This is all the more urgent, for you know how late it is; time is running out. *Wake up*, for our salvation is nearer now than when we first believed."**
>
> (Romans 13:11, NLT, Italics Mine)

Section C:

Prepare Yourself...

YOUR TRUE GOOD - SECTION INTRO

> "And we know that for those who love God
> all things work together for good,
> for those who are called according to his purpose."
>
> (Romans 8:28)

That awesome verse in Romans is so massively powerful, edifying, and comforting. There we learn that all things in our lives are divinely orchestrated together for God's glory and our good.

Accordingly, it's been used to bless an untold number of Christians, dealing with many varieties of life issues, all throughout the last 2,000 years.

Unfortunately, it's also been widely abused by quoting it out of context. When this happens, people are left to self-define the word "good".

As D.A. Carson says quoting his father: "a text without a context becomes a pretext for a proof text[37]". Much disaster can result from this type of eisegesis, especially with a verse so strong.

What is <u>Good</u>?

You see, we *think* we know what's *really* "good" for us, and thus we're tempted to interpret this Scripture in a way that caters to our personal desires. But our sinfulness and finite minds render us incapable of attaining that truth on our own. Instead, we're told: **"Trust in the LORD with all your heart, and do not lean on your own understanding. In all your ways acknowledge him, and he will make straight your paths"** (Proverbs 3:5-6).

Just as a 4-year old thinks it's in his best interest to stay up late eating candy, the teenager thinks his parents have no clue what they're talking about, and many adults have a litany of national policy changes they'd immediately implement were they elected president, we are all tempted to think we know everything, but we really don't.

That's why it's so incredibly important for us to understand what our *true* good is and how *God* defines that phrase! He reveals this in the very next verse:

> **"For those whom he foreknew he also predestined to be conformed to the image of his Son"**
>
> (Romans 8:29a)

Thus, what's *truly* good for us, what's *really* in our best interest, what *God* is working toward in us...is making us more like our Lord Jesus Christ!

This will happen *regardless* of the life events and circumstances that may be required for God to achieve that righteous end. Our Heavenly Father is *omnipotent*, that is, He alone is sovereign over *everything* that happens to us. Accordingly, God's going to lovingly and meticulously arrange every single piece of minutiae in our day-to-day existence, in every season of our lives...to make us think, feel, and act progressively more like His holy Son.

Thus, we must fully imbibe that this also includes our marital status! Whatever marital status will make you more like the Lord Jesus Christ (be it single, married, or widowed) that is where you will be placed. If and when it will make you more like Jesus to be married, you will be married. Right now, it will make you more like Jesus to be single; so, you have been placed in singleness. It's that simple.

We must take great comfort in the fact that, as God's children, wherever we are at this moment is exactly where God wants us. Knowing this, we must place all of our trust in the Lord and His plan for our lives, receiving the indescribably deep peace that comes from this complete acquiescence to God.

Maturation...

These truths must bring contentment. However, this doesn't mean they're supposed to make us complacent and passive, quite the contrary actually.

In the context of this book, if you are single and you desire to get married, among other things, you need to be prayerfully seeking what God wants you to learn and how He wants you to grow before He will flip the switch and "change the seasons".

Single Christian, God's goal for your life is not your personal happiness. His goal is growth in your personal holiness! God doesn't say "be happy, for I am happy". Rather, He commands us thus: **"You must be holy because I, the LORD, am holy. I have set you apart from all other people to be my very own"** (Leviticus 20:26, NLT, cf. 1 Peter 1:13-25).

This mustn't bring a frown to your face, for with holiness comes joy unspeakable! You see, joy and happiness are two entirely different things. Happiness is "you-centered"; joy is "God and others-centered". Happiness is earthly; joy is holy. Happiness is of the flesh; joy is of the Spirit **(cf. Galatians 5:22)**. The Lord both commands and gives this joy, which we'll discuss deeper in a later chapter.

For now, instead of "kicking against the goads" of God's sanctification, it's time to submit. Rather than asking God, "Why am I single right now?," it's time to ask God, "How am I going to become more like your holy Son, my Lord and Savior, right now?"

Remember this: **"A single rebuke does more for a person of understanding than a hundred lashes on the back of a fool"** (Proverbs 17:10, NLT).

Thus, we've all been left with a choice to make.

We can either respond wisely to God's reproof; letting Him sanctify, grow, and strengthen us, thus moving everything forward in our hearts and lives.

Or, we can act like the hard-headed fool who has to receive 101 "lashes" from God's refining hand before he will change, thereby delaying all growth in maturity and sanctification in our lives.

Obviously, there's only one acceptable option.

The practical questions...

So how must this season of singleness make us more like our Lord, Savior, and King Jesus Christ?

Just how must we vigorously and proactively pursue spiritual growth during this season of life?

How must our singleness make us more holy?

How must you use this time to prepare yourself, not only for marriage, but to *be* a godly spouse?

Answering those questions is the focus of this section. So let's dive into God's Word for those answers and be changed by them. As Solomon wrote:

> "For everything there is a season,
> a time for every activity under heaven.
> *Yet God has made everything beautiful for its own time."*
> (Ecclesiastes 3:1,11, NLT, italics mine)

STRENGTH...

**"The name of the LORD is a strong tower;
the righteous man runs into it and is safe."**
(Proverbs 18:10)

Let's go back in time and picture this true historical event, as recorded in **1 Samuel 30**.

There, David was the commander of an army and the husband of not one, but two wives. He was returning home with his soldiers after a successful campaign of raids. Life was pretty good, right?

But when David arrived back home, he found that an enemy army had kidnapped his wives.

Suddenly, David found himself in a very tough situation. He'd just been made effectively "single".

To make matters worse, the wives and children of all of David's men had been kidnapped as well!

Since he was their leader, **"David was greatly distressed, for the people spoke of stoning him, because all the people were**

bitter in soul, each for his sons and daughters" (1 Samuel 30:6a).

You think being single by yourself is hard? Well, imagine six hundred warrior men, freshly returned from victorious battles, now holding you responsible for their new "singleness" as well!

That is the exact situation where David, who would later go on to become King of Israel and a blessed ancestor of our Lord Jesus Christ by the way, now found himself. So how did David respond?

Did he get drunk to drown his sorrows?

Did he turn to some other sin to ease his pain?

Did he cowardly run away from his men?

Did he go looking for some new women?

With no friends around, did he attempt suicide?

Did he ask his broken men for advice?

No! David was a true man of God, so for him there was but only one acceptable way to respond:

"David strengthened himself in the LORD his God."

(v. 6b)

There was no alcohol abuse. There was no debauchery. There was no cowardly fleeing. There was no promiscuous dating. There was no suicide attempt. There was no turning to human "wisdom".

There was only this: David **"said to Abiathar the priest, 'Bring me the ephod!'"** (v. 7a, NLT). Now the ephod was basically a vest of sorts, worn by the priests such as Abiathar, when serious and focused counsel of the LORD was to be sought through prayer. Thus, in immediate response to his crisis, **"David inquired of the LORD"** (v. 8) as to what course of action he should take, fully acquiescent to obey whatever the LORD commanded of him.

Faced with catastrophe and "sudden singleness," multiplied 600-fold, David turned to the LORD *alone*. In doing so, among many other things, David gave every "single" man and woman of God who would come after him a perfect example to follow. Thus, my brethren, let's espouse this godly man's wisdom.

This is one of the paramount lessons we need to learn from our current life state. Our singleness must make us *strong in the Lord*! This is yet another way that it will grow and bless us immeasurably.

There's a great old saying: "You don't know Jesus is all you need, until Jesus is all you have." One of the beautiful designs of being single is that it forces us to rely on God for emotional and spiritual support 24/7, and this is a very beautiful thing. This truth has been one of the greatest lessons God has taught me through my own singleness.

While it's undeniable that we all need strong Christian fellowship in our lives, our ultimate source of strength must forever be the Lord Jesus!

I love my brothers and sisters immensely, but I've learned the truth that we cannot rely completely on others, as they are all frail sinners just like we are. I've learned that we can only rely fully on God for the strength to handle *anything*.

Jesus is the only One who will *always* be there for you. When you wake up alone in your bed from a nightmare at 3 AM, when you have an argument with a close friend, when an immediate family member gets sick, Jesus is there. He is there not only to give you strength, He is there to *be* your strength!

Beloved, please remember, your current singleness is *by divine design*, to grow you in the image and likeness of our Lord Jesus Christ. And one of our Lord's character traits was a complete and utter reliance on his Father for strength in *everything*.

That is just as was prophesied about Him: **"And he shall stand and shepherd his flock in the strength of the LORD, in the majesty of the name of the LORD his God. And they shall dwell secure, for now he shall be great to the ends of the earth. And he shall be their peace"** (Micah 5:4-5a).

So if King Jesus leaned on our Abba for strength in all things, how much more must we learn to do the same? So let's imbibe *now*, as singles, the truth in these words of our Lord: **"For apart from me you can do nothing"** (John 15:5).

This is a highly valuable lesson that many other people of God have learned throughout history.

As **Habakkuk** wrote, when writing about his own difficult earthly trials: **"GOD, the Lord, is my strength; he makes my feet like the deer's; he makes me tread on my high places"** (v. 3:19a).

As **Jeremiah** wrote, when facing the Babylonian captivity: **"O LORD, my strength and my stronghold, my refuge in the day of trouble"** (v. 16:19a).

As was written of John the Baptist: **"the child grew and *became strong in spirit*, and he was in the wilderness until the day of his public appearance to Israel"** (Luke 1:80, italics mine). No doubt, being single and living in the wilderness made John one of the strongest men of God that's ever lived.

Paul learned this lesson, too. Speaking of his difficult "thorn in the flesh," a pain he couldn't handle on his own, a pain he'd repeatedly asked God to remove, he wrote, **"But he said to me, 'My grace is sufficient for you, for my power is made perfect in weakness.' Therefore I will boast all the more gladly of my weaknesses, so that the power of Christ may rest upon me"** (2 Corinthians 12:9).

You see, in the areas of weakness in your life, God's answers to your prayers for removal of an affliction may be similar. More specifically, if your singleness is an area of weakness and pain in your life, this might be one of the exact reasons why you're still single. God won't let you live in "strength" that's gained outside of Him - be it yourself, your spouse, or any other human relationship.

God teaches some of His children this lesson through marriage and some of them through singleness. Either way, He wants our strength to be in and from Him alone, for His glory and our good.

Paul understood this, hence this was his response to the Lord's gracious refusal to remove his "thorn": ***"For the sake of Christi*, then, I am content with weaknesses, insults, hardships, persecutions, and calamities.** For when I am weak, then I am strong"* (2 Corinthians 12:10, italics mine).

When *Paul* was weak, *Christ* was strong, in and for him. Single Christian, please personalize this passage. For example, if singleness is a thorn in your flesh, then read the passage like this: "Therefore I will boast all the more gladly of my singleness, so that the power of Christ may rest upon me. For the sake of Christ, then, I am content with singleness. For when I am weak, then I am strong."

Once again, this is another major reason why I love and am so thankful for the blessing of my current singleness, because it *keeps me growing stronger in the Lord daily*! I'd much rather be single right now and learning to live in my perfect Lord's strength alone, than getting married before I've learned this lesson, and as a result, being reliant on a fallible human spouse for strength. And just to be clear, I'm not saying that a spirit of "utter co-dependence" is by nature present in all marriages. What I am saying is that your current singleness must be wisely used to allow God to grow your heart's total dependence on Him alone!

In "strengthening ourselves in the LORD our GOD" as David did, God also prepares us to be his "strong hand" to our brethren. Because we have everything *we* need in Jesus, we can be used as a conduit of God's strength. You can't share something you don't have an excess of, but when your strength is from God, it's *limitless* and *outflowing*!

This truth is not to dissuade you from growing many human relationships. Rather, it's so you understand where you must base your personal trust and to understand what your role should be in those relationships, the role of bless-*er*! You must use this time to learn to be God's strength to others, so that He may strengthen them through you!

Just as our Lord Jesus Christ said: **"It is more blessed to give than to receive'"** (Acts 20:35b).

This lesson, that our current life state is not only for our own good but also for the good of our brethren, is something we also learn from Paul.

Speaking of the multitudinous painful trials he faced in Asia, he wrote: **"Indeed, we felt that we had received the sentence of death. But** *that was to make us rely not on ourselves but on God who raises the dead"* (2 Corinthians 1:9, italics mine).

And what was a result of this learned strength in the Lord? It wasn't only for his personal benefit. Rather, by God's design, it was so he could extend that benefit and be God's strong hand for others! For this Paul praised God: **"Blessed be the God and Father of our Lord Jesus Christ, the Father of mercies and God of all comfort,** *who comforts us in all our affliction, so that we may be able to comfort those who are in any affliction, with the comfort with which we ourselves are comforted by God"* (2 Corinthians 1:3-4, italics mine).

Indeed, as the Lord said to Peter when he was about to face one of his greatest trials, **"I have prayed for you, Simon, that your faith may not fail. And** *when you have turned back, strengthen your brothers*" (Luke 22:32, NIV, italics mine). That is, when his own strength in the Lord had been increased through this fiery trial, Peter could in turn "strengthen his brethren". We see the consummation of this promise to Peter, when after his repentance, the Lord commanded him three times:

"Feed my sheep."

(John 21:15-17)

For you personally, if it be God's will, your future family will be among the many "sheep" you will be able to feed. Regardless of the recipients of your ministry though, you must first remember a very important truth about life. As The Lord Jesus Christ said: **"In the world you will have tribulation"** (John 16:33B). Thus, life's storms are not a matter of *if*, but only a matter of *when* they occur. Accordingly, you must *respond* to those storms in some way. *How* you respond is what matters most.

In **Matthew 7**, the Lord exhorts us: **"Everyone then who hears these words of mine and does them will be like a wise man who built his house on the rock. And the rain fell, and the floods came, and the winds blew and beat on that house, but it did not fall, because it had been founded on the rock"** (vv. 24-25). Sadly, when faced with stormy seas, the worldly turn to alcohol and other drugs or sinful activities for the "strength" to deal with those issues. They are those of whom the Lord spoke when He said: **"And everyone who hears these words of mine and does not do them will be like a foolish man who built his house on the sand. And the rain fell, and the floods came, and** the winds blew and beat against that house, and it fell, and great was the fall of it"** (vv. 26-27).

In that extolling, we see that if our lives are based in the strength of the Lord we will not fall, even when the winds are most fierce. For **"the LORD gives his people strength"** (Psalm 29:11a, NLT). This is why you must learn to build *your* life on "The Rock" right now, so you can build *your family's* life on The Rock if and when that time comes!

The truth is crystal clear. Any source of "strength" outside of God will always fail greatly. So as God's people, we must build our houses on the only immovable bedrock Foundation. We must base the strength we need to conquer the giants in our lives solely in the Lord our God! Brethren, we must **"Trust in the LORD forever, for the LORD GOD is an everlasting rock"** (Isaiah 26:4).

The Whole Armor...

"Be strong, all you people of the land, declares the LORD.
Work, for I am with you, declares the LORD of hosts"

(Haggai 2:4b)

How then do we learn and grow in the strength of the Lord practically? God teaches us how through Paul in **Ephesians 6**. There, we receive this firm command: **"be strong in the Lord and in the strength of his might"** (v. 10).

Paul then explains, step-by-step, how this happens practically. He says: **"Put on the whole armor of God, that you may be able to stand against the schemes of the devil"** (v. 11). Before we discuss those individual pieces of "armor," and how to correctly use them, it's very important to understand the historical context under which Ephesians was written.

Paul wrote Ephesians around 60 AD from a Roman prison.

Thus, he was very familiar with Roman soldiers and warfare, and his illustrations reflect what would have been contemporaneously common knowledge at the time. Knowing the historical context of the writing helps us to understand Paul's illustrations better. That being said, though "physical" weapons are used as easy to understand descriptives, it must be remembered that our battles are *spiritual*: **"For we do not wrestle against flesh and blood, but against the rulers, against the authorities, against the cosmic powers over this present darkness, against the spiritual forces of evil in the heavenly places"** (v. 12). So let's take a look at the specific items we'll need to wear to truly **"be able to withstand in the evil day, and having done all, to stand firm"** (v. 13b).

Transcendent Couture: **"Stand therefore, having fastened on the belt of truth"** (v. 14a). The Greek word translated as "belt" here, *perizōsamenoi*, really means a "girdle"[38]. This is very important for understanding this verse, as for a Roman soldier, the girdle was what held all the pieces of their armor in place. Thus, it was the "foundation stone" for the "house" of their equipment.

Accordingly, we must "fasten on" both the knowledge of God's word *and* the knowledge that God's word is absolute and unequivocal truth as the foundation for our lives. This is the *first* step in growing in the strength of the Lord.

Just knowing God's word is not enough, unless we truly and wholeheartedly imbibe the fact that *anything* in contrast with God's word is utter falsehood. In this way, **"we will no longer be infants, tossed back and forth by the waves, and blown here and there by every wind of teaching and by the cunning and craftiness of men in their deceitful scheming"** (Ephesians 4:14). As our brother Cephas wrote in **2 Peter**, **"we did not follow**

cleverly devised myths when we made known to you the power and coming of our Lord Jesus Christ, but we were eyewitnesses of his majesty. *And we have something more sure, the prophetic word"* (vv. 1:16,19a, italics mine). This is major, as Peter is there saying effectively this: "yes, we saw Jesus' glorious transfiguration with our own two eyes, but more important than just believing our testimony, believe *God's word* that testified about him long before we were even born because *that* is truth". If our apostolic brother decreased the value of his own words in comparison to God's word, how much more must we do the same with the words of all men? Just as we discussed in the first chapter of this book, *any* unbiblical view thrown at you must be trashed immediately.

Before you can even begin to grow in the other graces of Godly strength, you must first *forsake* the other paradigms and false sources of strength that come your way. You must also *forget* the way you used to deal with problems and issues.

To grow in God's strength from now on, you must firmly resolve to take *all* of your problems to God. This means that in your current storms, you must no longer "self-medicate" the way you may once have. By the very nature of the process, there will be "growing pains" involved, but the results will be more than worth it all. Just as it's painful to work out at the gym, you do it anyway because the resultant increases in strength merits the endurance.

Where you may have turned to some secular media source in the past, you must now turn to God's word *alone* for wisdom. Where you may have turned to some sinful activity in the past, you must now turn to prayer instead. Where you may have hung out with non-Christians in the past for a fun night out, you must now seek that only among Christians.

Where you may have sought contentment through human relationships in the past, you must now learn to get this from the Lord alone. In the context of this book, this is *the* most important grace of Godly strength in which to grow. To understand this better, let's go to **John 4** and study the eternally famous interaction between our Lord Jesus Christ and the Samarian "woman at the well".

There, the Lord told that woman, **"Go, call your husband, and come here"** (v. 16). He already knew that she wasn't actually married, but He was testing her in order to illustrate a point and to prove who He was. **"The woman answered him, 'I have no husband.' Jesus said to her, 'You are right in saying, 'I have no husband'; for you have had five husbands, and the one you now have is not your husband. What you have said is true'"** (vv. 17-18).

Knowing these facts helps us to comprehend more deeply the earlier part of their conversation, after Jesus had asked the woman for a drink of water and she had responded in awe that the request was made: **"Jesus said to her, 'Everyone who drinks of this water will be thirsty again, but whoever drinks of the water that I will give him will never be thirsty again. The water that I will give him will become in him a spring of water welling up to eternal life.' The woman said to him, 'Sir, give me this water, so that I will not be thirsty or have to come here to draw water'** (vv. 13-15).

It's obvious that she immediately perceived what the Lord was talking about, that he wasn't merely speaking of satiating her physical desire for H^2O. She had spent her life seeking contentment, seeking "living water" through many adulterous relationships and she was, at that moment, still doing the same. She had been through many different guys, many different false saviors, and they had all left her "thirsty". Now, here was one offering her *true* salvation; before her stood a *true* Savior.

She had to inquire further, saying, **"Our fathers worshiped on this mountain, but you say that in Jerusalem is the place where people ought to worship"** (v. 20). Her inquiry was far more than a mere question of where to go to church. She was really asking, "How do I *receive* this salvation of which you speak?" The Lord's response perfectly illustrates the only real bifurcation of humanity and gives the answer to the deepest query of her soul, and every other soul on the planet. He said, **"You worship what you do not know; we worship what we know, for salvation is from the Jews. But the hour is coming, and is now here, when the true worshipers will worship the Father in spirit and truth, for the Father is seeking such people to worship him"** (vv. 22-23). The Samarians, and all others outside of God, sought salvation through physical relationships, but real salvation comes only through one's spiritual relationship with God.

Satisfying the desires of her flesh would never save her soul. All the physical affection and attention a man could give would never bring her peace, make her content, or complete her life. The salvation, tranquility, contentment, and completeness she desperately wanted would be gained only through acquiescence to the one speaking to her.

Christian, the same truth applies to us. You can have all the physical relationships in the world, all the attention of the opposite sex, all the affection of another person. But it will not make you complete; it will not save you. Only Jesus can do this for you. For only your relationship with Him can give you the love and affection your soul desires.

Every day, we receive lies to the contrary. We're told, "Once you get married, you'll have everything you need, you'll be complete, you'll have the strength to face anything". Don't believe those falsities. Because beloved, in Christ, you're *already* there. In Him, you have everything you need — you're complete. He alone will truly give you the strength you need to conquer *anything*.

That is the truth.

Impenetrable Holiness: "**and having put on the breastplate of righteousness**" (Ephesians 6:14b). The Greek word used for "breastplate" here, *thōraka*, is the etymological root of the English word "thorax"[39]. It literally meant the piece of chain-mail soldiers wore to protect their physical heart. Accordingly, we here learn that it's our righteousness that protects our spiritual hearts. This is both the positional righteousness we have in Christ and the experiential righteousness we walk in because we are His!

This is the second step of our growth in strength; it's our second series of workouts. The first step, being in God's word and forsaking all other sources of knowledge, automatically leads to this second step. This happens because our Lord prayed to our Father for us, **"Sanctify them in the truth; your word is truth"** (John 17:17). It happens because **"the word of God is living and active, sharper than any two-edged sword, piercing to the division of soul and of spirit, of joints and of marrow, and discerning the thoughts and intentions of the heart"** (Hebrews 4:12). Thus, being in the Word of God is indubitably sanctifying for the Christian. It's automatically going to produce more experiential righteousness in your life. In turn, it makes your heart stronger in the Lord and arms you with ever-increasing self-control.

We learn more about what this means practically by looking at another place where Paul uses the Greek word *thōraka*. In **1 Thessalonians** he wrote, **"since we belong to the day, *let us be*** *self-controlled,* **putting on faith and love as a breastplate**" (v. 5:8a, italics mine). It's our *righteous self-control* that protects our hearts from evil, and this illustration used by Paul is nothing new. Amazingly, the LORD our God Himself, when coming to redeem His people from evil around them, was described by **Isaiah** thus: **"The LORD saw it, and it displeased him that there was no justice. He saw that there was no man, and wondered that there was no one to intercede; then his own arm brought him salvation, and his righteousness upheld him. He put on righteousness as his breastplate"** (vv. 59:15b-17a). Wow! If God arms *himself* with "a breastplate of righteousness" when going out to war against his enemies, how much more must we do the same in our spiritual battles?

Wearing this "spiritual chain-mail" will make us stronger than any temptation thrown our way. By continually walking in the statutes of our Lord, and having his word written on our hearts, we wear impervious armor against sin and darkness. So we must always wear the breastplate of the knowledge of our complete, definitive sanctification in our Lord Jesus Christ and the ever-increasing experiential sanctification God the Holy Spirit brings forth in our lives.

Let us be like our brother **Job**, who in pontifical reminiscence about the original days of God's favor on his life, described himself like this: **"I put on righteousness, and it clothed me"** (v. 29:14a).

Combat Boots: **"and, as shoes for your feet, having put on the readiness given by the gospel of peace"** (Ephesians 6:15). Roman soldiers put nails in their boots to help them grip the ground in combat. These shoes helped them remain grounded, immovable, and steadfast in battle. This is the same type of lower body armor the Philistine giant Goliath wore, as described in **1 Samuel: "He also had bronze greaves on his legs"** (v. 17:6). Both Roman and Philistine soldiers weren't truly ready to go out to war until they had protected their feet and legs. As a golfer, even with all of my other equipment set, I'm not truly ready to play until I've put on my spikes.

In the same way, we don't have the readiness to go out and battle for the souls of men until we've firmly fastened on the "gospel of peace," the immutable truth that in Christ we are totally and completely at peace with God **(Romans 5:6-11)**. Just as our Lord Jesus Christ commanded his disciples to **"wear sandals"** when he sent them out two-by-two to preach the gospel (Mark 6:9), just as God commanded every Israelite to keep "**your sandals on your feet"** when eating the Passover meal which foreshadowed the new covenant gospel (cf. Exodus 12:11), we must figuratively do the same.

Having fortified our feet by strengthening ourselves in God's true gospel of grace, our feet become ready to take that truth to the world, and our feet become beautiful. As **Isaiah** wrote: **"How beautiful upon the mountains are the feet of him who brings good news, who publishes peace, who brings good news of happiness, who publishes salvation, who says to Zion, "Your God reigns"** (v. 52:7).

Fireproof Shield: **"In all circumstances take up the shield of faith, with which you can extinguish all the flaming darts of the evil one"** (Ephesians 6:16). The Greek word used for shield here, *thyreon*, means the big, heavy, oblong, full-door-size shield Roman soldiers carried to protect their entire bodies from arrows[40]. In effect, it protected not only the body, but all of the other pieces of armor the soldier wore as well. I love how Paul said to "in all circumstances" carry this shield. As Christian soldiers, we're never really in "peace time," as our enemy doesn't sleep. Accordingly, we must never be lax in our strong faith in the Lord. Just because we may be in a calm before a storm, this doesn't mean we can put our shields down, as that is the exact moment when fiery arrows may be shot our way. These "flaming darts," which are all manner of evil thoughts and temptations to evil, come at us in a myriad of ways, often where and when we least expect them. Our steadfast faith, which is our unshakable confidence in God and who we are in Him, allows us to render benign those flaming arrows. When those darts are sent our way, our faith allows us to see them for what they are, rather than entertaining, accepting, and internalizing them. When they hit our shield of faith, they simply fall to the ground, their flames extinguished.

As Paul also wrote: **"pray that we may be delivered from wicked and evil men, for not everyone has faith. But the Lord is faithful, and he will strengthen and protect you from the evil one"** (2 Thessalonians 2:3-4, NIV). Indeed He will, because He is faithful. Our faith in Him becomes our strength and protection. So let us echo the words of our brother David: **"You give me your shield of victory; you stoop down to make me great. My shield is God Most High, who saves the upright in heart"** (2 Samuel 22:46, Psalm 7:10, NIV).

Head Gear: **"And take THE HELMET OF SALVATION"** (Ephesians 6:17a, NASB). Roman soldiers often had emblems placed on their helmets. These emblems reminded them of who they were, what they were fighting for, and most importantly, *for whom* they were fighting. Because of this, their helmets didn't merely provide physical, cranial protection for their gray matter.

Rather, they also provided constant reminders for their minds that their authority was that of a higher power, in that case the Roman Empire. This gave them the hope of ultimate victory in battle. In a war, one of the major targets the enemy tries to hit is the head. In this case, we can think of it as the doubts and worries that try to enter our minds. We must "wear" the sacrosanct truth of our salvation as a helmet, protecting our assurance. On the cross, Jesus said **"Tetelestai,"** which means, **"It is finished"** (John 19:30). The **"chastisement that brought us peace"** (Isaiah 53:5) was completed at that moment. The salvation for which God had predestined us **(cf. Ephesians 1:5, Romans 8:29-30)** was accomplished. And God appropriated this finished work to us the moment we were born again by faith in Christ the King. This means it's a done deal; it's unchangeable and undeniable. So when our flesh tries to condemn us, when it tries to make us doubt, when it tries to make us worry about some sin we've committed or something we haven't done...the "helmet of salvation" protects us **(cf. Ephesians 2:8-9, Mark 3:28, Hebrews 10:29-23)**. As John MacArthur says, regarding the Helmet of Salvation: "the believer must be as conscious of his or her confident status in Christ as he or she would be aware of a helmet on the head[41]." Accordingly, our minds must always be protected by this truth, which is our "emblem of hope"! Because our victory has been secured on the cross at Calvary, nothing and no one can truly defeat us. One of the greatest attacks of the enemy is tempting one of God's children to doubt their salvation. Once a child of God has allowed the enemy this foothold, they open themselves up to other avenues of attack, namely temptations to sin. Christian, this must not be you, so put on your helmet! In this way, you will be made perpetually victorious accordingly. Your helmet will allow you to see the attacks on your salvific hope for what they are, nothing but heinous lies of the evil one. So when those attacks come, let these words be more emblems on your helmet of salvation: **"Who shall bring any charge against God's elect? It is God who justifies. Who is to condemn? Christ Jesus is the one who died—more than that, who was raised—who is at the right hand of God, who indeed is interceding for us"** (Romans 8:33-34).

The Sharpest Sword: **"and take the sword of the Spirit, which is the word of God"** (Ephesians 6:17b, NLT). The Greek word used for sword here, *machairan*, is the etymological root of the English word "machete"[42]. This allows us to visualize the type of physical sword being described. It was shorter than what we commonly, contemporaneously refer to as a sword, as it was basically a long dagger. It was used for active thrusting in close quarters, hand-to-hand combat, rather than being used for defensive cutting like a long sword that kept an enemy at bay. This is very important to note, as this sword is the only *offensive* weapon described in our "armor of God". Holy Scripture is *theopneustos*, which is the Greek word for "God-breathed"[43], as God the Holy Spirit "breathed" it all out through the prophets and apostles. Accordingly, while every other piece of spiritual armor we're commanded to wear is protective and preparatory in nature, the word of God transcends everything else. Again, as the writer of **Hebrews** penned: **"the word of God is *living* and *active*, sharper than any two-edged sword, *piercing* to the division of soul and of spirit, of joints and of marrow, and *discerning* the thoughts and intentions of the heart"** (v. 4:12, italics mine). This is why we must be in God's word constantly, learning it like the back of our hands, replacing our thoughts with God's thoughts. As the Psalmist wrote: **"How can a young man keep his way pure? By guarding it according to your word"** (Psalm 119:9). It is

God's will and desire for us to know his word thoroughly. As our brother **Jeremiah** prophesied of us: **"This is the covenant I will make with the house of Israel after that time," declares the LORD. "I will put my law in their minds and write it on their hearts. I will be their God, and they will be my people"** (v. 31:33, NIV). Again, as our Lord Jesus Christ prayed to our Father for us: **"Make them holy by your truth; teach them your word, which is truth"** (John 17:17, NLT).

The word of God not only protects us from every attack, it *actively* arms us for waging war against the evil one, both for ourselves and for the souls of men. It's so amazingly powerful and life altering, that all who hear it have no choice but to be changed in some way. That is why its preaching is the only thing that truly bifurcates humanity **(cf. John 12:48)**. Indeed, when we know and share the word of God, we become **"the aroma of Christ to God among those who are being saved and among those who are perishing, to one a fragrance from death to death, to the other a fragrance from life to life"** (2 Corinthians 2:15-16a). Accordingly, it is our God Himself who arms us with His omnipotent word, to fight His battles and win His victories. Just as the LORD said to and through **Jeremiah**, speaking about the unrepentant and false prophets, **"behold, I am making my words in your mouth a fire, and this people wood, and the fire shall consume them. Is not my word like fire, declares the LORD, and like a hammer that breaks the rock in pieces?"** (vv. 5:14b,23:29). Speaking through **Hosea**, the LORD spoke of his disciplinary actions toward His people: **"Therefore I cut you in pieces with my prophets, I killed you with the words of my mouth"** (v. 6:5). Amazing in the grandiosity of its power, isn't it?

Armed with this sword, we can echo the words of our brothers. With Paul, we can say: **"the weapons of our warfare are** not of the flesh but have divine power to destroy strongholds. We destroy arguments and every lofty opinion raised against the knowledge of God, and take every thought captive to obey Christ"** (2 Corinthians 10:4-5). With **Isaiah** we can say God **"made my mouth like a sharp sword; in the shadow of his hand he hid me; he made me a polished arrow; in his quiver he hid me away. The grass withers, the flower fades, but the word of our God will stand forever"** (vv. 49:2,40:8). So, let us arm ourselves with the most powerful weapon in existence, to offensively fight and win the battles to which we've been called, for we are soldiers of God and we know that **"no soldier gets entangled in civilian pursuits, since his aim is to please the one who enlisted him"** (2 Timothy 2:4). Brethren, through steadfast, daily, prayerful study, let us keep the sword of the Spirit at the ready and boldly march forward, knowing the truth God spoke of His word when He said: **"it shall not return to me empty, but it shall accomplish that which I purpose, and shall succeed in the thing for which I sent it"** (Isaiah 55:11).

The Completed Warrior: **"And pray in the Spirit on all occasions with all kinds of prayers and requests. With this in mind, be alert and always keep on praying for all the saints"** (Ephesians 6:18, NIV). Having clothed us with all the pieces of armor needed to **"be strong in the Lord and in his mighty power"** (v. 6:10, NIV), Paul now concludes this didactic discourse with the command that allows all of those pieces to remain effective...prayer. And he didn't leave us to self-define "prayer," oh no, he teaches us the kind of prayer we truly need. We are, first of all, taught to pray "in the Spirit," meaning praying with the empowering help of the Holy Spirit. We can't do this on our own! We're told: **"the Holy Spirit helps us in our weakness. For example, we don't know what God wants us to pray for. But the Holy Spirit prays for us with groanings that cannot be expressed in words. And the Father who knows all hearts knows what the Spirit is saying, for the Spirit pleads for us believers in harmony with God's own will" (Romans 8:26-27, NLT).

The Lord also teaches us to pray with importunity, that is, with unwavering constancy and perseverance. As recorded in "The Parable of the Persistent Widow" in **Luke 18**, **"Jesus told his disciples a parable to show them that they should always pray and not give up. And will not God bring about justice for his chosen ones, who cry out to him day and night? Will he keep putting them off? I tell you, he will see that they get justice, and quickly"** (vv. 1,7-8a, NIV). We can't just pray a few times about something, not receive a quick answer, and then just give up our supplication! No, we need to be like that widow who wouldn't stop petitioning the judge until he gave her an answer! God is more faithful to us than any human judge, so how can we not be faithful in presenting our requests to him, for any and everything? As Paul also wrote, from a Roman jail cell by way of reminder, **"do not be anxious about anything, but in everything by prayer and supplication with thanksgiving let your requests be made known to God"** (Philippians 4:6). We're then commanded to "be alert," meaning we need to constantly be looking for new areas of needed prayer, for ourselves and for everyone else. We're commanded: **"Never stop praying. Devote yourselves to prayer with an alert mind and a thankful heart"** (1 Thessalonians 5:17, Colossians 4:2, NLT). This means that even when our brethren don't specifically ask us to pray for them, if we see a Godly need in their lives, we must pray for them anyway. This should happen both corporately and privately, and we see great examples of this from our apostolic brothers. As we read in **Acts**, after the Lord's ascension to heaven, **"They all met together and were constantly united in prayer"** (v. 1:14a, NLT). Throughout his epistles, we see Paul dropping reminders like this to his readers: **"I have not stopped thanking God for you. I pray for you constantly"** (Ephesians 1:16, NLT). His ministry to those from whom he was geographically separated was not only through the written word; it was also through the accompanying prayer. So let the ministries, to which we've been called, whatever they may be, follow the same pattern of prayer. This prayer should not only be for our brothers and sisters, but for all men. As we're commanded: **"I urge you, first of all, to pray for all people. Ask God to help them; intercede on their behalf, and give thanks for them. Pray this way for kings and all who are in authority"** (1 Timothy 2:1-2a). In this way, our strong and mighty armor of God will be kept perpetually effective and powerful. We must always pray in the Holy Spirit, with praise and thanksgiving, for any and everything, for everyone including ourselves, proactively seeking how we can be a blessing and be blessed through this precious communion with our almighty, holy God.

Armed for Strength...

"David became more and more powerful,
because the LORD God of Heaven's Armies was with him."
(2 Samuel 5:10, NLT)

As God's precious chosen people, His strength is ours. We've just learned how to walk in this strength, so now let us do this always. As our Lord said to **Joshua: "Have I not commanded you? Be strong and courageous. Do not be frightened, and do not be dismayed, for the LORD your God is with you wherever you go"** (v. 1:9). As our Lord said through David: **"Wait for the**

LORD; be strong, and let your heart take courage; wait for the LORD!" (Psalm 27:14). As our Lord said through **Isaiah: "you whom I took from the ends of the earth, and called from its farthest corners, saying to you, "You are my servant, I have chosen you and not cast you off"; fear not, for I am with you; be not dismayed, for I am your God; I will strengthen you, I will help you, I will uphold you with my righteous right hand"** (vv. 41:9-10).

As the Lord said to his people through **Joel: "Let the weakling say, "I am strong!"** (v. 3:10b).

Brethren, once again, please learn this strength *now*, while you're single. You don't need a spouse and kids; you only need God. It isn't about not wanting that family; it's about understanding the truth that God is and always will be *everything* you need. In living out this truth, you will be prepared to strongly and courageously lead and raise a godly family in a fallen world, with the strength and courage of our strong and mighty God!

Beloved, having prepared yourself in this way, regardless of earthly plight, you will always be a godly leader. This means that even if your future wife finds a lump under her breast, even if your husband falls in battle, even if your child is snatched from your hands...you will be able to sing. With **Isaiah**, you will sing: **"Behold, God is my salvation; I will trust, and will not be afraid; for the LORD GOD is my strength and my song, and he has become my salvation"** (v. 12:2). With Moses and the people of Israel you will sing: **"The LORD is my strength and my song, and he has become my salvation; this is my God, and I will praise him, my father's God, and I will exalt him"** (Exodus 15:2).

Possessing this strength and grace will grow not only all of your Christian relationships, but your secular, evangelical relationships as well. Our witness to non-believers is not merely with our words, but with our behavior and actions around them. If they see that we react in a godly way to all the situations we encounter, they will see the beauty and reality of our Savior and be drawn to Him. As King Jesus said: **"In the same way, let your light shine before others, so that they may see your good works and give glory to your Father who is in heaven"** (Matthew 5:16).

In every area of your life, you are an ambassador for Christ, whether you realize it or not. As Christians, God **"has made us his captives and continues to lead us along in Christ's triumphal procession. Now he uses us to spread the knowledge of Christ everywhere, like a sweet perfume. Our lives are a Christ-like fragrance rising up to God. But this fragrance is perceived differently by those who are being saved and by those who are perishing. To those who are perishing, we are a dreadful smell of death and doom. But to those who are being saved, we are a life-giving perfume"** (2 Corinthians 2:14-16A, NLT).

Now then my dear brothers, let us all henceforth **"Be watchful, stand firm in the faith, act like men, be strong"** (1 Corinthians 16:13). Now then my dear sisters, please henceforth be that Godly **Proverbs 31** woman who **"is clothed with strength and dignity, and she laughs without fear of the future"** (v. 25, NLT). Now then my dear brethren, let us all henceforth personally live out the realization of the LORD our God's perfect prophecy through **Zechariah: "By my power I will make my people strong, and by my authority they will go wherever they wish. I, the LORD, have spoken!"** (10:12, NLT). *That* is being conformed to the image of our Lord Jesus; *that* is your true good.

DISCIPLINE

> "All athletes are disciplined in their training.
> They do it to win a prize that will fade away,
> but we do it for an eternal prize."
>
> (1 Corinthians 9:25, NLT)

Picture this: it's Monday morning, 6:30 AM, your alarm just went off. Immediately, you have to get your kids up, get them in the shower and dressed. At 7:15, you're chasing your 2-year-old around the house because he absolutely refuses to wear clothes today. You still have to make breakfast and lunch for your 6-year-old before she goes to school. And then you have to get everyone in the car, drop your spouse off at work, the kids at school and daycare, and then go to your own busy office. You work all day, then pick the kids and the spouse back up, and get home to make dinner. After dinner comes homework with your 6-year-old and then the nightly ordeal of getting your 2-year-old to go to bed. Then finally, you have about thirty minutes of private time to minister to your spouse. Before you know it, it is 10 PM, time to go to bed...and you still have not spent any real quality time with the Lord in prayer or reading His word.

Such a scenario is an all too common reality for many. And this could be *your* life in the future, if you don't learn and cultivate spiritual discipline right now, while you're still single. These disciplines are very important in your life, for by them you grow in godliness. They are not to be construed as legalistic in any way. They are means by which you can become more Christ-like "organically," with much freedom and joy in the Holy Spirit.

You have been saved by God's grace alone, through faith alone, in Christ alone. And now, in light of that marvelous fact, it's time for you to **"Supplement your faith with a generous provision of moral excellence, and moral excellence with knowledge, and knowledge with self-control, and self-control with patient endurance, and patient endurance with godliness, and godliness with brotherly affection, and brotherly affection with love for everyone"** (2 Peter 1:5b-7, NLT).

Private Prayer...

> **"And rising very early in the morning,**
> **while it was still dark,**
> **he departed and went out to a desolate place,**
> **and there he prayed."**
>
> (Mark 1:35)

God deserves the first-fruits of our lives in everything. Accordingly, this means that He deserves our first waking moments of every day. Our Lord Jesus Christ knew that as soon as everyone else woke up, He would be extremely busy for the rest of the day. So He got up before everyone else in order to spend time talking to His Father. We all need to follow His perfect example. As He told us:

"apart from me you can do nothing."

(John 15:5c)

It's extremely important to know that you can't face one single day on your own. You *need* the Lord's strength to face each day. Thus, one of the first things you should do on any given morning is ask Him for strength and to guide and bless your day. Do not try to do it without Him, because you can't!

This means that right now, at this point in your life, you must make it a priority to strongly build this habit into your life. If you don't already have a strong practice of Morning Prayer, now is the time to change that. It will not be this easy to do later in your life. So please pray and ask God for the discipline and desire you need to spend time communing with Him as your first activity every morning.

As you do this, please remember Biblical Christianity is not a "religion" in the modern connotation of that word. That is, we are not commanded to recite some ritualistic, effusive prayers all day long. Indeed, the Lord Jesus Christ actually condemned this type of prayer **(cf. Matthew 6:7, Mark 12:40)**. We're not *earning* our way back to God with our prayers. Rather, we come to God as His own *children* **(cf. Romans 5:9-11)** and thus we get to call on Him as "Abba! Father!" **(cf. Galatians 4:4-7)**.

Thus, we must speak to Him as our *true* Father. He is our perfect, loving, holy, just, eternal creator Father. In doing so, you must always remember that He **"knows what you need before you ask him"** (cf. Matthew 6:8). You're not surprising Him with any of your prayers. God doesn't *need* your prayers, but He loves to *work through* them for His glory.

In practical terms, you must start cultivating two different types of prayer into your lifestyle.

Get Some Kneepads...

> **"He got down on his knees three times a day and prayed and gave thanks before his God, as he had done previously."**
>
> (Daniel 6:10b)

First, you should begin to practice regular times of deep, private, "on your knees" prayer. This is the type of prayer that characterized the life of our brother Daniel as described in the verse above. It's the type of prayer the Lord Jesus commanded when He said: ***"when* you pray, go into your room and shut the door and pray to your Father who is in secret. And your Father who sees in secret will reward you"** (Matthew 6:6, italics mine). Carefully note that the command is *when* you pray, not *if* you pray. Indeed, prayer is one of our greatest blessings, for it is the grand privilege of direct, personal communion with the Lord of the universe!

Our brother James, physical brother of our Lord Jesus, was affectionately called "Old Camel Knees". He earned this nickname because he spent so much time in deep prayer that his knees were literally calloused and hardened like a camel's knees!

Although we may never achieve the awesome levels of prayer that "James the Just" embodied, it should nonetheless be a goal for which we strive.

The Endless Conversation...

> **"Never stop praying."**
>
> (1 Thessalonians 5:17, NLT)

Second, you should learn to practice the "spontaneous, on the fly" type of prayer that is done all throughout your day. This is prayer that happens while you're driving, while you're working, while you're socializing, etc. This is a moment-by-moment acknowledgement of your need for God and His grace. It is your admission to God that you cannot handle your life by yourself. It is also prayer for others that you come in contact with and see throughout your day. It is prayer for the salvation of that unsaved coworker you're speaking with at the water cooler. It is prayer for blessings on that homeless person you just saw on the road.

Think about it like this: Picture a long drive with a close friend. You're not conversing every second, but you are conversing all throughout the trip. If you had long periods without interaction, it would be an awkward ride . And remember, **"there is a friend who sticks closer than a brother"** (Proverbs 18:24b), our perfect Lord, who never leaves our side! So let's continually seek His face accordingly. That's what it means to truly "pray without ceasing," conversing with the Lord all throughout your day, making Him the focal point of every activity, for He is to be our closest & best friend!

To reiterate, this constant prayer is another spiritual discipline you must learn and ingrain right now, while it's still relatively easy for you. That way, if and when you have that car full of fighting kids on your way home from a busy day at work, you will already know how to immediately **"give all your worries and cares to God, for he cares about you"** (1 Peter 5:7, NLT). If and when you are tempted to argue with your spouse, you'll know to instead **"pray in the Spirit at all times and on every occasion"** (Ephesians 6:18a, NLT).

Prioritization...

> "Pray then like this: Our Father in heaven,
> hallowed be your name. Your kingdom come,
> your will be done, on earth as it is in heaven."
>
> (The Lord Jesus Christ, Matthew 6:9-10)

In our pursuit of ever-stronger prayer lives, we must remember that our Lord has already taught us how we are to pray by giving us a model for prayer. In what is called "The Lord's Prayer," which I think would be more accurately described as "the disciple's prayer," Jesus shows us that we are to always open our prayers by worshipping God and asking for *His* will to be done. It's only after that praise and thanksgiving unto the Lord that we are to start presenting our own requests.

Now, secondarily, I want to challenge us all to take this correct prayer format to the next level, by praying for others *before* you begin lifting up supplication for yourself. Praying for your brothers and sisters is one of the strongest ways to be a blessing to and for them. As Paul wrote to the church at Rome: **"God knows how often I pray for you. Day and night I bring you and your needs in prayer to God"** (Romans 1:9a, NLT). There we see the kind of heart we should espouse, one that never stops praying for our dear brethren. Thus, **"With this in mind, be alert and always keep on praying for all the Lord's people"** (Ephesians 6:18b, NIV). Pray for their sanctification, protection, wisdom, understanding, fruitfulness, growth, and blessing. Pray for their practical needs too, as you're led. Then you can proclaim like Samuel: **"As for me, far be it from me that I should sin against the LORD by failing to pray for you"** (1 Samuel 12:23a, NIV).

Additionally, we've received this exhortation: **"I urge you, first of all, to pray for all people. Ask God to help them;**

intercede on their behalf, and give thanks for them. Pray this way for kings and all who are in authority so that we can live peaceful and quiet lives marked by godliness and dignity. This is good and pleases God our Savior, who wants everyone to be saved and to understand the truth" (1 Timothy 2:1-4, NLT). This means we are to be praying not only for other Christians, but also for the spiritual and physical needs of the unsaved. The passage we just read above was written in a time and place where persecution against Christians was very strong, especially by the political leadership. Thus, Paul was exhorting Timothy to pray for the leaders who were actively (and sometimes violently) oppressing them. Knowing this, how much less of an excuse do we have in our day and age for not doing the same? For most of us, the "persecution" we face is nothing compared to what those first-century brethren faced. Hence, let's just simply pray for anyone and everyone, especially those whom God has appointed to leadership.

Gratitude & Culmination...

> "Let your roots grow down into him,
> and let your lives be built on him.
> Then your faith will grow strong in the truth you were taught,
> and you will overflow with thankfulness."
>
> (Colossians 2:7, NLT)

In every aspect of your prayer life, seeing through gospel glasses will inundate you with gratitude and praise for the Lord. Thank God *every* single day for the truths of the gospel, never letting them become "stale" to you, and always remembering exactly *why* and *how* you belong to the holy God of the universe. Because the gospel is an immutable truth, this means you *always* have much to be thankful for, regardless of any life conditions.

The gospel allows us to be authentically thankful for not only the unalterable fact of our salvation in Christ, but also for the promised future glory to come! That is how we can truly obey the command to **"Be thankful in all circumstances, for this is God's will for you who belong to Christ Jesus"** (1 Thessalonians 5:18). On top of always expressing this "gospel gratitude" to God, we all have so much more for which to be thankful. Every single good thing, no matter how infinitesimal it may seem, comes straight from God's hand. From the first cup of coffee each morning, to the noontime sun that shines on your face, to the food on your plate at dinner, it's all given by God's grace. So our lifestyles must be filled with **"giving thanks always and for everything to God the Father in the name of our Lord Jesus Christ"** (Ephesians 5:20).

Therefore my brothers and sisters please, at this time of your lives, permanently ingrain the beautiful spiritual discipline of a strong private prayer life. And remember: **"do not be anxious about anything, but in everything by prayer and supplication with thanksgiving let your requests be made known to God. And the peace of God, which surpasses all understanding, will guard your hearts and your minds in Christ Jesus"** (Philippians 4:6-7).

Corporate Prayer...

> "They all met together and
> were constantly united in prayer"
>
> (Acts 1:14a, NLT)

For you personally, ingraining the spiritual discipline of corporate prayer must be about learning how to unite with the other members of Christ's Body and being **"filled with the Holy Spirit, singing psalms and hymns and spiritual songs among yourselves, and making music to the Lord in your hearts"** (Ephesians 5:18b-19, NLT).

Group prayer is far more than just one person praying and everyone else saying "amen" at the end. True corporate prayer involves each person actively praying along with the person leading the prayer. You must learn how to do this in a way that is God-focused, self-forgetful, and wholehearted.

Just like with every other corporate spiritual discipline, you must learn to divorce yourself from the activity of group prayer. As the Lord Jesus Christ admonished us, **"When you pray, don't be like the hypocrites who love to pray publicly on street corners and in the synagogues where everyone can see them"** (Matthew 6:5a, NLT). Group prayer is *not* about you. It's not about how much Bible you know, your eloquent speech, or your wisdom. Accordingly, corporate prayer is *not* about how much Bible others in the group know, how eloquently they speak, or how wise they are. Rather, group prayer is about being conjoined with other children of God *as one*, lifting up your praises and your supplications unto the Lord.

Group prayer is not only about praying *with* each other, it's about corporately praying *for* each other. As we've been instructed: **"Is anyone among you sick? Let him call for the elders of the church, and let them pray over him, anointing him with oil in the name of the Lord. And the prayer of faith will save the one who is sick, and the Lord will raise him up"** (James 5:14-15a). This is yet another call to humility, as it means not only praying for your brethren in a group setting, but confessing your own needs to that same group and allowing them to pray for you. That is why we've been commanded thus: **"Therefore, confess**

your sins to one another and pray for one another, that you may be healed. The prayer of a righteous person has great power as it is working" (James 5:16).

With modern technology, this type of group prayer doesn't always have to be done in person. And though this shouldn't be the primary form of corporate prayer we practice, it's nonetheless an amazing blessing we must fully utilize for the purposes of group prayer. Most churches have a "prayer warrior" email list. In case you're not familiar, this is a list of all prayer requests that have been submitted by members of the church for others to lift up to the Lord. The church compiles these and sends out a regular email with these requests, and the "prayer warrior" team receives and makes intercession for these daily. This can and should be done both congregation-wide, as well as within small fellowship groups. The more pressing, highly urgent, life-threatening prayer requests should be sent to the entire congregation and the more private, personal accountability-related prayer requests should be confined to the email list of small group fellowships. If your church or small group doesn't have one, start one! With modern technology, this is not a difficult task. So team up with a church elder or another member of your small group and get to work on this great ministry!

As an aside, it's worth noting that before you can be prepared to pray well with your future spouse, you must learn how to regularly pray with others. This is yet another way that learning to fully and correctly engage in group prayer will be a huge blessing in your life. These times of corporate prayer are very powerful, edifying, and are the most intimate way human beings can ever interact. When God's people unite together and pray in one mind to the Lord, their relationships grow much deeper and stronger than they ever could otherwise. An older Christian brother I know, whose been married for many years, once said that praying with his wife is far more intimate than *anything* they share physically[44]. Indeed, praying together is one of the great blessings of a Christian marriage.

Therefore, now is the time to start truly praying *with* your eternal family, not just *among* them. It's time to permanently ingrain this discipline. By it, may you bless and be blessed by your brethren. By it, may you one day lead a family that "prays together and stays together". And by it, may your future marriage far surpass every physical intimacy.

Time in the Word...

> **"Take the helmet of salvation
> and the sword of the Spirit,
> which is the word of God."**
>
> (Ephesians 6:17, NIV)

It is also very important to cultivate a lifestyle of copious amounts of time in God's Word. Again, this is a discipline that you must learn and train right now at this time in your life. The fastest way to grow in your relationship with the Lord is to spend time in His word. Remember, we are commanded to, **"like newborn infants, long for the pure spiritual milk, that by it you may grow up into salvation"** (1 Peter 2:2). We should be *craving* God's Word constantly. A baby won't grow without milk, and likewise we won't grow without God's Word. The primary way God communicates with us is through His Word. Thus, if you don't have a daily habit of spending time there, you are cutting off this vital source of life-giving milk and hindering your own spiritual growth. Remember: **"the word of God is living and active, sharper than any two-edged sword, piercing to the** division of soul and of spirit, of joints and of marrow, and discerning the thoughts and intentions of the heart" (Hebrews 4:12). As such, we need God's word *daily*.

Additionally, how can you ever expect to teach God's Word to your future children, or use it to minister to your future spouse, unless you know it yourself? This is yet another reason why it's so important to learn, and learn from, this discipline right now. You won't have this much time to read God's Word when you have a newborn to deal with.

Thus, learning to spend regular time in the Word means not only cursory reading, but also learning to deeply study and meditate on God's Word. We should emulate the psalmist who said: **"I will meditate on your precepts and fix my eyes on your ways"** (Psalm 119:15). When we prayerfully study God's Word and ask the Holy Spirit to illuminate the Scriptures we're reading, we're given an understanding deeper than ever before. When we take a piece of Scripture and deeply meditate on it, we can learn exactly what God is trying to teach us there.

Practically, this means setting aside a scheduled portion of each day specifically for reading the Word of God. Put it high on your priority list and forsake unimportant things like watching television, if necessary, in order to make this happen. Treat it like you would a routine mealtime, for **"man does not live by bread alone, but man lives by every word that comes from the mouth of the LORD"** (Deuteronomy 8:3b). Realize that you *can't* live without it; that you *need* it just like you need oxygen and water. Breathe God's Word in, drink it up, and **"let God transform you into a new person by changing the way you think. Then you will learn to know God's will for you, which is good and pleasing and perfect"** (Romans 12:2b, NLT).

Remember the psalmist's refrain: **"Your word is a lamp to my** feet and a light to my path" (Psalm 119:105). And he reminds us why reading God's Word is so important for sanctification: **"How can a young man keep his way pure? By guarding it according to your word"** (Psalm 119:9). The Lord Jesus Christ often quoted from and referred to God's Word in His ministry. This means that, being fully God and fully human, He read and studied the Word throughout His life. If God Himself studied the Holy Scriptures, how much more must we? God's word is better than life. So let's make the discipline of reading and studying it such an ingrained part of our lives that we can't possibly imagine its neglect. Let's, right now, cultivate a strong love of communing with God through His Word.

Time in Fellowship...

> "Iron sharpens iron,
> and one man sharpens another."
>
> (Proverbs 27:17)

One of the first things that often gets sacrificed by a new burgeoning family is time at church with other believers. You know the story...A newly married couple gets busy with a new baby and they let their mid-week ministries and other fellowships slip. This causes weakened relationships and also a loss of accountability. This is why it's very important to strengthen all of those relationships right now, so that they will be strong enough to survive and grow through the changes to come. In this way, you will always have godly accountability, which you will especially need for your future marriage. You need your brothers and sisters in the body of Christ. This is yet another reason we've received this command: **"Let us not give up meeting together, as some are in the habit of doing, but let us encourage one another-**

and all the more as you see the Day approaching" (Hebrews 10:25, NIV).

That Day is coming rapidly, so fellowship time needs to be something you're already prioritizing on your weekly schedule. This doesn't happen automatically. It must be proactively cultivated and prayed over. Once again, this is a discipline you will have less time to build once you have a family.

Remember, being in fellowship is not only to be blessed, it's so you can be a blessing to others.

So let's make sure, right now, to build strong fellowship into our lives, making it a discipline so infused with importance that it won't be forsaken.

Time In Private Worship...

> **"Since we are receiving a Kingdom that is unshakable, let us be thankful and please God by worshiping him with holy fear and awe."**
>
> (Hebrews 12:28, NLT)

Resolve to spend time each day simply worshipping God for who He is, for His greatness, for His majesty. Do this in the privacy of your mind and heart. Meditate on the Lord, divorce yourself and others from these times of focalized worship, and gain a deeper personal understanding of Him. From His Word, receive a perpetually higher view of Him. Then, worship Him for His omnipotence, His eternality, His Triunity, His creativity, His perfection, His omniscience, His sovereignty, His omnipresence, His immutability, His Justice, His Holiness, His Faithfulness, His love, His patience, His *everything*.

Cast your crown before His throne, bow your head on the floor, and just praise Him. Revere Him. Be humbled by his awesomeness. Tremble at His power. Let everything and everyone else melt away.

You will be forever changed by these intimate times with the Lord of all. You will be abased. You will be filled with joy. You will want to go scream His name from the rooftops in lavish acclaim. You will desire to loudly and profusely proclaim His name among the nations. You will no longer harbor any timidity about exalting Him publicly. You will want to lift Him up high and in the assembly. You will endeavor to make His name great *everywhere*.

You will walk out of your personal "worship closet" ready to lead and point others to God. You will want your conversations to be about Him. Your heart will sing, your soul will magnify the Lord.

Instill this discipline *now* and thus be prepared to lead a family that worships the King of Kings as Moses did, by singing: **"Great and marvelous are your works, O Lord God, the Almighty. Just and true are your ways, O King of the nations. Who will not fear you, Lord, and glorify your name? For you alone are holy. All nations will come and worship before you, for your righteous deeds have been revealed"** (Revelation 15:3-4, NLT). Amen.

Time in Corporate Worship...

> "All the believers devoted themselves to the apostles' teaching, and to fellowship, and to sharing in meals (including the Lord's Supper), and to prayer."
>
> (Acts 2:42, NLT)

At your next Sunday service, notice how many families are walking in late. They walk in late because, especially on weekend mornings, it's hard to get a whole family up and ready, in the car, and on the way. It takes a lot of time, and if one isn't adequately prepared, their family is late for church, or, even worse, they miss church completely.

I say this not to judge any of those families, but only so that you and I may learn from that scenario. Godly men and women are people of discipline. This means that, if it takes two hours to get your family ready on a Sunday morning, you're up early enough to get them ready and make it to church on time. And of course, this is a discipline that must be learned and cultivated in your life right now.

A general rule in the corporate world is that 15 minutes early is "on time". So if the executives of this world can hone this discipline for money-making, how much more so should the people of God for the purpose of engaging in corporate worship?

Hearing the word of God preached by someone whom He has called and gifted to do so is a tremendous blessing, one that should never be neglected. And neither should the accompanying corporate worship. We are commanded: **"teach and admonish one another with all wisdom, and as you sing psalms, hymns and spiritual songs with gratitude in your hearts to God"** (Colossians 3:16, NIV). So we all need to cultivate increasingly strong obedience to this command, a discipline that will remain until The Lord Jesus calls us home.

Practically, this simply means learning to deny your flesh when it wants to sleep past the alarm clock's buzzing. It also means denying your flesh when it wants to stay up late watching television or eating, in order that you may be more prepared to arise early the next morning. It means being a *man* or *woman* of God, and thus having your "house" in order. Even if your "house" is only a room at this point, how can you expect to keep a family disciplined if you can't even do this for yourself yet?

As Paul describes a consummate man of God, **"He must manage his own family well and see that his children obey him, and he must do so in a manner worthy of full respect"** (1 Timothy 3:4). As he describes the same type of woman, **"Therefore, I want younger women to marry, have children, manage their households, and give the adversary no opportunity to accuse us"** (1 Timothy 5:14, HCSB). And the whole "but that's a pastoral epistle, talking about those desiring church leadership" cop-out excuse is rendered invalid, as deeper study of those epistles reveals that all men and women of God are called to evince that same character!

Thus, it's time to "get it together," so you can get your family together when that time comes. Now, I obviously don't romanticize any part of this earthly life. I know that in this fallen world even the most disciplined spouse/parent will run into obstacles. But those are beyond our control. What we can and must control is our obedient spiritual discipline that will render those obstacles benign.

Evangelism...

"But you will receive power when the Holy Spirit has come
upon you, and you will be my witnesses in Jerusalem
and in all Judea and Samaria, and to the end of the earth."
(The Lord Jesus Christ, Acts 1:8)

In a previous chapter, we discussed evangelism in detail. So here I merely present another imploration for you to ever-increasingly make obedience to this command an instilled discipline in your life. Remember, the Lord both commands and empowers your evangelism of his gospel **(cf. Mark 16:15).**

Evangelism is one of the primary reasons you are still on this planet and this doesn't change, regardless of any changes in your marital status. As the great Charles Spurgeon aptly said, "Every Christian is either a missionary or an impostor."

Being busy with a spouse and kids, or anything else in life, does not in any way exempt a Christian from *always* sharing the Good News. Every unbeliever around you *needs* to hear the Truth, and that right *quickly*! So once again, this is a discipline that you must proactively cultivate immediately. You must ingrain a steadfast practice of regularly sharing the gospel and make it one of the highest priorities of your life. If this doesn't become an instilled habit right now, it will be that much harder once you have familial responsibility.

Remember, just as with any other activity, you get better at evangelism by doing it over and over again. So you have to drop all fear **(cf. 2 timothy 1:7)**, you must repent of any shame you may feel **(cf. Romans 1:16)**, and prayerfully walk forth boldly in obedience **(cf. Proverbs 28:1)**. As a reminder, you are sharing the greatest news ever delivered. It is the "gospel of the grace of God" **(cf. Acts 20:24)**!

Accordingly, please make it a goal to share the gospel with at least one person *daily*, whether it is through personal interaction, phone, or Internet. Ask God for opportunities. Pray for the boldness to walk through those opened doors. Don't worry about what words to use, the questions you will receive, or how people will think of you. Just pray wholeheartedly and then **"do not be anxious how you are to speak or what you are to say, for what you are to say will be given to you in that hour. For it is not you who speak, but the Spirit of your Father speaking through you"** (Matthew 10:19-20).

This doesn't mean you shouldn't study and learn God's Word

inside and out, as you absolutely must, but remember that in evangelism it's always God who empowers your words and opens the hearts of the elect who hear them. It's God's will for you to share His truth, so you know He will always carry you along as you obey Him. When you habitually and steadfastly bring the Good News, you get better and better at it, and you see and walk through more and more open doors. This is a beautiful thing.

Therefore, Christian, I once again beseech you to embrace this discipline posthaste. Let it become such a huge part of your life that it will remain atop your priority list regardless of any future familial responsibilities. Then evangelism will be something you do *with* your future spouse, not something that loses priority when that time comes.

Service...

> "For even the Son of Man came not
> to be served but to serve others"
>
> (Mark 10:45a)

Serving is something you most likely have plenty of time for right now. At this time, you probably have the privileged blessing of "picking and choosing" from the plethora of service opportunities available to you, but that might not always be the case. It may not always be so easy or "convenient" for you to serve the body of Christ. Nonetheless, service is something that should always be a big part of your life until the Lord calls you home.

There are multitudinous opportunities for you to serve. So please prayerfully seek the Lord's will and guidance in the areas where He desires your service. Then obey those calls without hesitation.

The only way to make your service be a lifelong ministry is to make it a big part of your life *right now*. As we discussed in a previous chapter, you must maximize your current free time by prolifically serving God and His people. In doing so, you will receive the joy of servanthood, learning firsthand the truth that **"It is more blessed to give than to receive"** (cf. Acts 20:35). Redeem the time you've been given in a way that glorifies God.

Remember, your future family will in itself *be* a ministry of service. So learning how to do this joyously and fervently at this time in your life will bring a double blessing. You will have ingrained a lifestyle of serving the Lord and you will be prepared to serve your future family in a way that will bless them and draw them closer to our God.

Fasting...

> **"But *when* you fast,
> comb your hair and wash your face."**
> (Matthew 6:17, NLT, Italics Mine)

The Lord Jesus Christ said *when* we fast, not *if* we fast. This implies that fasting should be a part of our lives. Fasting is not some sort of legalistic asceticism; it is spiritual worship via self-denial.

Fasting honors God by showing Him that we value Him above satisfying our physical appetites. By this discipline, spiritual growth explodes, wisdom is gained, and your relationship with the Lord grows.

Being that fasting is one of the more difficult spiritual disciplines to ingrain, it's an especially important one to learn immediately. Think about it practically. Right now, as a single, your fasting neither affects nor is affected by someone else's life.

However, once you're married and have kids, your fasting will be harder to maintain because your eating habits will be influenced by your family's. It is a lot easier to deny yourself food when you are not around others all day who are eating. It gets harder when you are trying to prayerfully fast while still preparing a meal for your family.

Get where I'm going with this? Learn how to bring your stomach and its desires under your complete control *right now*, and it will be so much easier to maintain this discipline even with a family.

Therefore, let us never be like those whose **"god is their belly"** (cf. Philippians 3:19). Rather, let us be those who understand the truth that **"'All things are lawful for me,' but not all things are helpful. 'All things are lawful for me,' but I will not be enslaved by anything. 'Food is meant for the stomach and the stomach for food'—and God will destroy both one and the other"** (1 Corinthians 6:12-13a). As our Lord Jesus Christ told us, **"For life is more than food, and your body more than clothing. Food doesn't go into your heart, but only passes through the stomach and then goes into the sewer"** (Luke 12:23, Mark 7:19a).

Thus, it's time to prayerfully study what God's Word says about fasting and proactively cultivate obedience to those teachings. Doing so, we'll never be slaves to our bellies. Rather, our bellies will become our slaves, allowing us to deny them even when others don't. Let's be like Paul, who wrote: **"I discipline my body like an athlete, training it to do what it should"** (1 Corinthians 9:27a, NLT).

Giving...

"But as you excel in everything—
in faith, in speech, in knowledge, in

all earnestness, and in our love for you—
see that you excel in this act of grace also."

(2 Corinthians 8:7, ESV)

Paul wrote those words to the church at Corinth almost as a challenge. He had just informed them that the churches in Macedonia, who were much poorer than the Corinthians, had given above and beyond their financial means to support the saints. So now he was basically saying, "You guys are much wealthier, and you've already proven your faithfulness in other areas, so now prove it here too". Just as Paul wrote next, **"I am not commanding you to do this. But I am testing how genuine your love is by comparing it with the eagerness of the other churches"** (2 Corinthians 8:8, NLT).

Accordingly, I'm going to issue a challenge here, both to you and to myself. Brethren, for most of us as singles this is a time in life when we have the most (ostensibly) "disposable" income. So, at this stage in your life, given less familial responsibility and since you can more freely do so, how is your giving?

This is a grace and a discipline that must be eagerly fostered through prayer and true gratitude to God. Our flesh wants to hoard and store away. Our flesh says that what we earn through work is "ours," as if we somehow have sole rights over these provisions, but that is wrong. That's why the Lord admonishes us: **"Beware lest you say in your heart, 'My power and the might of my hand have gotten me this wealth.' You shall remember the LORD your God, for it is he who gives you power to get wealth"** (Deuteronomy 8:17-18a). Remember, *every* single thing we have is a gift of God through unmerited grace. Indeed, **"A person cannot receive even one thing unless it is given him from heaven"** (John 3:27). For no matter how hard you work, it's God who gives you the body, mind, time, and opportunity to work. Therefore, all is of Him.

So here comes the challenge. Let's learn to give freely, generously, and joyously *right now*. Let's learn to trust God so deeply and honestly that we don't hold back when the tithing plate passes, when the homeless person on the street asks for money, or when we receive those ministry-funding requests in the mail. For if you can't do this now, when your faithful giving only affects you for the most part, how can you expect to excel in this grace when you have the financial responsibility of providing for a family? You must learn to trust in God's provisioning hand so fully, that when the time comes, your giving isn't hindered or doubtful because of any concerns about your family's care.

Beloved, as Paul wrote, **"The point is this: whoever sows sparingly will also reap sparingly, and whoever sows bountifully will also reap bountifully. Each one must give as he has decided in his heart, not reluctantly or under compulsion, for God loves a cheerful giver. And God is able to make all grace abound to you, so that having all sufficiency in all things at all times, you may abound in every good work"** (2 Corinthians 9:6-8). Do you really trust God? You trust Him with the salvation of your eternal soul, the most important aspect of your entire existence. But do you doubt Him when it comes to relative trivialities like having your earthly needs met? If so, it's time to grow. It's time to "step off the ledge" and start trusting that God will catch you...because He surely will.

I want you to take a little time and Google "Answers to Prayer from George Muller's Narratives". There, you will find awesome examples of God's always perfect faithfulness to provide for His children. Our brother Mr. Muller ran multiple orphanages and *never* physically solicited giving from the public. Instead, he went into his prayer closet and asked God to provide exactly what was needed to continue operating. *Every single time*, God perfectly provided what was needed by divinely orchestrating amazing occurrences. For example, one time the orphans needed milk, but they couldn't afford to buy any that day. Mr. Muller prayed and then a milk truck broke down in front of the orphanage, compelling the truck driver to give all the milk to the orphans rather than letting it spoil[45]. Our God is beyond magnificent, isn't He? The same God who met all of George Muller's needs, and those of the vast amount of children under his responsibility and care, is the same God who promises to do the same for you and your future children.

So *right now*, at this time in our lives, I challenge us to authentically obey this command and thus receive its commensurate promise: **"'Bring the whole tithe into the storehouse, that there may be food in my house. Test me in this,' says the Lord Almighty, 'and see if I will not throw open the floodgates of heaven and pour out so much blessing that there will not be room enough to store it. I will prevent pests from devouring your crops, and the vines in your fields will not drop their fruit before it is ripe,' says the Lord Almighty. 'Then all the nations will call you blessed, for yours will be a delightful land,' says the Lord Almighty"** (Malachi 3:10-12, NIV).

Therefore, let us cheerfully give generously, trusting the Lord, not holding back what we have freely and graciously received from the God of whom it is written: **"He who did not spare his own Son but gave him up for us all, how will he not also with him graciously give us all things?"** (Romans 8:32). Let's henceforth fully trust our Savior to meet our every need, so that we'll always fully trust Him to meet every need of our future families.

Forgiveness...

> "And Jesus said to him,
> "Why do you call me good?
> No one is good except God alone."
>
> (Mark 10:18)

If you haven't truly learned this lesson yet, *now* is the time to get this education...the knowledge that there are *no good people*. It is extremely important to understand and imbibe the truth of this text. You need to truly know that *no one* is good, except God alone. One of the fundamental truths of the Gospel is that *none* of us is good **(Romans 3:23)** and thus, Jesus had to come and be good and perfect for us **(2 Corinthians 5:21)**! None of us could ever save ourselves and not one of us could ever live a truly perfect life on our own!

What this means practically, in the context of this chapter, is that even as redeemed sinners, people are still going to sin against you. And this is okay, as you will doubtless sin against others as well. Indeed, one need only read the book of **1 Corinthians** to understand the reality of Christians sinning against each other. Thus, you must understand that no human being is ever going to be a perfect companion to you...not your pastor, *not your future spouse, not your future kids*, not your friend who has been a Christian for 20 years, no one.

This truth is very important because, as we'll talk about later, you must not romanticize your future married life, or any human relationships for that matter. Just like you, everyone you know and interact with was once a slave to sin and it's only by God's amazing grace that you and they have been saved and set free. And just like you, everyone you know still lives in a fallen body in a fallen world, and thus our human relationships will not be perfect. But the beautiful truth that singleness will teach you is, God is *always* perfect! And in the Lord Jesus Christ, God's grace and forgiveness toward you is complete, eternal, and perfect. For this reason, you must learn *right now*, as a single Christian, how to completely, wholeheartedly, and instantly forgive those who sin against you. To do so, you must always see *everyone* through gospel glasses...

Even in strong Christian relationships, including a Godly marriage, disagreements and small arguments are bound to occur in this fallen world. Your flesh's desired response is to lash out in anger and try to "win" all arguments, by any means necessary. When we're wronged and wounded by another's words or actions, our flesh wants to return that pain. When someone hurts us, especially someone close to us, we desire to be bitter and angry with them. We desire to pour out our wrath upon them for offending us. But gospel glasses will empower us to **"Let all bitterness and wrath and anger and clamor and slander be put away from you, along with all malice. Be kind to one another, tenderhearted, forgiving one another, as God in Christ forgave you"** (Ephesians 4:31-32).

As Christians, we are called to a different response when we are wronged, *especially* when that trespass is committed by our brethren. The Lord Jesus Christ commanded us: **"Pay attention to yourselves! If your brother sins, rebuke him, and if he repents, forgive him, and if he sins against you seven times in the day, and turns to you seven times, saying, 'I repent,' you *must* forgive him"** (Luke 17:3-4, italics mine). Paul repeated this command when he wrote: **"Bear with each other and forgive whatever grievances you may have against one another. *Forgive as the Lord forgave you*"** (Colossians 3:13, NIV, italics mine). This unconditional, unlimited forgiveness of sin against us is something only Christians can do, as it's the forgiveness we have received in our Lord Jesus Christ!

This is no small matter! To understand why, take some time right now and go read "The Parable of the Unforgiving Servant" in **Matthew 18:21-35**. The Lord's words there are very stern and serious: **"For if you forgive others their trespasses, your heavenly Father will also forgive you, but** *if you do not forgive others their trespasses, neither will your Father forgive your trespasses"* (Matthew 6:14-15, italics mine). This is yet another reason why our gospel glasses must *always* be worn, because they will purify our motives for forgiveness and make them wholehearted and *truly* gracious. As the Lord Jesus Christ said to the Pharisee, when speaking of the forgiven "sinful woman of the city" who had anointed his feet with costly ointment: **"Therefore I tell you, her sins, which are many, are forgiven—for she loved much. But he who is forgiven little, loves little"** (Luke 7:47). This was not to say that the Lord's people receive different *levels* of forgiveness from Him. Rather, it was to demonstrate that because the Pharisee, in his pride, did not *see* his own sin as the penitent woman saw hers, the Pharisee didn't *serve* Jesus as the woman did. The woman served the Lord with all her heart *because* she had received his forgiveness, *not* to earn his grace. On another occasion, when something similar happened, the Lord rebuked the Pharisees thus: **"Those who are well have no need of a physician, but those who are sick. I came not to call the righteous, but sinners"** (Mark 2:17b). This was not to say that anyone is truly righteous and without need of forgiveness on their own merit, as the Pharisees thought of themselves. Rather, it was to demonstrate that the Lord came to save those who *see* their sin, and thus *acknowledge* and confess their sin to receive the Lord's forgiveness.

Christian, as these verses teach us, the truth is crystal clear. There's *only one* acceptable response to the forgiveness we've graciously received in Christ Jesus...forgiven people *must* forgive. Accordingly, this forgiveness of others is something you *must* practice and cultivate *right now,* in *all* of your relationships. As you grow in this grace, you will be ever more prepared and fully able to obey our Lord's command: **"if *anyone* slaps you on the right cheek, turn to him the other also"** (Matthew 5:39b, italics mine). In this way, when you receive the inevitable "slaps" of your future spouse and children, you will be able to gladly show them your other cheek. This will be an immense blessing in your future marriage, as you will better be able to sanctify and bless your spouse as you won't be overcome by the fleshly temptation to "win" every argument and disagreement. Rather, *you* will be the one who is able to *always* give the *grace* that is necessary to resolve conflicts. Unfortunately, so many marriages suffer deeply, and some are even destroyed completely, because of one spouse's inability or unwillingness to forgive a transgression of their spouse. Sadly, I've even read about the *suicide* of this man who was unable to forgive the harsh words his wife spoke to him in while arguing.

Christian, this must not be you! Once again, at this time in your life, you *must* grow so deeply in the gospel of God's grace that *your* grace mirrors that of our Heavenly Father as exemplified in "The Parable of the Prodigal Son". After sinning against his father, that sinful son **"arose and came to his father. But while he was still a long way off, his father saw him and felt compassion, and ran and embraced him and kissed him"** (Luke 15:20). *That* is the gospel grace you must possess, grace so powerful that it *runs* to forgive others *before* they have even repented! *That* is being conformed to the image of our Lord Jesus Christ...your *true* good.

Denouement...

> "the Spirit God gave us does not make us timid,
> but gives us power, love and self-discipline"
>
> (2 Timothy 1:7, NIV, italics mine)

Brethren, all these spiritual disciplines were merely cursorily described for brevity's sake. As you grow in each grace, there's still much more to learn about them all. So please prayerfully study each one of them as your walk with the Lord grows.

Also, once again beloved, please misconstrue none of this chapter. Not one of these spiritual disciplines is in any way to be pursued legalistically. All must be pursued as a *response* to God's completely unmerited grace you've received by faith in our Lord Jesus Christ, *not* to earn that grace. As always, we must earnestly seek obedience *because* we are eternally accepted, not to *become* accepted.

As Paul wrote, **"For the grace of God has appeared, bringing salvation for all people, training us to renounce ungodliness and worldly passions, and to live self-controlled, upright, and godly lives in the present age, waiting for our blessed hope, the appearing of the glory of our great God and Savior Jesus Christ, who gave himself for us to redeem us from all lawlessness and to purify for himself a people for his own possession who are zealous for good works"** (Titus 2:11-14). The *grace* of God is what must compel us to obedient spiritual discipline, *not* the law or wrath of God, but the gospel of our Lord's *grace*!

Through gospel glasses, we are compelled to vigorously pursue these areas of spiritual growth. Without our gospel glasses on, we cannot truly grow in spiritual discipline because we will fail to remember the price our Lord Jesus Christ paid for our souls, as well as the change that knowledge originally actuated in our lives! Accordingly, **"those who fail to develop in this way are shortsighted or blind, forgetting that they have been cleansed from their old sins"** (2 Peter 1:9, NLT).

Thus, though you should always prayerfully pursue these practices, *when* you fail at one, simply repent and move forward. Indeed, **"The godly may trip seven times, but they will get up again"** (Proverbs 24:16a, NLT). Seeing yourself through gospel glasses, a vision of a saved sinner still in the process of experiential sanctification appears, and you will realize that every failure has already been paid for on the cross at Calvary. So carry not your failures, for our Lord has already carried them on His own back. Every place you fall short, our Lord didn't! Hence, even though all of these disciplines require much *work* on the part of our bodies, our souls must always *rest* in the truth of the gospel.

Brothers and sisters, let's all grow up into truly Godly men and women. Let's be the self-disciplined people our Lord calls and empowers us to become. And let's do this *now*, wisely maximizing the time God has graciously given us in our singleness.

In these ways, we will not only become better at glorifying and serving our Lord, we will be ever more prepared to lead a family that does the same.

Indeed, speaking of spiritual growth, including these disciplines, our God has graciously promised:

> **"The more you grow like this,**
> **the more productive and useful you will**
> **be in your knowledge of our Lord Jesus Christ."**
>
> (2 Peter 1:8, NLT)

WORK

> "As a door turns on its hinges,
> so does a sluggard on his bed.
> How long will you lie there, O sluggard?
> When will you arise from your sleep?"
>
> (Proverbs 26:14,6:9)

Ah, that old bedside alarm clock, such a small, seemingly insignificant machine. Atop it rests yet another minuscule piece of plastic, ostensibly even less significant, colloquially known as the "snooze" button. For some, it's their best friend; for others, their worst enemy. For Christians, however, how we use this button can mean the difference between starting the day in obedience or sin.

You see, from the *beginning*, we were created to work. This was *a* purpose of our creation, though certainly not the only or primary purpose, and that has not changed to this day. What *has* changed, however, is the *type* of work to which we are called. To understand this and how it applies to *us* specifically, let's jump into a little history lesson.

In the beginning of creation we read: **"When no bush of the field was yet in the land and no small plant of the field had yet sprung up—for the LORD God had not caused it to rain on the land,** *and there was no man to work the ground,* **then the LORD God formed the man of dust from the ground and breathed into his nostrils the breath of life, and the man became a living creature. And the LORD God planted a garden in Eden"** (Genesis 2:5,7-8a; italics mine). As we know, the Garden of Eden was *perfect*. The Hebrew word for "Eden" itself alludes to "pleasure and delight"[46]. The word translated as "Eden" in the Septuagint (the Greek translation of the Hebrew Old Testament), is *"paradeisos"*; which very obviously transliterates into the English word "paradise". It was physically beauteous and lush, horticulturally exquisite, odoriferous, and filled with food so delectable that I'm sure nothing on earth compares today. Most importantly though, it was a place uncontaminated by sin! And thus, it was a place where the LORD God Himself walked **"in the garden in the cool of the day"** (Genesis 3:8). Indeed, Eden was a place where there was to be no separation between God and man.

After the creation of this magnificent place we read: **"Then the LORD God took the man and put him into the garden of Eden to** *cultivate* **it and keep it"** (Genesis 2:15, NASB, italics mine). The Hebrew word translated as "cultivate" in this text is *abad*, which means literally "to work"[47]. But it's actually translated as "serve", or a form thereof, *200 times* in the Bible. It's also been translated as "till," "dress," and other *verbs*[48]. It's the same word translated as "work" in our **Genesis 2:5** text on the last page. Thus, we see man was never meant to live in idleness. We were not created to spend our days "chilling". We were not created to be sedentary.

Now, not only was Adam himself put in Eden to "till, cultivate, dress" the land, but also **"the LORD God said, 'It is not good that the man should be alone; I will make him a *helper* fit for him'"** (Genesis 2:18, italics mine). Hence, Adam did not "work" the land alone, for he now had "help". Even in this place of stainless innocence, human beings were serving the Lord through their physical activity. And since this was indeed a land of bliss, the work of Adam and Eve was doubtless a source of pleasure in itself. The "happy couple" was always busy and enjoying every minute of their work. It was a task most pleasurable, for it was not a task of pain, toil, or sweat. They were just being who they were created to be and doing what they were created to do.

But then, disaster happened. A moment that brought an end to all of this perfection...the Fall of man. The couple succumbed to the temptation of the evil one and *everything* changed, including their work. So now, because of their transgression, the LORD God said to Adam: **"cursed is the ground because of you; in pain you shall eat of it all the days of your life; thorns and thistles it shall bring forth for you; and you shall eat the plants of the field. *By the sweat of your face* you shall eat bread"** (Genesis 3:17b-19a, italics mine).

The very definition and practical implications of *work* had now changed for Adam and all of his physical offspring, down through the millennia until the end of this world. Because now, work was no longer an unequivocal joy. Work was no longer "painless". The tasks of man had now become labor. The very sweat pouring out of man's skin as he toiled for his living was, in itself, a testament to the judgment under which he was now living.

Hence, this is the "working world" in which we find

ourselves today. The physical unpleasantness of "post-Fall" work notwithstanding, we are nonetheless commanded to partake of this activity for many different reasons. Thus, The Bible condemns laziness as sin and commands work in its stead.

So let's study some of the admonitions regarding this, concentrating especially on the specific ways that we as singles are most tempted to laziness and how we can achieve victory over this sin.

But my expenses are low...

"The soul of the sluggard craves and gets nothing, while the soul of the diligent is richly supplied."

(Proverbs 13:4)

For us, one of the main ways this temptation creeps in is thinking that we don't have to start "working hard" until we *have* a family. This attitude most strongly tempts those singles that are still living under their parents' roof. They can be tempted to think: "I don't have any major responsibilities, so there's no reason to work too hard, or to take work too seriously." This is wrong, for many reasons as we'll study, but let's start with the first practical reason. On this particular point, I'm going to address the brothers and sisters separately.

Brothers, if you want a wife and kids someday, you *must* be working hard to prepare for that right now. To quote our Proverb here, if "your soul craves" a family, laziness won't get you there! Truly Godly women will be looking for truly Godly men. And one of the attributes of a Godly man is a strong work ethic. Godly women will seek this trait, not so they can have a rich husband and live a life of luxury, but for assurance that they and their offspring will be provided for and supported. If you're lazy right now, Godly women will *not* assume you'll start to espouse a strong work ethic after marriage, regardless of what you may tell them. As Solomon observed, laziness is not something that can remain hidden for very long, as it will always bear fruit: **"I passed by the field of a sluggard, by the vineyard of a man lacking sense, and behold, it was all overgrown with thorns; the ground was covered with nettles, and its stone wall was broken down. Then I saw and considered it; I looked and received instruction. A little sleep, a little slumber, a little folding of the hands to rest, and poverty will come upon you like a robber, and want like an armed man"** (Proverbs 24:30-34). Thus, working hard has to be something you're doing *right now*, so any woman you pursue will *know* she's going to have a provider. So she will *know* that her children will never go without.

In addition, the hard work you're doing right now, in your desire for a family, is not only to attract a Godly woman. It's also to prepare your body, mind, and soul for the exponentially larger work ethic you will be called to adopt once you actually *have* that family. Before you can be prepared to support a wife and kids, you must be good at supporting yourself. This will not happen unless you're stepping up and accepting that responsibility right now. Remember, if you seek the great blessing of a "quiver full of arrows" **(cf. Psalm 127:4-5)**, it must be done with the understanding of the level of work and responsibility that will entail. My dear brothers, if that is your desire, you must prepare yourselves by heeding this admonition: **"if anyone does not provide for his own, and especially for those of his household, he has denied the faith and is worse than an unbeliever"** (1 Timothy 5:8).

Now, sisters, just as Eve worked the garden with Adam, you are also called to work hard. We see an amazing portrait of a

Godly woman painted in **Proverbs 31**. So let's take a look at some of the ways in which God describes the truly godly woman:

> She **"works with willing hands"** (v.13b)

> **"She rises while it is yet night
> and provides food for her household
> and portions for her maidens."** (v. 15)

> **"with the fruit of her hands
> she plants a vineyard."** (v. 16b)

> She **"makes her arms strong"** (v. 17b)

> **"Her lamp does not go out at night.
> She puts her hands to the distaff,**
>
> **and her hands hold the spindle."** (v. 18b-19)

> **"She makes bed coverings for herself"** (v. 22)

> **"She makes linen garments and sells them"** (v. 24)

> **"She looks well to the ways of her household**
>
> **and does not eat the bread of idleness."** (v. 27)

Sounds like a pretty amazing woman, doesn't she? Sisters, this is who are you are called to be as well, especially if you want a family someday. While it will be your husband's responsibility to support your family financially, it's easy to see that your work responsibilities will be no less numerous or important. And thus, just as with the brothers, these are responsibilities you must be preparing for right now. My dear sisters, if you desire the "heritage" and "reward" of children **(cf. Psalm 127:3)**, please heed the wisdom of the Proverb above. Please practice "diligence," that your soul may be "richly supplied". May your hard work be rewarded like the Godly woman we just studied: **"Give her of the fruit of her hands, and let her works praise her in the gates"** (Proverbs 31:31).

But I love to sleep...

**"Love not sleep, lest you come to poverty;
open your eyes, and you will have plenty of bread."**

(Proverbs 20:13)

A second way the laziness temptation creeps in for us is in pure love of leisure and rest, a.k.a. sloth. Because we don't all have to get up early on our days off to make breakfast for kids, or get a spouse ready for work, this temptation is pervasive. However, we're commanded against slothfulness all throughout Scripture. Let's take a look at some examples and see their specific applications for us.

"Take a lesson from the ants, you lazybones. Learn from their ways and become wise! Though they have no prince or governor or ruler to make them work, they labor hard all summer, gathering food for the winter. But you, lazybones, how long will you sleep? When will you wake up?" (Proverbs 6:6-9, NLT). It can be tempting to just gloss over this verse and think, "Ya, ya, ya, I *know* I have to work or I'll go without". But that would be doing this text, and its amazing wisdom, a severe injustice. Just as with the rest of God's word, in our mining of the depths of its teaching, we never seem to exhaust the supply. So let us espouse its wisdom.

Of primary noteworthiness is one unavoidable fact, one that we would do well to understand. As we'll study in a moment, ants are amazing creations of God, blessed with industriousness so indomitable it puts every other insect to shame. However, as awe-inspiring as they are, there is a creature that has been given dominion over them **(cf. Genesis 1:28)**. A creature that daily treads their nests under foot without a second thought because he far outweighs them in worth and importance **(cf. Psalm 8:3-8)**. A creature so amazingly blessed that it bears the image of Almighty God Himself **(cf. Genesis 1:27)**. This creature, my brethren, is you and I!

And thus, how humbling for us, that in our sinfully slothful pride we are sent to so lowly a creature as an ant to learn its wisdom. How shameful for us, that we must learn avoidance of "poverty" and "want" from an almost infinitesimal creature. How disreputable for us, that a creature with no "prince, governor, or ruler," has become an instructor of industry to a creature knowledgeably under the subjugation of the King of Kings!

But alas! It was no arbitrary decision that Solomon chose to use the ant over other insects as an example. It was by design, as we're sent to "Ant University" for two reasons: humility and knowledge. For God **"teaches us more than the beasts of the earth and makes us wiser than the birds of the heavens"** (Job 35:11). So let's matriculate and make sure we're studious enough to graduate *cum laude*.

The ant is one of the most industrious and hard working of all creatures, not only out of immediate necessity, but also out of foresight! They gather and store food not only to meet the day's needs, but to meet those of the future also. To store their food they build small, rainproof cells, then they proactively care for those stored provisions. Should a piece of their corn somehow get wet, they remove it from its cell and bring it outside to dry, in addition to biting off both of its ends to prevent its growth.

Ants not only work incessantly, but in doing so, they work *as a team*. In fact, they work together so cohesively for the common good that their colonies have even been referred to as "super organisms". Though they're not the strongest of creatures, they traverse relatively vast distances to gather food, helping each other carry their bounty on the way back home. It gets better than that though. For instance, when an ant finds a new path to a food source, it will leave a trail of pheromones on the way back to the colony so other ants can follow that path. If that path gets blocked, the ants will disperse and explore different paths until a new route is discovered, at which point it's also marked with pheromones for the good of the colony. There is no self-serving labor here.

This "selflessness" is further exemplified by the way ants tend to their offspring. They exercise a most diligent care there. They carry their babies out of the nest on sunny days for the healthful sustenance that star gives and return them to their nests upon a sign of rain, making sure to dutifully and protectively cover the nest hole once their kids are safely inside. Ants not only protect their own progeny, they also work together to corporately protect the colony's newborn larvae. They do this by forming "bivouacs". In this process, thousands of ants cohesively build a nest out of their own bodies, adjoining their legs together in a massive "fort-like" protective cell. *Inside* this cell, worker ants feed the larvae and the more "buffed" ants carry them to *new* bivouacs as they're built.

Ants help each other not only *in* labor, they also teach each other *how* and *where* to labor. They do this through a ridiculously awesome process called "tandem running". There, a more experienced ant will teach a neophyte forager how and where to go for food. It works like this: the more knowledgeable ant will have its pupil run behind it, slowing down when the pupil falls behind, and picking up the speed when their pupil gets too close. And thus, the pupil quickly learns how to forage.

These creatures not only work hard, they also use *wisdom* about where they work. This is exemplified by the way their nesting sites are carefully selected. They will expeditiously abscond a site as soon as a threat is detected. In addition, they will not build a nest where they find dead ants, to avoid possible diseases or pests that might linger there.

When ants want to build a nest up in a tree, tons of worker ants will line up and collectively transform themselves into a "bridge". They then use this "ant bridge" to pull leaves together. Once the leaves are touching each other, the older ants will impel their larvae to make silk, which is used to fuse the leaves together. These bridges also have other uses for ants, such as when a colony runs into a large gap underground. In vegetation or over water, they will "chain" themselves together to make a bridge for traversing the ravine. In a flood, ants conjoin to form floating "ant rafts".

Ants are also excellent "gardeners" when nesting on the ground. They will go out and forage for leaves and bring them back to the colony. Once there, the ants will cut the leaves into tiny stalks, chew them up, and spit them out into "gardens" of fungi. These gardens are then carefully cultivated. The ants excrete symbiotic bacteria to kill external, unwanted bacteria that may hurt their fungi. If they detect that a certain leaf type is harming their garden, they'll no longer use those.

Indeed, ants are marvelous creations of God[49].

Okay, now that we're all ready to *dominate* the "Insect" category during our next round of Trivial Pursuit, let's break down everything we've practically learned from the ants about work. The Ants:

Are Indefatigably Assiduous.
That is, they are tireless, diligent workers.

Are Long-Sighted.
That is, they work for "long-term" benefits, not only temporal.

Are Collaborative.
That is, they work as a team, not as self-seekers.

Are Altruistic.
That is, they are charitable and work philanthropically.

Are Conscientious Parents.
That is, they work carefully and meticulously.

Are Pedagogical.
That is, they teach others how to work well.

Are Sagacious.
That is, they use wisdom in how and where they work.

Are Prudent.
That is, they work cautiously, to protect their interests.

Are Adroit.

That is, they are resourceful and clever workers.

Thus, we now know that our command to "go to the ant and consider her ways" extends far beyond what a mere perfunctory reading would imply. God made these creatures astonishing workers. Let's truly espouse and evince what we've learned here that we may never suffer "poverty" or "want". May the work ethic of the ant no longer surpass ours.

But I support myself...

"Let each of you look not only to his own interests, but also to the interests of others."

(Philippians 2:4)

A third way the temptation to laziness creeps in for us is by harboring the misconception that we're called to work only for ourselves or our biological families. There are some singles that don't have or want a family right now; who possess a strong work ethic, but think that their "providential" responsibility ends with themselves. That is incorrect.

Remember, as Christians we are called to care for the needs of the poor and needy **(cf. Deuteronomy 15:7, Ezekiel 16:49, Proverbs 14:31, James 2:15-16, 1 John 3:17)**. Being single does not relieve us from the responsibility to work for others. In fact, as we talked about in Section B - Chapter 2, our ministry size can and should be much bigger than that of a typical married Christian. The amount of people we serve and care for should exceed that of a typical married head-of-household breadwinner. Now this doesn't always mean we take care of others monetarily, as sometimes it's pure service to and for them. And this is all work. The more and the harder we work, the more and better we can be a blessing.

As Christians, we are admonished to: **"Bear one another's burdens, and so fulfill the law of Christ"** (Galatians 6:2). The Greek word translated as "bear" here is *bastazó*, which means "to carry away, to take up"[50]. Now obviously, the primary context of this verse means bearing each other's spiritual and moral failings. But, in "so fulfilling the law of Christ," this extends much farther than that in our universal call to love and charity. The Greek word translated as "burdens" in our text here is *baros*, which means "a trouble, a weight, a load, a heaviness"[51]. Thus, we can understand this verse is a command to "take up and carry away one another's weights and troubles". This is a command that cannot in idleness be obeyed. *Bastazó* is a *verb*, which means this "burden carrying" is something we must actively (and proactively) be doing always. This of course requires us to *work* in service of our brethren, not just in serving ourselves.

As our brother James wrote: **"If a brother or sister is poorly clothed and lacking in daily food, and one of you says to them, 'Go in peace, be warmed and filled,' without giving them the things needed for the body,** *what good is that?***"** (James 2:15-16, italics mine). So again, we see our work must also be used to benefit our brethren. This happens both directly, through physical service to and for them, and indirectly, by working hard at our jobs to earn money to help those in need. If God has given you a good paying job as a single, this is probably one of the *exact* reasons why that blessing was bestowed on you. As Paul said of the regenerate thief: **"let him labor, doing honest work with his own hands, so that he may have something to share with anyone in need"** (Ephesians 4:28b). That text reiterates the fact that every blessing we've been given is to be shared and used outwardly toward our fellow man. This includes the fruits of our labors;

thus, it's yet another reason why our labors should be ceaseless.

But I have a lot of money...

"There were no needy people among them,
because those who owned land or houses would sell them
and bring the money to the apostles to give to those in need."

(Acts 4:34-35, NLT)

There's a fourth way we as singles can be tempted to laziness. And this one applies specifically to those who don't financially need to work. Maybe you're very young, just out of high school and still living at home. Maybe you have wealthy parents who insist on supporting you fully. Or maybe you're a widow(er) recipient of a large life insurance settlement. Regardless, no matter what external, personal monetary provision you receive or have received, it's still no excuse for not working hard.

Let's read some words from the second epistle to Thessalonica: **"Now we command you, brothers, in the name of our Lord Jesus Christ, that you keep away from any brother who is walking in idleness and not in accord with the tradition that you received from us. For you yourselves know how you ought to imitate us, because we were not idle when we were with you, nor did we eat anyone's bread without paying for it, but *with toil and labor we worked night and day*, that we might not be a burden to any of you. *It was not because we do not have that right, but to give you in ourselves an example to imitate.* For even when we were with you, we would give you this command: *If anyone is not willing to work, let him not eat.* For we hear that some among you walk in idleness, not busy at work, but busybodies. Now such persons we command and encourage in the Lord Jesus Christ to do their work quietly and to earn their** own living" (2 Thessalonians 3:6-12, italics mine). If you're in the aforementioned financial situation, then just like Paul, Silvanus, and Timothy, you have the "right" to make use of those provisions and not work hard. However, those three Godly men *laid down* this right in order to give us "an example to imitate". They gave us the Godly example of "singing for your supper," that is, of "earning your keep". They even formalized the command to all, saying that "if you don't work, you don't eat," pure and simple. That's why they also urged the saints at Thessalonica *"to work with your hands,* **as we instructed you, so that you may walk properly before outsiders** *and be dependent on no one"* (1 Thessalonians 4:11c-12, italics mine). The fact that they mentioned this in *both* letters, both times referring back to instruction they had personally given the Thessalonians while they were there, underscores the command's importance.

Now, none of this is to in any way condemn the personal use of financial gifts from the Lord. Rather, it's to reiterate the admonishment that having those gifts is in no way an excuse for laziness in one's life. If anything, it should make one *busier* in their service, as that person has the resources to be a massive blessing to many. As Paul wrote to the Corinthians, who had abundant material blessings: **"For I do not mean that others should be eased and you burdened, but that as a matter of fairness your abundance at the present time should supply their need, so that their abundance may supply your need, that there may be fairness. As it is written, "Whoever gathered much had nothing left over, and whoever gathered little had no lack." And God is able to make all grace abound to you, so that having all sufficiency in all things at all times, you may abound in every good work. You will be enriched in every way to be generous in every way, which through us will produce thanksgiving to God"**

(2 Corinthians 8:14-16;9:8-11). Single Christian, if that passage describes you, may God lead you to work and give generously like the saints at Corinth.

Remember, if you are a materially wealthy Christian, you're not the first one and there have been many before you. And thus, Paul's following command to the original "Christians of means," applies to you as well. **"As for the rich in this present age, charge them not to be haughty, nor to set their hopes on the uncertainty of riches, but on God, who richly provides us with everything to enjoy.** *They are to do good, to be rich in good works, to be generous and ready to share,* **thus storing up treasure for themselves as a good foundation for the future, so that they may take hold of that which is truly life"** (1 Timothy 6:17-19, italics mine; verse 19 refers to *eternal* rewards, which we'll soon study). If that's you, then work hard, enjoy it, and thank God for the blessing. Just as Solomon said: **"Everyone also to whom God has given wealth and possessions and power to enjoy them, and to accept his lot and** *rejoice in his toil*—**this is the gift of God"** (Ecclesiastes 5:19, italics mine).

But I don't like working...

> "So I saw that there is nothing
> better than that a man should
> rejoice in his work, for that is his lot."
>
> (Ecclesiastes 3:22a)

A fifth way singles can be subject to the temptation of laziness is a paucity of finding enjoyment in work. When a single person considers work drudgery, sloth will always be knocking at the door, especially if that person is relatively unburdened financially. For when work, service, or any activity is performed by a person begrudgingly, that person will always seek to minimize the amount of time spent on that task. In addition, labor practiced in this way will suffer lack not only quantitatively, but *qualitatively* also. As we just discussed, our command to work is irrespective of our financial independence. Knowing that we *all* must work and serve, we, by extension, know that a lack of delectation in this area will only hinder our ability to obey this command efficaciously.

Now, before we can jump into the practical steps for overcoming this particular temptation, one thing needs to be made clear. Blaise Pascal put it well when he said: "All men seek happiness. This is without exception. Whatever different means they employ, they all tend to this end. The cause of some going to war, and of others avoiding it, is the same desire in both, attended with different views. The will never takes the least step but to this object. This is the motive of every action of every man, even of those who hang themselves[52]." Thus, just as we noted with other sins, it's the *object* of our delights that must change, not the delighting itself. In experiential sanctification our desires change, becoming aligned with God's desires for us. This means that what gives us pleasure and joy changes.

And in this particular case, let's understand this practically. It means that for those who used to love sleep and rest, you should now love to work and serve as a born again child of the Lord.

This is nothing new. Heed Solomon's words, written thousands of years before the modern "gentleman of leisure" existed: **"There is nothing better for a person than that he should eat and drink and find enjoyment in his toil"** (Ecclesiastes 2:24a). The Hebrew word translated as "toil" there is *amal*, which means "grievous effort, travail[53]". And how can we *enjoy* something defined as "unpleasant"? Our passage here answers that as well. You see, the enjoyment *comes from God!* Let's dive a little deeper into this principle in order to gain a stronger practical comprehension of this truth.

Toward the end of his life, using the same Hebrew word we just learned, the wisest sinner that ever lived asked rhetorically: **"What gain has the worker from his toil?"** (Ecclesiastes 3:9). He answered thus: **"I have seen the business that God has given to the children of man** *to be busy with.* **I perceived that there is nothing better for them than to be joyful and to do good as long as they live; also that everyone should eat and drink and** *take pleasure in all his toil—this is God's gift to man"* (Ecclesiastes 3:10,12-13, italics mine). So we see, the "busyness" of our labor is a gift from God!

The Three Keys...

> **"This also, I saw, is from the hand of God, for apart from him who can eat or who can have enjoyment?"**
>
> (Ecclesiastes 2:24b-25)

How specifically do we practically enjoy the gift of work? There are many ways. Here I present three major keys in ascending order of importance.

The first key...

> **"And since I, your Lord and Teacher, have washed your feet, you ought to wash each other's feet."**
>
> (John 13:14, NLT)

The first key to enjoying work is something we, by now, are very familiar with studying. And that is *humility*. Pride says: "This *type* of work is beneath me." Or even worse, "Work itself is beneath me." Humility says: "I'm so blessed to be able to work. Some couldn't work even if they wanted to and God has given me the gift of busy hands. Boredom isn't a problem for me." The Psalmist used the same Hebrew word we recently learned, *amal*, when he wrote about God's response to some who had rebelled against Him: **"Therefore He humbled their heart with labor"** (Psalm 107:12, NASB). So we see, God has actually used work as a way to *abase* people in the past. Indeed, only prideful hearts think they're above labor. And thus, hard work is best enjoyed *and* performed with a humble heart. One's work is most effective and gratifying when their attitude is: "I'm not above work, it's something I'm called to do. It's one of the reasons God put me here". A humble heart understands that work is "his lot" and he must thus, **"accept his lot and rejoice in his toil—this is the gift of God"** (Ecclesiastes 5:18b,19b). Knowing this, the humble person seeks to perform their work as outstandingly as possible, because of their understanding that labor is one of the very reasons for their creation.

As we've studied previously, enjoyment of *anything*, including life itself, cannot be found without "lowliness of mind". So if your pride is not allowing you to enjoy your labor, it's time to humble yourself or God will do it for you **(cf. 1 Peter 5:6, James 4:6,10)**. My dear brethren, please remember these words of our Lord: **"Whoever exalts himself will be humbled, and whoever humbles himself will be exalted"** (Matthew 23:12).

The second key...
> **"Their trust should be in *God, who richly gives us all we need for our enjoyment*."**
> (1 Timothy 6:17B, NLT, Italics Mine)

The second key to enjoying work is through the blessing of some little neurotransmitters in our bodies called "endogenous morphines", colloquially known as "endorphins". In case you're not familiar, these are chemicals that, through physical activity, are released into the brain and spinal cord from the hypothalamus and into the blood from the pituitary gland[54]. Upon release, these chemicals produce feelings of pleasure and well-being, and thus increase the enjoyment of whatever activity is serving as a catalyst for their dispensation.

Thus, the harder and more strenuously we work, the more endorphins then get released, and the better we feel. This is a beautiful, wonderful blessing. We don't have to "muster up" enjoyment of work, as the labor *in itself* can become a source of immense gratification. Understanding this leads us to glorify and thank God for this benefaction.

Just as Solomon said: **"Whatever your hand finds to do, do it with your might, for there is no work or thought or knowledge or wisdom in Sheol, to which you are going"** (Ecclesiastes 9:10). The Hebrew word translated as "might" there is *koach*, which means "power, ability, strength, efficiency"[55]. The directive of this verse comes during a section of **Ecclesiastes 9** known as that chapter's "five imperatives". There, shortly after Solomon reiterates the universality of death for men **(cf. vv. 1-6)**, he gives these commands. He says, *because* you're going to die and you know it, do these things. He says to follow these five imperatives *because* only the living can do them, as the dead can't do a single thing. He thus commands enjoyment of life, and through our verse here, he reaffirms that this includes our work. Now obviously, because of progressive revelation, Solomon's reference to "Sheol/Hades" here meant a physical, earthly grave, though he does allude to an afterlife of consciousness in **Ecclesiastes 12:7**. Regardless, the principle remains the same: go enjoy your God-given life and all of its blessings, including work, because **"God has already approved what you do"** (v. 7). This passage also has a correlation with **John 9:4**, where the Lord Jesus Christ said: **"We must work the works of him who sent me while it is day; night is coming, when no one can work"**. Together, these verses also remind us that we must practice a ministry of *presence* in our lives[56]. That is, wherever God has us in life, we must make the most of everything. This is in direct contrast to a ministry of *passivity*, where a person just lazily lets life go past them. So let's work hard, knowing that the more vigorously we labor, the better we'll feel.

The third key...

> **"And whatever you do, in word or deed,**
> **do everything in the name of the Lord Jesus,**
> **giving thanks to God the Father through him."**
>
> (Colossians 3:17)

The third and most important key to enjoying work is *motivation*, of which there are two types. They're distinct, yet intricately intertwined. Given the importance of motivation, let's study each type separately, in ascending order of significance.

The Earthly Motivation...

> **"In all toil there is profit, but**
> **mere talk tends only to poverty."**
>
> (Proverbs 14:23)

This type of motivation makes work enjoyable because of the day-to-day benefits our labor produces. The practical blessings of hard work are self-evident. As Solomon wrote: **"A slack hand causes poverty, but the hand of the diligent makes rich"** (Proverbs 10:4). We see the truth of this proverb confirmed throughout the world everyday. Even for non-Christians, those who are living only under God's *common* grace, their diligent work is rewarded. This is especially true in first-world countries, where meritocratic, capitalist societies reign. We've all seen the people who, through sheer grit and determination, rise from poverty to wealth. Accordingly, as Christians, our hard work promises earthly rewards as well. And though our attitude toward this must by nature be different from the unbeliever's, it's nonetheless something we should use as a motivational tool.

So we must understand that using the temporal, immediate remuneration of our work as a motivation for enjoying that labor is not in itself sinful. For **"The laborer deserves his wages"** (cf. Leviticus 19:13, Deuteronomy 25:4). Indeed, as long as we're glorifying and thanking God for it, this attitude is a good thing because **"A worker's appetite works for him; his mouth urges him on"** (Proverbs 16:26). Work, enhanced by the knowledge that it will stock your refrigerator that will result in caloric energy for more service, is a good thing. Work, enhanced by the knowledge that it will put gas in your tank that will allow you to make it to church and ministry, is a good thing. Work, enhanced by the knowledge that it will allow you to have a roof over your head, which will give you a place to study your Bible and rest for more service, is a good thing. In this we see that labor, just like many other activities, receives its sanctity or sinfulness based on the attitude of the heart performing the action, not necessarily the action itself. For **"Everything is pure to those whose hearts are**

pure" (Titus 1:15a, NLT). So, as long as your appetites are pure, your labor will be also.

Using this motivation as a reason for enjoying work also compels us to *diversify* our labors. As we're taught: **"In the morning sow your seed, and at evening withhold not your hand, for you do not know which will prosper, this or that, or whether both alike will be good"** (Ecclesiastes 11:6). This is the concept contemporaneously known as "don't put all your eggs in one basket". When it comes to our work, it means that we should seek to excel in multiple areas, all to the glory of God.

In these ways, the earthly motivation for a strong work ethic becomes yet another driving force in our fight against the laziness temptation.

The Heavenly Motivation...

> **"Work with enthusiasm, as though you were working for the Lord rather than for people."**
>
> (Ephesians 6:7, NLT)

Now, the most important motivation for work, and also the most important key to enjoying labor, is *heavenly* motivation. Let's explore this concept.

As Paul wrote: **"Slaves, obey in everything those who are your earthly masters, not by way of eye-service, as people-pleasers, but with sincerity of heart, fearing the Lord. Whatever you do, work heartily, as for the Lord and not for men, knowing that from the Lord you will receive the inheritance as your reward. You are serving the Lord Christ"** (Colossians 3:22-24). Now obviously, the immediate context of those verses pertains to those in "earthly slavery," and their correspondent servitude of their earthly "masters". However, this passage has a very strong practical application for all Christians, as it radically transforms our paradigms regarding work. Heretofore, we may not have seen our work as being *directly* "unto the Lord," but now we know the truth.

The Greek word translated as "heart" in verse 22 is *kardia*, which means "the volitional center of our lives[57]". To better understand the strength of this word, it must be noted that in its 158 appearances in the New Testament, *not once* does it refer to the physical organ in our chests that pumps blood. Rather, in *every* instance, it is *only* used as a metaphorical reference[58]. Likewise, the Greek word translated as "heartily" in verse 23, *psuché*, means "the human soul, the self, the breath of life[59]".

Recall how Solomon admonished us to work with all of our "power & strength" in **Ecclesiastes 9:10**, which we studied earlier. Paul steps in and strengthens this command in the New Testament, for we are now directed to work with all of our "volition & soul". Solomon's incitement for his admonishment was sheer physical pleasure, due to the fleeting nature of bodily life. Paul's incitement trumps that immeasurably, as we are now told to work "as for the Lord," above all other reasons. Accordingly, Paul has also written elsewhere, **"So, whether you eat or drink, or whatever you do, do all to the glory of God"** (1 Corinthians 10:31).

By this contrast, we see the jump from the physical to the spiritual, from the temporal to the eternal, from the earthly to the heavenly, and from the self-centered to the God-centered. This is beautiful, as it not only increases and improves our work ethic, it increases our enjoyment of work tremendously. In addition to the multitudinous corporeal benefits of labor we've discussed, we can now have *eternal* benefits in mind to spur us on to enjoyable, quality work. Thus, always remember this truth: **"But on the** judgment day, fire will reveal what kind of work each builder has done. The fire will show if a person's work has any value. If the work survives, that builder will receive a reward" (1 Corinthians 3:13, NLT).

What shall we say then?

"Therefore, my dear brothers and sisters, stand firm.
Let nothing move you.
Always give yourselves fully to the work of the Lord,
because you know that your labor in the Lord is not in vain."
(1 Corinthians 15:58, NIV)

As we've just studied, work is a command and a blessing. Accordingly, a strong work ethic is a character trait we must not only be espousing and evincing in ourselves, but a trait we must be looking for in a Godly spouse. So, resolve to henceforth mortify laziness completely and always work hard. First and foremost, do it out of obedience to the Lord. As we've just studied, laziness is not "something we need to work on". It is sin to be repented of, just as it was for that city destroyed by fire from heaven: **"Sodom's sins were pride, gluttony, and** *laziness, while the poor and needy suffered outside her door"* (Ezekiel 16:49, NLT, italics mine).

Secondarily, do it to maximize your rewards in this life and in the *true* life to come, remembering the truth that **"we must all appear before the judgment seat of Christ, so that each one may receive what is due for what he has done in the body, whether good or evil"** (2 Corinthians 5:10).

My dear brethren, **"let us not grow weary of doing good, for in due season we will reap, if we do not give up. So then, as we have opportunity, let us do good to everyone, and especially to**

those who are of the household of faith" (Galatians 6:9-10).

Finally beloved, may the lives we live and the work we do allow us to truly echo the words of our blessed Lord and Savior Jesus Christ, who said:

"My Father is always working, and so am I."
(John 5:17, NLT)

Section D:

The Wait…

"ALTAR" THE ALTAR - SECTION INTRO

> **"For whoever would save his life will lose it, but whoever loses his life for my sake and the gospel's will save it."**
> (The Lord Jesus Christ, Mark 8:35)

Sisters, picture your wedding day. The flowing white dress, the veil. Your dad walking you down the aisle, teary-eyed. Your friends and family smiling ear-to-ear as you walk past them. You're wearing "something old, something new, something borrowed, something blue, and a silver sixpence in your shoe[60]." At the end of the aisle, you step up onto the altar and turn to look your godly, soon-to-be husband in the eyes. Your heart melts, you start crying, it's perfect...just like you always imagined.

Brothers, picture your wedding day. The perfectly tailored tux, the wing-toed shoes. You're standing at the altar. Your godly, soon-to-be bride is being walked down the aisle about to be handed over to you forever. Your lifelong best friend is standing behind you, serving as your best man, whispering encouraging thoughts in your ear as the organist plays "Here Comes the Bride[61]". It's all absolutely perfect...just like you always imagined.

Now, my brothers and sisters, close your eyes and picture that day never happening. Take a minute right now and think deeply about that possibility.

Did that thought depress you? Does that picture seem unimaginable to you? Would that make you question God's love? If that wedding day never happens, will it steal your joy?

If your answer to any of those questions was "yes," then this chapter might be hard for you to read. Nonetheless, if you found yourself nodding your head up and down as you read any of those questions, you *need* to hear this. So I beseech you, *please* prayerfully read this chapter. These truths will cleanse your heart and bless you immensely.

Iconoclasm...

"Little children, keep yourselves from idols."

(1 John 5:21)

Will it rob your peace? If God never gives you one of His children as a spouse, will it hinder your service to Him? Will it affect your evangelistic witness for His Kingdom?

Our brother John Calvin aptly said, "The human heart is an idol factory[62]". You see, an object of desire doesn't need to be made of steel or gold to become an idol. For *anything* that comes before God in your heart or mind is an idol. Anything that makes your love or service for God conditional, has taken His place in your heart. If there's anything in your life that makes you say to God in your heart of hearts, "Lord, without this, I'll question Your love for me, and my service of You," *that* is your idol.

For many single Christians, their biggest temptation to

idolatry comes through their desire for marriage. As we've discussed, there's nothing at all ungodly about a desire for marriage, if it's truly for godly reasons. As Paul wrote, **"if you do get married, it is not a sin. And if a young woman gets married, it is not a sin"** (1 Corinthians 7:28a, NLT).

Epithumeo...

> **"Whoever loves father or mother more than me is not worthy of me, and whoever loves son or daughter more than me is not worthy of me."**
>
> (The Lord Jesus Christ, Matthew 10:37)

A heart desire becomes idolatrous when it grows to the point that it passes into the realm of "lust". You see, the Greek word above, *epithumeo*, is often translated as "lust" in the New Testament. And it means far more than just the mere modern English connotation would imply, as it means *any* type of desire that consumes your life, not merely those related to sexual passions[63].

Beloved, do you spend more time fantasizing about your marriage and future spouse than you do about serving the Kingdom of God? Do you spend more time thinking about the names of your future physical offspring than you do about the names of the spiritual children whom you could disciple?

Be completely honest with yourself here. Remember, repentance starts with acknowledgment of sin, then confession and prayer for deliverance.

So if marriage is indeed an idol in your life, you can't overcome it simply by *trying* to think about it less. No, you must confess to God the idol and ask for His forgiveness and cleansing. God has already promised the answer to that heartfelt prayer, for

"If we confess our sins, he is faithful and just to *forgive us our sins and to cleanse us from all unrighteousness*" (1 John 1:9, Italics Mine).

A.T.A.P.A.T...

> "If you refuse to take up your cross and follow me, you are not worthy of being mine."
>
> (The Lord Jesus Christ, Matthew 10:38, NLT)

My pastor likes to use this phrase, "A-Ta-Pat". It's an acronym for "Any Thing, Any Place, Any Time[64]". He uses it to describe what the attitude of our hearts should be toward the Lord. We should be willing to do anything God says, in any place, at any time. Commensurately, we should be willing to *lay down* any thing, in any place, at any time. That is the ideal for all Christians, so it should be our goal.

In the passage from the holy gospel of Matthew that opened this chapter, we read the Lord's stern words regarding *anything* or *anyone* coming before Him in our lives. Those words are sobering and convicting, and by them we understand the importance of placing nothing and no one ahead of our Lord.

We all need to be truly "sold-out" servants of Christ the King. We must be like the saints our brother John described in **Revelation**, who **"loved not their lives even unto death"** (cf. v. 12:11a).

Brethren, please remember always these words of our Lord Jesus Christ: **"'You must love the LORD your God with all your heart, all your soul, and all your mind.' This is the first and greatest commandment"** (Matthew 22:37-38, NLT). *All* our hearts, *all* our souls, and *all* our minds. Our lives simply have no room for two kings because **"No servant can serve two masters, for either** he will hate the one and love the other, or he will be devoted to the one and despise the other"** (Luke 16:13a).

Through gospel glasses, we see that God's love for us is *unconditional*. Thus, our response should be the same type of love and obedience for Him. Our hearts need a love for God that is irrespective of life circumstance because that's how God loves us.

Beloved, God has *already* proven His love for you on the cross at Calvary! Hence, if we are questioning His love because of some fact of our lives, we're sinfully neglecting that fact! So don't try to make God prove something that He's already proven!

Before the Lord saved you, your marriage, or something else, may have dominated your thoughts and heart. For **"You know that when you were pagans you were led astray to mute idols, however you were led"** (1 Corinthians 12:2). But now, that can no longer be true of your life. You must remember what happened when you first became a Christian, **"how you turned to God from idols to serve the living and true God"** (1 Thessalonians 1:9b).

What must now be true of our lives is a heart like our brother **Isaiah**, who when called by God said, **"Here am I! Send me"** (cf. v. 6:8).

The Ultimate Sacrifice...

"When they came to the place of which God had told him, Abraham built the altar there and laid the wood in order and *bound Isaac his son and laid him on the altar,* **on top of the wood."**

(Genesis 22:9, italics mine)

We all know the story of Abraham and his son Isaac. The child Abraham had been waiting on for years, his promised son, had finally been given to him. And now here he was, just a short time later, being asked to give this son right back to the Lord. In unwavering faith and obedience, Abraham stepped forward and offered up his biggest blessing on the altar to God. Because of his sacrifice, Abraham was blessed immensely, for not only was Isaac's life preserved, but in so doing God also made them both a blessed ancestor of the Lord Jesus Christ!

Now of course, there are many Christological foreshadows and parallels to be gleaned from this story. This is not mere allegory; this was a true historical event. Abraham giving up his own son was a foreshadowing of God the Father giving up His own Son, the Lord Jesus Christ (**cf. Hebrews 11:17-18**). The grammatical-historical context, when espousing a literal hermeneutic, is about Abraham's trust and obedience in YHWH, and the 'type' in this episode points to the Messiah ('anti-type') who will be born from this child of promise, which is Isaac.

However, there's also another important lesson for all singles to learn here. Let's break it down.

> **"After these things God tested Abraham and said to him, "Abraham!" And he said, "Here am I."**
> **He said, "Take your son, your only son Isaac, whom you love, and go to the land of Moriah, and offer him there as a burnt offering on one of the mountains of which I shall tell you."**
> (Genesis 22:1-2)

Abraham was a man of God. He had faithfully waited a *long* time for this blessing. Finally, the blessing had come; yet, Abraham still didn't love Isaac more than God. His response to this test showed a heart of love for, and complete trust in, God, exemplified by the fact that he KNEW the Lord could, and would, raise his son from the dead (**cf. Hebrews 11:19**). God already knew Abraham's heart, but this test showed Abraham that he was indeed a man of God, and its shown *us* what the heart of a godly man looks like. So we must learn from him.

Abraham teaches us that our hearts should never love the gift more than the Giver. We should never desire the blessing more than the Blesser. In the context of this chapter, we should never desire marriage outside of God's will. We must be willing even to give up our desire for marriage, if that is the call of the Lord. An overwhelmingly strong desire, the "epithumeo," is what can make marriage idolatrous for the single, obviously not marriage itself. The *consuming lust* for marriage is to be repented of, as it is an idolatrous desire of the heart.

On this point we must delve a little deeper. It must be categorically stated that not all desires are inherently lusts, nor do all desires become lust. We find a great example of this in Psalm 21:1-2: **"O LORD, in your strength the king rejoices, and in your salvation how greatly he exults! You have given him his heart's desire and have not withheld the request of his lips. *Selah"*.** Here we see an overwhelming godly desire for *God's* strength and *God's* salvation, and thus this desire was not a sinful lust. A desire only becomes sinful when it's self-centered, rather than God-centered, and especially so when a lack of the object of a desire causes discontentment. I have seen this temptation arise in my own life, with golf. Because it was such an idol in my life before Christ, it's a temptation I have battled regularly. I've been tempted to identify myself by my golf scores and to become discontented when I don't perform as I think I deserve. Of this I must always repent immediately.

This is why we must align our desires with what God desires for us. When the deepest desires of our heart are selfish, and anything other than God-centered, we are treading on dangerous ground. Dangerous because, when we inevitably don't receive these desires, we will multiply our sin with the resultant unhappiness and lack of joy. This is why the psalmist declared: **"Delight yourself in the LORD, and he will give you the desires of your heart"** (Psalm 37:4). When our deepest desires, our *delights*, are in the Lord, we know we will receive them. And thus, we will be truly joyous and thankful people! God wants us to be joyful and He wants this joy to be in HIM. It's why we are commanded to **"Rejoice *in the Lord* always; again I will say, Rejoice"** (Philippians 4:4, italics mine).

As our brother **Habakkuk** said: **"Though the fig tree should not blossom, nor fruit be on the vines, the produce of the olive fail and the fields yield no food, the flock be cut off from the fold and there be no herd in the stalls,** *yet I will rejoice in the LORD*; **I will take joy in the God of my salvation"** (vv. 3:17-18, italics mine). Our hearts must mirror his. Then, even if our fig trees (marriage, etc.) should not blossom, we'll still rejoice!

If we truly desire to glorify the God of our salvation, we must rejoice in and enjoy Him above all else. As our brother John Piper says: "God is most glorified in us when we are most satisfied in Him[65]". It doesn't glorify the Lord, or draw unbelievers to Him, when the world sees us constantly lamenting our earthly plight. So, not only is desiring God above all else the only way to true lasting joy, it's also one of the best witnesses a Christian can live.

One of the purposes of trials and tests is to show *us* where our hearts are. God already knows our hearts, and everything else about us, but trials show us where our hearts truly are. If you question God's love for you because of your singleness, this may be the exact reason why you're still single; to show you that marriage has become an idol for you. If that's you, please repent and trust in the Lord as Abraham did:

> **"Then Abraham reached out his hand and took the knife to slaughter his son."**
>
> (Genesis 22:10)

Abraham didn't just trust in the Lord, as in solely mentally, his actions followed through. Biblical trust ALWAYS bears fruit (**cf. James 2:14-26**). Abraham put his only child on the altar of the Lord. For many singles, their greatest imaginable blessing and biggest prayer is for a Godly spouse.

However, Abraham teaches us that we *must* be willing to put even our greatest blessings on the altar, which of course includes marriage.

That is, we must be willing to give it *all* over to God and submit to His will! We must relinquish any ostensible "control" over our lives and recognize His complete sovereignty. We must repent of any and all idolatry in our lives. In doing so, we will doubtless be blessed, just as Abraham was.

> **"And the angel of the LORD called to Abraham a second time from heaven and said, 'By myself I have sworn, declares the LORD, because you have done this and have not withheld your son, your only son, I will surely bless you, and I will surely multiply your offspring as the stars of heaven and as the sand that is on the seashore. And your offspring shall possess the gate of his enemies, and in your offspring shall all the nations of the earth be blessed, because you have obeyed my voice.'"**
>
> (Genesis 22:15-18)

Again, the promises made to Abraham there were

Christological and prophetic in nature, but the lessons we learn also apply to other areas of our lives. In putting our greatest desires on the altar before God and saying, "Lord, Your will be done," we are free to receive God's greatest blessings. We are no longer tied to the idols of selfish desire, but instead are able to enjoy the deep contentment and joy of a life fully submitted to and reliant on God. A life that walks in the **"the peace of God, which surpasses all understanding"** (cf. Philippians 4:7).

None of this is to say that this will always be an easy task, as our flesh fights back against us. This is why our brother Peter exhorted us: **"Dear friends, I urge you, as aliens and strangers in the world,** *to abstain from sinful desires, which war against your soul"* (1 Peter 2:11, italics mine). This might be a daily battle and sacrifice, but it's one we are called to make. As our Lord said: **"If anyone would come after me, let him deny himself and take up his cross** *daily* **and follow me"** (Luke 9:23, italics mine).

Free to Lay Freedom Down...

> "Do we not have the right to take along a believing wife, as do the other apostles and the brothers of the Lord and Cephas? Nevertheless, we have not made use of this right, but we endure anything rather than put an obstacle in the way of the gospel of Christ."
>
> (1 Corinthians 9:5,12b)

Brethren, don't get any of what I'm saying in this chapter twisted. Don't read any legalism into it because there is none intended. Nothing written here is to hinder your absolute freedom to pursue marriage. However, everything written here is to encourage you to place any desires for marriage in the correct *priority*, namely, by *laying down* those desires in complete submission to our Lord Jesus Christ. I'm merely encouraging you to say in your heart, "Lord, when and if it's your will for me to get married, awesome, please give me wisdom to see that. But until then, here's my life, use it as you will".

Just as Paul says in the passage above, he absolutely had the right to get married, but he laid that right down because his priorities were straight. He valued his mission for Christ much higher than any personal desires. My exhortation is for you to do the same in your heart of hearts. Place God and his mission for your life where it belongs, at the highest peak of your mountain of priorities. Then just let Him take care of every lower peak on that mountain, including your marriage.

Our Qinah King...

> **"Do not worship any other god, for the LORD,
> whose name is Jealous, is a jealous God."**
>
> (Exodus 34:14)

The Hebrew word above, *Qinah*, literally means "jealousy". It's used 44 times in the Old Testament and it has also been translated into words like "passion, zeal, rivalry, envy, and anger". In the context of our passage above, and in other places where it's used about God and His people, it's best understood to mean "ardent, zealous love, like the jealousy of a husband[66]". Knowing this definition gives us a deeper comprehension of the meaning of the passage above. So try reading it like this: "Do not worship any other god, for the LORD, whose name is jealousy, loves you with an ardent zeal, as a husband loves his wife."

This will remind us that God loves us intimately and personally. We were created to serve Him, love Him, and be in deep communion with Him **(cf. Romans 11:36)**.

His Holy Spirit indwells us, and because of this, **"He yearns jealously over the spirit that he has made to dwell in us"** (James 4:5). The context of that James verse is Christians desiring and asking for worldly, selfish things, and the sinful discontentment that arises from not receiving those requests **(cf. James 4:1-4)**. What it means is that anything, which would come between the Lord and us, will be removed or be delayed in coming.

Hence, we must espouse the truths described in this chapter, as we do not know when, or even if, God will bless us with marriage. What we *do* know is that we must divorce our true contentment, joy, and satisfaction from marriage and anything other than God himself. That is the purpose of this final section.

So like Abraham, let's obey the Lord's voice and move forward boldly, doing whatever He calls us to do, knowing that God works all things together for His glory and our good **(cf. Romans 8:28-30)**. Let's always remember that we have but one Holy Triune God. And He is the God of both the married and the single.

> **"Therefore, my beloved, flee from idolatry."**
> (1 Corinthians 10:14)

PURITY

**"Run from sexual sin!
No other sin so clearly affects the body as this one does.
For sexual immorality is a sin against your own body."**

(1 Corinthians 6:18, NIV)

The human body is the absolute pinnacle of God's creation. It is beautiful beyond measure. And thus, its allure is understandable. However, this does not make impurity acceptable in our lives.

As we've studied, we're no longer who we were, we're no longer of the flesh. For **"Flesh gives birth to flesh, but the Spirit gives birth to spirit"** (John 3:6). We were physically born into the flesh, into sin, but God has **"washed away our sins, giving us a new birth and new life through the Holy Spirit. He generously poured out the Spirit upon us through Jesus Christ our Savior"** (Titus 3:4b-6, NLT). This means we no longer have to acquiesce to the desires of our flesh.

Beloved, I'm in no way trivializing the battle that this sin brings. For many single Christians, this is the biggest war they fight against; it's their largest and most powerful temptation. Defeating this sin isn't easily or automatically done.

What I *am* here to tell you is this: victory over this sin is not only possible, it's both commanded and empowered, through the power of the Holy Spirit! The immutable truths of the gospel both promise and deliver this! **"For sin is the sting that results in death, and the law gives sin its power. But thank God! He gives us victory over sin and death through our Lord Jesus Christ"** (1 Corinthians 15:56-57, NLT).

So let's jump deep into God's word, to learn why purity is such a large battle for us, and most importantly, how the Lord sets us free and gives us victory over this large enemy.

The Conflict Within...

"The spirit is willing, but the flesh is weak."

(Mark 14:38b, NIV)

As a Christian, with your new nature and new heart, you desire to follow all of God's commands. But your flesh, the old nature, the old heart, doesn't want to give up or die easily. **"For the desires of the flesh are against the Spirit, and the desires of the Spirit are against the flesh, for these are opposed to each other, to keep you from doing the things you want to do"** (Galatians 5:17).

Living in a fallen body in a fallen world, the new you is at war not only with your own flesh, but also with the godless society around you. The fact that we're called to purity, while we live in a world that despises it, was perfectly captured by Paul when he wrote: **"God's will is for you to be holy, so stay away from all sexual sin. Then each of you will control his own body** and live in holiness and honor—not in lustful passion like the pagans who do not know God and his ways" (1 Thessalonians 4:3-5, NLT). The Holy Spirit tells you to obey and serve God, while your flesh, and everything and everyone around you, tell you to do the opposite. So, you're walking around with that proverbial angel whispering in your right ear and that demon whispering in your left.

If you've been acquiescing to the enemy whispering in your left ear, then you know exactly what Paul was describing when he wrote: **"For I know that nothing good dwells in me, that is, in my flesh. For I have the desire to do what is right, but not the ability to carry it out. For I do not do the good I want, but the evil I do not want is what I keep on doing"** (Romans 7:18-19). Every Christian knows that battle and that failure. We all know what happens right after that, as the cry of our heart becomes: **"Wretched man that I am! Who will deliver me from this body of death?"** (Romans 7:24).

But check it out beloved, Paul doesn't just leave us hanging there, wallowing in sin. Oh, no! In that very same book of Romans, and in his other epistles, Paul describes the keys to victory over that "wretched old man" inside. He gives us the principal truths we so desperately need for experiential sanctification. These are not new truths. They are bigger expansions and deeper expositions of *the truth* of the gospel! So let's dive in and clean our gospel glasses for better vision through them.

The Eternal Victory...

> "the Law has become our tutor to lead us to Christ,
> so that we may be justified by faith."
>
> (Galatians 3:24, NASB)

Beloved, before we jump into the practical aspects of experiential victory over impurity (and all sin), we must first revisit some "gospel groundwork". Through gospel glasses, we see this fact: the law could never save you; it never had the power.

We can easily see this all around us, even with human laws. America has a law book thick enough to sit on; yet, our prisons are still filled with people. God gave His Ten Commandments to humanity thousands of year ago; yet, people everywhere disregard and disobey these laws.

So, it's easy to see the law is not the answer because *the answer is Jesus!* **"Is the law then contrary to the promises of God? Certainly not! For if a law had been given that could give life, then righteousness would indeed be by the law. But the Scripture imprisoned everything under sin, so that the promise by faith in Jesus Christ might be given to those who believe"** (Galatians 3:21-22).

Thus, the primary purpose of the law was never to justify us before God. **"Therefore no one will be declared righteous in God's sight by the works of the law; rather, through the law we become conscious of our sin"** (Romans 3:20, NIV).

This is where the Israelites stumbled. It's why **"the people of Israel, who tried so hard to get right with God by keeping the law, never succeeded. Why not? Because they were trying to get right with God by keeping the law instead of by trusting in him. They stumbled over the great rock in their path"** (Romans 9:31-32, NLT). And who is that Rock? Christ the King!

The law is also where all the works-based false religions in the world miss the mark, especially the ones that ostensibly believe in the Bible or use their own specious "translation" of God's eternal Word. It's where they're totally sightless in their soteriology. "In their case the god of this world has blinded the minds of the unbelievers, to keep them from seeing the light of the gospel of the glory of Christ, who is the image of God" (2 Corinthians 4:4).

Those who think one can be justified before God by law keeping overlook this fact: the law produces rebellion. Think about it this way, in the Garden of Eden, Adam and Eve had just one law: "the LORD God commanded the man, saying, 'You may surely eat of every tree of the garden, but of the tree of the knowledge of good and evil you shall not eat, for in the day that you eat of it you shall surely die'" (cf. Genesis 2:16-17). For that first couple, there was only one "forbidden fruit," only one law of restriction. And what did that produce? Rebellion! "When the Woman saw that the tree looked like good eating and realized what she would get out of it—she'd know everything!—she took and ate the fruit and then gave some to her husband, and he ate" (Genesis 3:6, MSG). From the very beginning of time, "forbidden fruits," the breaking of God's laws, a.k.a. sins, by the very fact that they're forbidden, became alluring and appealing to us. That is why the law cannot, and will never, justify a person before God.

Beloved, this is by Divine design. "For Christ is the end of the law for righteousness to everyone who believes" (Romans 10:4). Through the law, and its inevitable transgression by humans, "God has consigned all to disobedience, that he may have mercy on all" (Romans 11:32). This is God's perfect design, so that we may never boast in ourselves or our good deeds. For "All of us have become like one who is unclean, and all our righteous acts are like filthy rags" (Isaiah 64:6a, NIV). God's salvific system is flawless. In it, "God has united you with Christ Jesus. For our benefit God made him to be wisdom itself. Christ made us right with God; he made us pure and holy, and he freed us from sin. Therefore, as the Scriptures say, "**If you want to boast, boast only about the LORD**" (1 Corinthians 1:30-31, NLT). God does all the work, and He gives it all freely by His grace for His eternal glory alone! "**Can we boast, then, that we have done anything to be accepted by God? No, because our acquittal is not based on obeying the law. It is based on faith**" (Romans 3:27, NLT).

The Lord God will be a debtor to no man. For "**When people work, their wages are not a gift, but something they have earned. But people are counted as righteous, not because of their work, but because of their faith in God who forgives sinners**" (Romans 4:4-5, NLT). God will let no man into His Kingdom because He *owes* it to them based on their righteousness. For then He'd have to share His glory with that man, which will not happen. As the Good Lord says, "**My glory I will not give to another**" (Isaiah 48:11b).

The law produces condemnation, but *the gospel* frees us from this! "**For God, who said, 'Let light shine out of darkness,' has shone in our hearts to give the light of the knowledge of the glory of God in the face of Jesus Christ**" (2 Corinthians 4:6). Through gospel glasses, we see that by trusting in Christ alone, we are not, and never will be, condemned. Check it: "**There is therefore now no condemnation for those who are in Christ Jesus**" (Romans 8:1). Hallelujah, praise the Lord!

Therefore, let us personally imbibe these truths wholeheartedly and exclaim with our brother Paul, "**As for me, may I never boast about anything except the cross of our Lord Jesus Christ**" (Galatians 6:14a, NLT).

Brethren, now that we've reiterated the gospel truth — our justification by grace alone through faith alone in Christ alone — let's learn how this *same* truth will practically sanctify us.

The Temporal Victory...

> "For sin shall not be master over you,
> for you are not under law but under grace."
>
> (Romans 6:14, NASB)

To me, this is one of the most powerful verses in all of Holy Scripture. For within its truth lies the key to victory over all sin, including impurity. So let's delve into that truth and be changed forever accordingly.

As we just studied, it's not the law that saved you. And now that you are saved, it's still not the law, or your flesh, that cleanses you or gives you victory over sin. Instead, **"the Scriptures declare that we are all prisoners of sin"** (Galatians 3:22a, NLT). So, the victory over our flesh does not lie in the law, or our striving in our own power to obey the law. Because here's the thing about your flesh and the law: **"the sinful nature is always hostile to God. It never did obey God's laws, and it never will"** (Romans 8:7, NLT).

This is why striving by the power of your flesh to keep the law will actually produce the *opposite* result — the *works* of the flesh! **"Now the works of the flesh are evident:** *sexual immorality,* **impurity, sensuality, idolatry, sorcery, enmity, strife, jealousy, fits of anger, rivalries, dissensions, divisions, envy, drunkenness, orgies, and things like these"** (Galatians 5:19-21a, italics mine).

But, as we've studied throughout this chapter, the Lord Jesus Christ has set us *free* from that old covenant of law that resulted in sin, that "ministry of death and condemnation"!

As Paul wrote: **"Now if the ministry of death, carved in letters on stone, came with such glory that the Israelites could** not gaze at Moses' face because of its glory, which was being brought to an end, will not the ministry of the Spirit have even more glory? For if there was glory in the ministry of condemnation, the ministry of righteousness must far exceed it in glory" (2 Corinthians 3:7-9).

As the author of Hebrews wrote: **"The old system under the law of Moses was only a shadow, a dim preview of the good things to come, not the good things themselves. The sacrifices under that system were repeated again and again, year after year, but they were never able to provide perfect cleansing for those who came to worship. For God's will was for us to be made holy by the sacrifice of the body of Jesus Christ, once for all time"** (Hebrews 10:1,10, NLT).

In Christ, we have now been *set free* to live righteously[67]! Because there is nothing that can condemn us, there are no more "forbidden fruits" for us, which makes sin lose *all* of its power. Sin is a defeated foe; it no longer has the allure it once had. Brethren, this is why we are commanded thus: **"Christ has truly set us free. Now make sure that you stay free, and don't get tied up again in slavery to the law"** (Galatians 5:1, NLT).

A New Law...

**"For the law of the Spirit of life has set you free
in Christ Jesus from the law of sin and death."**

(Romans 8:2)

Beloved, as we've seen, slavery to the law only results in slavery to sin! This happens because God is holy and we are not. He makes perfect laws and we break them. Before we knew Christ, these facts made us enemies of God; we existed in complete enmity with the holy Creator of the universe. Because of this, we willfully lived in sin against the Lord. We didn't need more obedience to the law; we needed someone to come and keep the law perfectly for us! We needed God's justifying love, the love we've now received in our Lord Jesus Christ!

You see, the astounding gospel truth of our eternal unity with God does not make us respond in rebellion. Rather, this *perfect* love makes us respond in love for God, love for others, and hatred of sin and evil. It's a beautiful and perfect system that testifies to God's greatness and glory. Through gospel glasses, we can see how God's perfect love for us is the only thing that results in the transformation of our hearts and minds, and reiterates why the law could never do this.

Check it out my brothers and sisters:

Enmity Begets Enmity...

Before knowing Christ, **"you were alienated from God and were enemies in your minds because of your evil behavior"** (Colossians 1:21, NIV).

And Love Begets Love...

"But now he has reconciled you by Christ's physical body through death to present you holy in his sight, without blemish and free from accusation" (Colossians 1:22, NIV).

Enmity Begets Enmity...

Before knowing Christ, we were all **"foolish, disobedient, led astray, slaves to various passions and pleasures, passing our days in malice and envy, hated by others and hating one another"** (Titus 3:3).

And Love Begets Love...

"But—"When God our Savior revealed his kindness and

love, he saved us, not because of the righteous things we had done, but because of his mercy. He washed away our sins, giving us a new birth and new life through the Holy Spirit. He generously poured out the Spirit upon us through Jesus Christ our Savior"** (Titus 3:4-6, NLT).

Enmity Begets Enmity...

Before knowing Christ, we **"were by nature children of wrath, like the rest of mankind"** (cf. Ephesians 2:3).

And Love Begets Love...

"But God is so rich in mercy, and he loved us so much, that even though we were dead because of our sins, he gave us life when he raised Christ from the dead. (It is only by God's grace that you have been saved!)" (Ephesians 2:4-5, NLT).

Enmity Begets Enmity...

Before knowing Christ, Paul's epic **Romans 1** diatribe condemning humanity was a portrait of our lives. As he wrote there: **"They are backstabbers, haters of God, insolent, proud, and boastful"** (Romans 1:30a, NLT).

And Love Begets Love...

"But God demonstrates his own love for us in this: While we were still sinners, Christ died for us. While we were God's enemies, we were reconciled to him through the death of his Son" (Romans 5:8,10a, NIV).

All of this overwhelming truth can thus be summed up in one perfect sentence penned through our apostolic brother John: **"We love, because He first loved us"** (1 John 4:19, NASB).

A New Walk...

> "But I say, walk by the Spirit,
> and you will not gratify the desires of the flesh."
>
> (Galatians 5:16)

At this point, you might be thinking, "Okay, we're free from the law, so how are we supposed to obey God now?" And God prophetically promised the answer to that question long ago: **"I will give you a new heart, and I will put a new spirit in you. I will take out your stony, stubborn heart and give you a tender, responsive heart. And I will put my Spirit in you so that you will follow my decrees and be careful to obey my regulations"** (Ezekiel 36:36-27, NLT). The old law, by the simple fact that we were condemnable transgressors of it, gave us stony hearts. But the new law, which is faith in our Lord and Savior Jesus Christ, who kept the law perfectly for us, has given us brand new hearts. Indeed, as we just studied, it's the only thing that could.

So now we know, it's *God the Holy Spirit* who gives us victory over sin, working out the truths and promises of the gospel experientially in our lives, making us obedient to God! Now we know, victory isn't gained by striving in our own flesh, as all of *our* efforts against sin only make it fight back stronger! Instead, seeing through gospel glasses, now **"We know that our old sinful selves were crucified with Christ so that sin might lose its power in our lives. We are no longer slaves to sin. For when we died with Christ we were set free from the power of sin"** (Romans 6:6-7, NLT).

You see, when we look at ourselves through gospel glasses, we see that we actually *died* with Christ on that old rugged cross at Calvary. As Paul wrote, **"I have been crucified with Christ. It is no longer I who live, but Christ who lives in me. And the life**

I now live in the flesh I live by faith in the Son of God, who loved me and gave himself for me" (Galatians 2:20).

That's right my brothers and sisters. You, the *old you*, is dead and gone. Accordingly, now **"We know that our old self was crucified with him in order that the body of sin might be brought to nothing, so that we would no longer be enslaved to sin. For one who has died has been set free from sin"** (Romans 6:6-7).

Paul continues this didactic discourse throughout the rest of that chapter of Romans. He wrote, when Christ died, **"he died once to break the power of sin. But now that he lives, he lives for the glory of God. So you also should consider yourselves to be dead to the power of sin and alive to God through Christ Jesus. Do not let sin control the way you live; do not give in to sinful desires. Do not let any part of your body become an instrument of evil to serve sin. Instead, give yourselves completely to God, for you were dead, but now you have new life. So use your whole body as an instrument to do what is right for the glory of God"** (Romans 6:10-13, NLT).

And after that, Paul wrote, **"You have been set free from sin and have become slaves to righteousness. I am using an example from everyday life because of your human limitations. Just as you used to offer yourselves as slaves to impurity and to ever-increasing wickedness, so now offer yourselves as slaves to righteousness leading to holiness"** (Romans 6:18-19, NIV).

Do you see how it all ties together beautifully? The gospel is just absolutely perfect! The law produced rebellion and made you a slave to sin. Then the Lord Jesus Christ saved you and set you free from that slavery! Now, your commanded response, your great freedom, and your blessed privilege, is to present yourself as a "slave to righteousness".

Paul summed this up better than I ever could when he wrote: **"The law of Moses was unable to save us because of the weakness of our sinful nature. So God did what the law could not do. He sent his own Son in a body like the bodies we sinners have. And in that body God declared an end to sin's control over us by giving his Son as a sacrifice for our sins. He did this so that the just requirement of the law would be fully satisfied for us, who no longer follow our sinful nature but instead follow the Spirit"** (Romans 8:3-4, NLT). Praise the Lord!

A Beautiful Mind...

The knowledge of all of this must transform our paradigms. It must transform how we see our behavior and ourselves. Seeing yourself correctly as God's child, you will be empowered to **"Imitate God, therefore, in everything you do, because you are his dear children"** (Ephesians 5:1, NLT).

Our Lord Jesus Christ saw many beautiful women in his lifetime, but not for one did he lust. Through the power of the Holy Spirit, "we have the mind of Christ" **(cf. 1 Corinthians 2:16)**. Accordingly, through submission to our new mind, and thus to God the Holy Spirit, we too can look upon beautiful people without a hint of lust. Remember, **"To the pure, all things are pure"** (Titus 1:15a).

This purity will not come by way of *you* "trying" harder. Overcoming lust is not just *hard* for you on your own; it's *impossible!* You *need* Christ to bear this fruit and make this change in you. As He said, **"Whoever abides in me and I in him, he it is that bears much fruit, for apart from me you can do nothing"** (John 15:5b).

So, what is required is for us to think like the children of God that we are, and to rely wholly on Christ for the heart purification we need. For **"It is the Spirit who gives life; the flesh is no help at all"** (John 6:63a).

Pastor Leonce Crump, in an epic exhortation to men of God, says: "Manning up is not just managing your sexual temptations! It's not just managing your sin! That's not what it means to be a man! Because you can try harder, and you can do better, and you can hang on longer...that's not manning up! Manning up is our ability to lay down all of our effort, and all of our trying, and all of our strength, and say I trust in Jesus! I trust in His perfection! I trust in His power! I trust in His resurrection! Because He's the only one that can get me through this! And He's the only one that can make me free![68]"

So you see, "self-control" really means complete submission to God's control. And thus, like the other Fruit of the Spirit, self-control comes from God and trusting Him, not from ourselves or our own efforts.

This is exactly what God promised through Ezekiel, who wrote: **"*I* will sprinkle clean water on you, and you shall be clean from all your uncleannesses, and from all your idols *I* will cleanse you. And *I* will give you a new heart, and a new spirit *I* will put within you. And *I* will remove the heart of stone from your flesh and give you a heart of flesh. And *I* will put my Spirit within you, and cause you to walk in my statutes and be careful to obey my rules"** (vv. 36:25-27, italics mine). Did you catch all the I's there? That's God speaking in the first person, proclaiming the changes *He* will make in our hearts and minds. None of this is our doing; it's all in and from *Him* alone. This is a very beautiful thing, and a truth we must wholeheartedly espouse.

Everyday Purity...

So how do we live this out practically? Let's take a look at that by imagining a couple of typical scenarios that bring the temptation to impurity.

First, let's picture this everyday occurrence. You're going through your daily routine and along the way you cross paths with a beautiful, scantily clad person. Sisters, maybe he's running down the road shirtless. Brothers, maybe she's just walking along wearing an extremely short dress. Either way, your flesh immediately starts screaming, "Look again!" Then, once you've given in to that second look, your flesh immediately tempts you to start conjuring up sexual scenarios between you and that person in your mind. You've just lost that battle because, as our Lord Jesus Christ said, **"everyone who looks at a woman with lustful intent has already committed adultery with her in his heart"** (Matthew 5:28). So what's the practical antidote?

Given the Biblical truths we've just studied in this chapter, here's the checklist of thoughts that should run through our minds immediately anytime this temptation arises:

1. I am the righteousness of God in Christ **(cf. 2 Corinthians 5:21)**.
2. Sin has no dominion over me because I'm not under law, but under God's eternal grace **(cf. Romans 6:14)**.
3. My flesh is dead and God has given me a new heart that allows me to live a pure life. **(cf. Romans 6:6-7, Ezekiel 36:25-27)**.
4. I have the mind of Christ. He never lusted for any person, so I don't have to lust at all. I'm not a slave to that evil and I've been set free from the power of lust. **(cf. 1 Corinthians 2:16, Philippians 2:5)**.
5. A quick prayer of: "Lord Holy Spirit, please take control here, and give me victory over this temptation. I give you control of my mind and heart".

Now, let's imagine a second scenario that brings the temptation to impurity for singles. This time, let's envision a Christian couple who are in a courtship. As they grow closer and closer to betrothal and marriage, their flesh grows increasingly impatient for a sexual consummation of the relationship. They hear lies in their mind like, "It's okay, you're going to get married anyway" or "You *can't* wait, it's *impossible*".

Once again, let's take a look at the practical Biblical countermeasures that will prevent acquiescence to this sin.

1. It's *not* okay. As Paul wrote to singles in courtship, **"if they can't control themselves, they should go ahead and marry. It's better to marry than to burn with lust"** (1 Corinthians 7:9).
2. You *can* wait. God not only commands it, He empowers it! **"For while we were living in the flesh, our sinful passions, aroused by the law, were at work in our members to bear fruit for death. But now we are released from the law, having died to that which held us captive, so that we serve in the new way of the Spirit and not in the old way of the written code"** (Romans 7:5-6).
3. Our bodies do not belong to us, so we can't use them to obey selfish passions. **"Or do you not know that your body is a temple of the Holy Spirit within you, whom you have from God? You are not your own, for you were bought with a price. So glorify God in your body"** (1 Corinthians 6:19-20).
4. God designed sex to be enjoyed, but *only* in marriage. Thus, remind yourselves of what's waiting for you *after* your wedding: **"The husband should give to his wife her conjugal rights, and likewise the wife to her husband. For the wife does not have authority over her own body,**

but the husband does. Likewise the husband does not have authority over his own body, but the wife does. Do not deprive one another" (1 Corinthians 7:3-5a).

5. Engage in regular prayer, both individually and corporately as a couple. In this prayer, ask God to take complete control of your minds and hearts, and to give you freedom and victory over this sin. Ask Him to bless and guide your courtship in every way, and hand it entirely over to Him.

The Ephemeral War...

"Beloved, I urge you as sojourners and
exiles to abstain from the passions of the flesh,
which wage war against your soul."

(1 Peter 2:11)

Brothers and sisters, I once again reiterate the fact that this is *not* an easy battle. I get that. The Greek word translated as "wage war" in the verse above, *strateuó*, is a *verb* that once again reminds us of the fact that our own flesh actively *fights* against us[69]! **"For the desires of the flesh are against the Spirit, and the desires of the Spirit are against the flesh, for these are opposed to each other, to keep you from doing the things you want to do"** (Galatians 5:17).

However, my dear beloved, I pray that the truths exposited in this chapter allow you to see the truth that this is a war that can be won! Though you may lose small battles here and there, once again remember: **"The godly may trip seven times, but they will get up again"** (Proverbs 24:16a, NLT). God and His word will lead you victoriously down the path of purity. For our success in this area lies in complete submission to the Holy Spirit, and in the embracing of the gospel truths we just studied.

God created sex and He gave you a sex drive. So you must trust that, in His time, God will bless you with the fulfillment of those desires in a way that glorifies and is obedient to Him. So now, as always, **"Delight yourself *in the LORD*, and he will give you the desires of your heart"** (Psalm 37:4, italics mine).

Beloved, you are sons and daughters of the living God. He has given you the imputed righteousness of our Lord and Savior King Jesus Christ. In doing this, God has freed you from both the condemnation *and* the power of sin. You're no longer under the law of sin and death, so sin should no longer have power in your life. **"For you have been called to live in freedom, my brothers and sisters. But don't use your freedom to satisfy your sinful nature. Instead, use your freedom to serve one another in love"** (Galatians 5:13).

Therefore, my brothers and sisters, know this: **"God's will is for you to be holy, so stay away from all sexual sin. Then each of you will control his own body and live in holiness and honor—not in lustful passion like the pagans who do not know God and his ways"** (1 Thessalonians 4:3-4, NLT).

And remember the eternal words of our Lord Jesus Christ:

"Blessed are the pure in heart, for they shall see God."
(Matthew 5:8)

COURTSHIP...

"An excellent wife, who can find?"

(Proverbs 31:10a, NASB)

I heard a tragic story about this young Christian girl from one of my pastors. She was around 30 years of age and was so terrified of being "alone" for the rest of her life that she married a man she didn't know everything about. She was a highly successful attorney, incredibly blessed in every way, and yet she didn't see these blessings. She didn't trust her loving Father in heaven, so she settled for a less-than-godly spouse. As it turned out, her new husband was very sketchy and he committed a felony after they got married. Because of California Bar regulations, since she was married to a criminal, she lost her license and ability to practice law in California.

This is a very extreme case, but nonetheless it underlies the necessity to trust God always and to never "step out on your own" in your desire for marriage. As we have studied all throughout this book, God has reasons for you to be single right now. You're not just "waiting in the wings" while He "looks" for someone for you. He's already predetermined your entire life, from conception to glorification, and this of course includes your marital status. And remember, He loves you and wants only what's best for you. Thus, just as in every other facet of your life, you must trust Him fully.

Beloved, the safest place to be is in God's will.

"Missionary" Dating?

"Do not be unequally yoked with unbelievers. For what partnership has righteousness with lawlessness? Or what fellowship has light with darkness?"

(2 Corinthians 6:14)

A common temptation for single Christians is the desire to "church date" an unbeliever who appeals to our flesh. A single Christian gets tired of waiting to meet another Christian, so they find someone they're attracted to and decide that they're going to "save" them through dating. It must be unequivocally understood that this is a sin.

But you might say, "They *will* get saved through my dating witness!" Well, God addresses that too:

"For how do you know, wife, whether you will save your husband? Or how do you know, husband, whether you will save your wife?"

(1 Corinthians 7:16)

That verse is addressed to new Christians who were already MARRIED to unbelievers. So if the married receive this warning, how much more must we as singles heed it? If the Lord says that there's no guarantee of a wife saving a husband, what makes you think you will save your boy/girlfriend?

Remember, God wants what's *best* for His kids, and that means *each other*. Think about it in human terms. I don't have kids, but I have nieces and nephews and I want only the best for them. I want them to marry the *best*, and of course that means only children of God. So if a sinful man like me can care about his family so much in this way, how much more does the perfect, holy, eternal God of the universe care for the good of His children? If you have a desire to get married, then that means it might be God's will for you to be married someday. And that means *right now* He might be preparing you for that person, and vice versa. So it's time to grow in godliness, not to "wallow in waiting." It is time to prepare to be a blessing to your future spouse.

You're NOT In Control, and It's a Beautiful Thing...

"Many are the plans in the mind of a man,
but it is the purpose of the LORD that will stand."

(Proverbs 19:21)

Most Christians have the "head knowledge" of God's complete sovereignty over their lives, but not all have fully imbibed this truth in their heart. This is of the utmost importance in the life of any Christian. You are *not* in control of whom you marry or when you get married. You are *not* even in control of whether you wake up tomorrow morning. So let go. This is a beautiful thing.

Even as redeemed people, we are all still sinners with extremely limited knowledge. So why would we want to be in control of our lives? Instead, let us submit fully to the will of our perfectly wise, omniscient, eternal, loving Father.

We know *nothing*: **"If anyone imagines that he knows something, he does not yet know as he ought to know"** (1 Corinthians 8:2). The more we learn, the more we realize what we don't know. As we grow in wisdom, we understand this better.

So let us live in childlike dependence on our Father. A child doesn't know *how* dinner is coming on any given day, they only know *that* dinner is coming. So they don't spend their day worrying about what they're going to eat that night, they just trust that daddy is going to provide for them and they enjoy their day. We must put on this same attitude in all areas of our lives, including dating.

Seek First The Kingdom...

> "Therefore do not be anxious, saying,
> 'What shall we eat?' or
> 'What shall we drink?' or
> 'What shall we wear?'
> For the Gentiles seek after all these things,
> and your heavenly Father knows that you need them all.
> But seek first the kingdom of God and his righteousness,
> and all these things will be added to you."
> (Matthew 6:31-33)

Your heavenly Father knows you need food, so He provides it. He knows you need clothing, so He sends it. And of course, He knows you desire to get married someday, so just like in everything else, He may give you another one of His children. But this will be done on *His* timetable, not yours. *He* says when it's the right time, not you. Espouse the truth of this passage...you don't receive blessings by concentrating on them. Only by chasing after

Him and pursuing His righteousness is one blessed. Putting any blessing before the Blesser is idolatry, pure and simple. Loving the gifts more than the Giver is one of the worst possible attitudes because then you've made yourself into a god. You've made your love for the Lord conditional, based on what He does in your temporal, earthly life. This is wrong.

"For the Gentiles seek after all these things"

The unbeliever worries about being an "old maid" or a "cat lady." She doesn't have a relationship with the Lord of Lords, so she has a giant void in her life that she tries to fill with human relationships, especially marriage. This must not be so for the children of God! I love Christian rapper Lecrae's paraphrase of this passage: "You pursue God, the rest He takes care of.[70]" And really, it's as simple as that. Verse 33 of Matthew 6 contains a promise from God, and His Word never returns void **(cf. Isaiah 55:11)**. Seek first His kingdom and His righteousness, and He will take care of *everything* else.

You are NOT of this world...

**"They are not the world,
just as I am not of the world."**

(John 17:16)

The world constantly bombards us with garbage. Women's magazines talk about "biological clocks" ticking, while men's magazines equate sexual prowess with the number of partners.

A hilarious paradox, isn't it? Women are told they *need* to get married and have kids before time runs out, and men are told they need to sleep with as many women as possible and avoid commitment.

Ahh, life in a fallen world, doesn't make any sense at all, does it?! But I digress, because all of this *does* make sense when you look at it through the lenses of God's Word!

> **"You used to live in sin,**
> **just like the rest of the world, obeying the devil—**
> **the commander of the powers in the unseen world.**
> **He is the spirit at work in the hearts**
> **of those who refuse to obey God."**
>
> (Ephesians 2:2, NLT)

The world is dead. As I've heard a pastor say: "We are walking among zombies daily." The world is fallen and cursed, and its end is to be burned. And thus are its inhabitants. The "course of this world," referenced in the aforementioned verse, is a course that people walk on the way to hell. It's a sinful course; a life lived in complete rebellion against God. It's a life lived following the "Zeitgeist," which is the German word for "the spirit of the age"[71]. And thus, by God's perfect justice, all who walk on this course are by nature children of wrath. The unbeliever walks around with a dead soul, just a slave to their passions until they pass away. That's why this world doesn't make any sense of itself. It's a world ruled by the evil one, the "prince of the power of the air". A world designed to keep dead people dead until they truly *die*!

> **"But God, being rich in mercy,**
> **because of the great love with which he loved us,**
> **even when we were dead in our trespasses,**
> **made us alive together with Christ—**

> by grace you have been saved—
> and raised us up with him and seated us with
> him in the heavenly places in Christ Jesus,
> so that in the coming ages he might show
> the immeasurable riches of his grace
> in kindness toward us in Christ Jesus."
>
> (Ephesians 2:4-7)

God has given *you* life! He has opened *your* eyes to the truth! You no longer walk on that course to hell. You are no longer a slave to your sinful passions. You are no longer of this world. You are no longer a slave to the Zeitgeist. You no longer have to let the sinful paradigms of this fallen world dictate how you live your life. Sisters, God knows all about your biological clock, for He created it, and He can transcend its natural limitations very easily...Remember Sarah? Brothers, you know God doesn't want lust ruling your life and He can give you victory over that sin. You were designed for one wife **(cf. Genesis 2:24)**, and if/when God wills, He will provide her!

Trusting As You Wait...

> "Trust in the LORD with all your heart,
> and do not lean on your own understanding.
> In all your ways acknowledge him,
> and he will make straight your paths."
>
> (Proverbs 3:5-6)

Our understanding is flawed. It's flawed by our sinful flesh and extremely limited by our finite minds. Thus, we can't trust ourselves. We can't trust our own minds or our own hearts. The Lord tells us: **"The heart is deceitful above all things, and** desperately sick; who can understand it?" (Jeremiah 17:9.) It's easy to see here, the only One we can trust is God. The only knowledge we can trust is His Word. So let us lean on Him and trust in His understanding alone. We must acknowledge Him first and foremost in our dating and desire for marriage, and He will make that path straight too.

Practically, this first of all means seeking God's will through prayer. Remember, the Lord indwells us and He will give us guidance if we seek Him through heartfelt conversation. Next, we must seek godly counsel. Talk to your pastor and your brothers and sisters in Christ who are stronger and more mature in the Lord. One way God blesses us with wisdom is through each other: **"Where there is no guidance the people fall, But in abundance of counselors there is victory"** (Proverbs 11:14). Oftentimes, when we meet someone new who attracts us physically, our sinful hearts become intoxicated and we don't see the object of our desire as they truly are. The Lord sees all and He will guide you through prayer. Your brothers and sisters have an objective viewpoint of that person you want to date and they will tell you the truth. So you must lean on the Lord and His people, and He will guide your dating.

"It's Not You, It's Me"...

"Love is never tired of waiting; love is kind; love has no envy; love has no high opinion of itself, love has no pride"
(1 Corinthians 13:4, BBE)

Pride is a sin that tempts all Christians and singles are certainly not immune. For us, one of the main ways where pride manifests itself is in dating. It is the attitude of: "I'm better than everyone else." It is the attitude of: "These people aren't good enough for me, I wouldn't marry a single one of them, so I'd rather stay single." Now, you should never settle for an ungodly spouse. However, this is not to be misconstrued with prideful avoidance of godly pursuers because you think they're not good enough for you. This is yet another major area where the world's philosophies and paradigms creep into our thinking. As we touched on in Section A - Chapter 3, you must learn to see people, especially potential mates, the way God sees them. The world sees the outside, the appearance, the status, and the money. But **"the LORD sees not as man sees: man looks on the outward appearance, but the LORD looks on the heart"** (1 Samuel 16:7). I think there are many single Christians who want to get married that are still single for this very reason. Indeed, being part of a singles ministry for several years now, I've seen this scenario play out in front of me many times. There are many who are not single for want of available godly mates. They are single because they think they're "too good" for all of them. If you're on mission in the Congo, or some other remote location, a legitimate lack of available godly mates is fully understandable.

But if you're a single, American Christian, it's really hard to say that there's "no one out there." In my church alone, one of the thousands of Christian churches in America, there are many amazing, single godly men and women. In visiting other churches, I know that this is true elsewhere.

Sisters, if you're waiting for your "Prince Charming" with the six-pack abs, seven-figure bank account, Masters Degree in Theology, son of a pastor...you're going to be waiting for a long time. Brothers, if you're waiting for your "perfect ten" supermodel, you are in that same boat.

As Paul admonished Corinth, **"For who regards you as superior? What do you have that you did not receive? And if you** did receive it, why do you boast as if you had not received it?" (1 Corinthians 4:7, NASB). You see, the problem doesn't lie in our "potential mate pool"; it lies in our prideful thoughts that we "deserve better." It lies in our sinful perfectionism. As we've studied, none of us are perfect, or even good **(cf. Luke 18:19)**, and thus none of us deserve perfect. If God were to never give us a spouse at all, we'd still have more than we deserve. Remember, the Lord told us how sinful we are, not how good we are **(cf. Luke 11:13, Mark 10:18)**. So, as with other social sins, this one is overcome not by changing the people you're meeting, but by changing your heart, by changing how you see them! Through gospel glasses you'll see that you *don't* deserve perfect, that you're *not* better than anyone else, and that *no one* is beneath you. A godly heart searches for a godly spouse and considers all other attributes secondary. It desires what God considers desirable.

A truly humble, gospel heart understands the gracious blessing of a godly mate. It knows that **"He who finds a wife finds a good thing and obtains favor from the LORD"** (Proverbs 18:22). That Scripture doesn't say "he who finds a perfect wife finds a good thing". So we know that a humble, gospel heart receives a spouse as a blessing, and for that it thanks the Lord. It doesn't look for "bigger and better". A truly humble, gospel heart is one that says: "God, I don't deserve one of your children at all, but you have given me one, and I thank you".

As our brother John Calvin says of our call to kill pride: "Christ's humility consisted in his abasing himself from the highest pinnacle of glory to the lowest ignominy: our humility consists in refraining from exalting ourselves by a false estimation. He gave up his right: all that is required of us is, that we do not assume to ourselves more than we ought. Since, then, the Son of God descended from so great a height, how unreasonable that we, who are nothing, should be lifted up with pride![72]" How unreasonable indeed!

Once again, victory lies in seeing everything and everyone through gospel glasses, which empowers that most dramatic paradigm shift, the one that only a Christian can truly experience...the radical transformation of *getting over yourself*!

Forget the "American Dream"

"Do not be conformed to this world,
but be transformed by the renewal of your mind"

(Romans 12:2)

The world tells you this is what you need to be whole and complete: a spouse, a house in the suburbs with a white picket fence, and 2.5 kids. The mass media says that if you don't have those things, plus a giant bank account, a nice car, and a country club membership, your life is lacking. The evil one controls the culture...so let's dispel those lies by seeing what God says you need!

"They are not of the world,
just as I am not of the world."

(The Lord Jesus Christ, John 17:16)

Reminder, in that verse, our Lord is speaking about you and me. *We* are not of this world! We know the truth. We see the lies inherent in popular culture. We have *real* life. *We* can know what we *truly* need. You have been **"ransomed from the futile ways inherited from your forefathers"** (cf. 1 Peter 1:18). This means that even if your own family is telling you to chase all the things of this world, you must not listen to them. Your life is no longer measured by material possessions. You're no longer living to please your parents or others; you're now living to please and serve the living God! What God values is more important than what the world values. Your identity is now in Christ, not in yourself or your "things." Our brother, Christian rapper Lecrae, puts it thus:

> "I'm not the shoes I wear, I'm not the clothes I buy,
> I'm not the house I live in, I'm not the car I drive,
> I'm not the job I work, you can't define my worth,
> By nothing on God's green earth,
> my identity is found in Christ![73]"

It's very important to imbibe the truth there. So much despair, depression and despondency over singleness is caused by basing your identity in marriage, kids and possessions. But that's not where your identity rests! So much sinful envy is caused by believing the lies that you are less blessed because you don't have what someone else at church has...of this we need to repent. The world says: keep up with the Joneses. The Lord says: **"Take care, and be on your guard against all covetousness, for one's life does not consist in the abundance of his possessions"** (Luke 12:15).

It will do us much good to remember whom Jesus was while on earth and how the world would have seen Him. Lecrae puts it thus:

> "He never got married,
> He was broke plus homeless,
> And yeah, that's the God I roll with![74]"

If Jesus were here today, think of how the world would see

Him. The world wouldn't call Him "successful". And it was no different at the time He walked this planet. The culture there shunned Him and thought lowly of Him. Remember that one of the first recorded things said about Him was a derision of His background: **"'Nazareth! Can anything good come from there?'** **Nathanael asked"** (John 1:46a, NIV). He was born in Bethlehem, which was not at all a noble place. He was born in a manger, among animals and straw, not in a fancy hospital with a midwife or a "pregnancy coach". We must know and remember who the Person was that we're trying to emulate and what His life was like.

Our brother Johnny Cash puts it best in the song lyrics below. Read it line by line slowly and really visualize the Lord's day to day earthly life...

"Here was a Man...A Man who was born in a small village, the Son of a peasant woman. He grew up in another small village. Until He reached the age of thirty He worked as a carpenter. Then for three years He was a traveling minister. But He never traveled more than two hundred miles from where He was born. And where He did go He usually walked. He never held political office, He never wrote a book, never bought a home, never had a family. He never went to college and He never set foot inside a big city. Yes, here was a Man. Though He never did one of the things usually associated with greatness...He had no credentials but Himself...He had nothing to do with this world except through the Divine purpose that brought Him to this world.[75]"

Does that sound like living the "American Dream" to you? No, of course not, because that's not why He was here. He was here to do the will of the Father and then go home, as should be our desire. This world is *not* our home! And while there is absolutely nothing wrong with wanting a spouse and kids, you must discern your motives. If it's for worldly dreams, it's time to repent. The Lord admonishes us thus: **"Do not love the world nor the things in the world. If anyone loves the world, the love of the Father is not in him"** (1 John 2:15).

You mustn't worry about or lament worldly position or background; rather, you must remember the following truth: **"For consider your calling, brothers: not many of you were wise according to worldly standards, not many were powerful, not many were of noble birth. But God chose what is foolish in the world to shame the wise; God chose what is weak in the world to shame the strong; God chose what is low and despised in the world, even things that are not, to bring to nothing things that are, so that no human being might boast in the presence of God. And because of him you are in Christ Jesus, who became to us wisdom from God, righteousness and sanctification and redemption, so that, as it is written, 'Let the one who boasts, boast in the Lord'"** (1 Corinthians 1:26-31). Any boasting in your life should have nothing to do with your worldly occupation, family, possessions, or achievements. **"Thus says the LORD: "Let not the wise man boast in his wisdom, let not the mighty man boast in his might, let not the rich man boast in his riches, but let him who boasts boast in this, that he understands and knows me, that I am the LORD who practices steadfast love, justice, and righteousness in the earth. For in these things I delight, declares the LORD"** (Jeremiah 9:23-24).

Espousing the correct attitude about this especially applies in dating. The world says to the ladies, "Marry the richest man you can find." The Lord says: **"Better is the little that the righteous has than the abundance of many wicked"** (Psalm 37:16). The world says to guys, "Marry the most beautiful, youngest girl who will have you." The Lord says: **"Charm is deceitful, and beauty is** vain, but a woman who fears the LORD is to be praised"** (Proverbs 31:30). You must get your values in line with what God values, with what God says is valuable. Once again, this means that in your prayers and search for a spouse, you're asking and looking for the godliest person, not necessarily the wealthiest or cutest.

The world says that your immortality lies in your accomplishments, your kids, your achievements, and your works...what it calls your "legacy." The Lord says: **"In the way of righteousness there is life; along that path is immortality"** (Proverbs 12:28, NIV). Your immortality does *not* lie in what you've done or your earthly legacy, it lies in the Lord Jesus Christ! It's not in your works, but in His! Our brother Jon Foreman from Switchfoot says it well: "We're so confident in our accomplishments, look at our decadence...(yet) all the riches of the kings end up in wills.[76]"

So where does your treasure lie? Does it lie in this temporal, fleeting world, or in life eternal with the Lord in His glorious kingdom? The answer to that question will determine your entire life paradigm.

A big part of the "American Dream" is the desire for retirement. The world says to stack money in the bank so you can retire as young as possible. But retirement is not a Christian principle. John Piper says it well regarding retirement: "20 years, perhaps, of leisure, ease...while the world...uncared for medically, uneducated, filthy water, poverty stricken, *unevangelized*...SINKS under the weight of healthy, 65 year old people playing bridge, and shuffleboard, and collecting shells, and fishing, and golfing their way into the presence of King Jesus! You're going to join them, unless, at this stage in your life...you make some very radical decisions, very radical commitments, very radical choices...about where your treasure is![77]"

Our savior, born in a small village in Israel, poor by every earthly standard...changed the world forever! So if you think that your worldly position or "status" is the determinant for your influence on this planet, think again. Johnny Cash puts it well regarding our Savior: "I think I'm well within the mark when I say that all of the armies that ever marched...All of the navies that ever sailed the seas...All of the legislative bodies that ever sat, and all of the kings that ever reigned...All of them put together have not affected the life of man on this earth...So powerfully as that one solitary life...Here was a Man.[78]" And remember the words of that God-Man: **"Truly, truly, I say to you, whoever believes in me will also do the works that I do; and greater works than these will he do, because I am going to the Father"** (John 14:12). Greater in quantity of course, *not* quality, for Jesus is God.

Don't Romanticize THIS Life...

> "Through many tribulations we
> must enter the kingdom of God."
>
> (Acts 14:22b, NASB)

A great danger for single Christians comes when they romanticize the married life. One thinks that once they have a spouse and kids everything will be perfect and they will be completely happy. But you must imbibe the truth...perfect, and thus perfect happiness, does not exist on this side of eternity. Married people have problems too, new and different problems you might not have even considered. Remember Paul's words: **"those who marry will have worldly troubles"** (cf. 1 Corinthians 7:28). While there are definitely blessings in marriage, there are issues as well. Even for two married Christians in the process of experiential sanctification by God, it's still a marriage of two sinners. It's still a union of two people living in fallen bodies, in a fallen world, each fighting their own flesh. And thus, conflicts and problems are inevitable.

All that "me" time that you currently enjoy, the worldly freedom, the extra money...will all be sacrificed on the altar of marriage. Not that any of those are on their own a cause for consternation, but you must understand that heaven isn't achieved in this life. It's waiting for us when we go to our true home, but for now, no matter what life state you're in, don't expect perfect bliss.

I write all of this not to condemn home-ownership, worldly success, or having a family...for those are all blessings. I write all of this to encourage you to discern your motives carefully for wanting all of these things. I write to encourage you to "let go" of the need for these things, in total abandonment to the Lord's will. Remember Paul's words: **"if we have food and clothing, with these we will be content"** and **"I have learned in whatever situation I am to be content"** (1 Timothy 6:8; Philippians 4:11). Therein lies the *real* "dream life"; therein lies contentment and joy in all circumstances. Define your success and identity by who you are in Christ, not in the world, remembering...

> "Identity is found in God we trust.
> Any other identity will self-destruct."[79]
> - Lecrae

The Directory of Desirability...

**"Do not let your adorning be external—
the braiding of hair and the putting on of gold jewelry,
or the clothing you wear—**

> **but let your adorning be the hidden person of the heart with the imperishable beauty of a gentle and quiet spirit, which in God's sight is very precious."**
>
> (1 Peter 3:3-4)

God knows what and who is best for you. In His word, God has given us a practical "checklist of godliness," which can be used as the basis for evaluating potential mates. Through this, God teaches us exactly what we should be looking for in a future spouse. Let's take a look at the attributes that God says should be most appealing to us. Though these come from what are called the "pastoral" epistles, they aren't meant to be descriptive only of pastors; they're meant to be the traits of all mature Christians.

Brothers, this is a description of the most truly beautiful women:

> They are **"dignified, not malicious gossips, but temperate, faithful in all things."**
>
> (1 Timothy 3:11, NASB)

> They live **"pure and reverent lives."**
>
> (cf. 1 Peter 3:2)

Sisters, this is the man of God whom you should seek:

> **"He must live a blameless life. He must not be arrogant or quick-tempered; he must not be a heavy drinker, violent, or dishonest with money. Rather, he must enjoy having guests in his home, and he must love what is good. He must live wisely and be just. He must live a devout and disciplined life. He must have a strong belief in the trustworthy message he was taught;**

then he will be able to encourage others with wholesome teaching and show those who oppose it where they are wrong."
(Titus 1:7-8)

He is "sober-minded, dignified, self-controlled, sound in faith, in love, and in steadfastness."
(Titus 2:2)

Now obviously my brethren, I live in the same fallen world you do, so I'm not saying you should expect to find someone who perfectly lives out every tenet of those texts already. What I *am* saying is, you must ask yourself these questions of any potential mates you are considering, "Are they *growing* in those areas?" and "Do they endeavor to *become* those people?"

Your future spouse will be someone you're going to live with, day in and day out, for, Lord-willing, the rest of your earthly life. I live in the same fallen body you do, so I know that physical beauty will have some value and merit, but those qualities must be subjugates of godly characteristics. Physical beauty changes, and money doesn't buy character or love. So you must be earnestly looking for someone you can see fulfilling God's commands for marriage as laid out in **Ephesians 5**:

"For wives, this means submit to your husbands as to the Lord. For a husband is the head of his wife as Christ is the head of the church. He is the Savior of his body, the church. As the church submits to Christ, so you wives should submit to your husbands in everything. For husbands, this means love your wives, just as Christ loved the church. He gave up his life for her to make her holy and clean, washed by the cleansing of God's word."
(vv. 22-27, NLT)

While a person's physical attractiveness may be the initial catalyst for a romance, that relationship must *not* move to the next stage unless you can honestly see your suitor becoming who God desires all of His children to become.

Accordingly, through this period, you must yourself be aiming for these same attributes to be evinced in your own life. I love this old saying:

> "God's not going to give you His best,
> Until He's made you your best"
>
> (Anonymous)

Ask, And It Will Be Given...

**"If you then, who are evil,
know how to give good gifts to your children,
how much more will your Father who is in heaven
give good things to those who ask him!"**

(Matthew 7:11)

It's quite simple, but often overlooked. The practical implications of this verse cannot at all be overstated: we must ask our Father for what we desire within His will. Again, if you have a desire to get married, then that means it's probably God's will for you to be married, someday. Sisters, if you want to get married, then *do not* worry about being an "old maid." Brothers, if you want to get married, then trust that God will *not* let you battle lust in singleness for the rest of your life.

Ask your Father for a godly spouse and trust Him fully to answer in His perfect timing.

All throughout Scripture, one of the common themes that

emerges is this: obey the Lord and be blessed; disobey and you pay the consequences, pure and simple. God is just and God is good, all the time. **"Don't be misled--you cannot mock the justice of God. You will always harvest what you plant"** (Galatians 6:7, NLT). So, if you want to be blessed by God, then you must obey Him.

> **"and whatever we ask we receive from him, because we keep his commandments and do what pleases him."**
> (1 John 3:22)

In the context of that third chapter of 1 John, we are commanded to love others, but it's not just obeying that command that pleases the Lord. As stated all throughout Scripture, God desires our obedience in all areas. And the beautiful thing is, for us as His children, **"his commandments are not burdensome"** (1 John 5:3b). They aren't burdensome because we love Him, and we love Him because He loved us first **(cf. 1 John 4:19)**. They aren't burdensome because they're given with *our* best interests in mind, not to place limits on our freedom, but to ensure our good. They aren't burdensome because, as the psalmist says of the Lord and His commands: **"My tongue will sing of your word, *for all your commandments are right"*** (Psalm 119:172, italics mine). So let us sing along with the psalmist: **"your commandments are my delight"** (Psalm 119:143b).

It's so amazing how the Lord not only paid for all of our sins Himself, but now that we have been reconciled to Him, He blesses us for obedience. Paul wrote: **"as servants of Christ, doing the will of God from the heart, rendering service with a good will as to the Lord and not to man, knowing that whatever good anyone does, this he will receive back from the Lord"** (Ephesians 6:6-8).

Doesn't that blow your mind? We deserve nothing but hell, but the Lord in His great mercy not only gives us eternal life for free, but also along with that clean slate, we are also now rewarded for our good deeds! Blessed be the name of the Lord!

So let us **"love righteousness and hate wickedness"** (Psalm 45:7a, NIV). For **"Whoever pursues righteousness and kindness will find life, righteousness, and honor"** (Proverbs 21:21). The Lord's word speaks for itself. Sow peace and righteousness...reap accordingly. So if you want the Lord's favor in all areas of your life, you must obey Him.

It bears summation: Ask your Father for your future spouse, placing all your trust in Him, acquiescing to His perfect will and choice for that person, in complete obedience remembering: **"the LORD God is a sun and shield; the LORD bestows favor and honor.** *No good thing does he withhold from those who walk uprightly"* (Psalm 84:11, italics mine).

And a godly spouse is most definitely a good thing…
a good thing absolutely worth waiting for.

WHEN?

"Who of you by worrying can add a single hour to his life?"
(The Lord Jesus Christ, Matthew 6:27, NIV)

In single Christians, the sin of anxiety can manifest itself in many ways; however, this happens most frequently in worries over marriage, two of which are the most prevalent. The temptation enters most often like this: "Am I *ever* going to get married?" and "Will I marry the *right* person?". We know that these worries are sinful. And just as it is with other sins, victory over anxiety lies in trusting God and standing on His irrefutable word. Accordingly, there are three texts that I believe are the most helpful for us to systematically destroy *all* worries, including those about marriage. Let's jump in and break them down.

First, The Red Letters...

The Lord Jesus Christ specifically addressed the sin of anxiety during the "Sermon on the Mount," so the best way to begin our study on this subject is by looking at His words. His exhortations about worry are recorded in **Matthew 6:25-34**. Let's unpack that passage verse by verse, applying those truths specifically to the temptations of marital anxieties and fully submitting to the Lord's commands there.

"Therefore I tell you, do not be anxious about your life, what you will eat or what you will drink, nor about your body, what you will put on. Is not life more than food, and the body more than clothing?" (v. 25). The Greek word translated as "be anxious about" is *"merimnate"*[80], which literally means to be divided and pulled apart in opposite directions by distraction. Knowing this definition helps us to more deeply understand the strength of this command. When we're worrying about a future marriage or spouse, we're taking our eyes and thoughts off Christ, allowing ourselves to be distracted by worldly cares. Contrast this with some specific commands we receive through the writer of **Hebrews: "Therefore, holy brothers, who share in the heavenly calling,** *fix your thoughts on Jesus***, the apostle and high priest whom we confess."** And *"Let us fix our eyes on Jesus,* **the author and perfecter of our faith, who for the joy set before him endured the cross, scorning its shame, and sat down at the right hand of the throne of God"** (vv. 3:1 & 12:2, italics mine). So try reading the text thus: "Therefore, do not be anxious about your life, when you will get married, or whom you will marry. Is not your life more than your marriage and your body more than a vessel for biological reproduction?"

Now, in our text, the Lord contrasts "life" with "food" and the "body" with "clothing". Taking note of this contrast is of the utmost importance in understanding this verse. The Greek word translated as "life" in our text is *psychē*, which means the human soul breathed into life by God[81]. This is a further reiteration that God gave us our very lives, through no merit or request of our own. The Greek word translated as "body" in our text is *"sōma,"* which means the physical flesh[82]. This is yet another reminder that God hand-wrote His signature on our cells, on our "flesh" that He made. So the contrast our Lord Jesus uses here begs two questions: "Will He, who gave you the desire for marriage, withhold a spouse to fulfill that desire?" and "Will He, who provides everything you need for godliness, fail to give you a godly spouse?" The answer to both questions is, of course, a very emphatic "no"! So why worry, ever?

"Look at the birds of the air: they neither sow nor reap nor gather into barns, and yet you're heavenly Father feeds them. Are you not of more value than they?" (v. 26). Let's think about this practically. What does the average bird do every morning that the average human, and sadly even the average Christian, doesn't? They sing! When was the last time you woke up and sang to God for His gracious provision of another morning, and for the sustenance He will provide because He woke you up that day? How often do we, instead of doing that, wake up and immediately resume our worries from the night before? As our text illuminates, this is sin. The birds have no refrigerator full of food to open when they wake up, no coffee makers ready to go, no breakfast restaurants to fly into, yet they lack all *"merimnate"* about the situation because God still feeds them everyday. And if He provides for the soul-less fowl of the skies, why should we ever doubt He will provide fully for we who eternally bear His image *and* call Him Abba? This happens because, even though we are witnesses to God's providential sustenance of His animal creations daily, we sinfully doubt our own value and worth in His eyes, whether we realize it or not. Let's dive deeper into the implications of this "sub-surface" doubt. The Greek word translated as "value" in our text is *"diapherete,"* which means to distinguish what is different between two parties, illustrating the fact that one party excels and surpasses the other[83]. Thus, more deeply espousing the fact that it is *we* who "excel and surpass" the avian benefactors of God's free daily provisions is yet another key to killing all worry about God's providence in our lives. The birds fly around **"careless in the care of God"** (cf. v. 26, MSG) all day long. Hence, it's time for us to learn how to do the same.

"And which of you by being anxious can add a single hour to his span of life?" (v. 27). The Greek words used in this verse can also allow it to be translated as: "And which of you by being anxious can add a single cubit to his stature?" (For reference, a "cubit" was a physical unit of measure roughly equal to 1.5 feet, or half a meter for my "metric" brethren)[84]. Knowing both of this verse's translations helps us to better comprehend its strength. We can't make ourselves grow taller anymore than we can make ourselves live longer, so why bother worrying about either our height or our lifespan, it's useless, and worst of all, it's sinful. For in His unchangeable will, God has already predestined both the length of our lives, including both our birthday and our death-day, as well as the length of our bodies. Accordingly, David was very astute when he wrote: **"O LORD, make me know my end and what is the measure of my days; let me know how fleeting I am! Behold, you have made my days a few handbreadths, and my lifetime is as nothing before you. Surely all mankind stands as a mere breath!"** (Psalm 39:4-5). The Hebrew word translated as "handbreadths" in that verse is *"tephach,"* which means the span of the spreading of a palm[85].

For a better understanding, try this: look down at your palm, spread it out, and check out its surface area. Your life is only as long as a couple of those in God's eyes! That being the case, we are left with two choices. We can be anxious about our "day of death," in a completely futile attempt to wrestle control of the length of our lifetime from God. Or, in adopting David's attitude, we can strive to make the most out of our earthly lives for the glory of God and the good of others by "numbering our days". Obviously, only the latter option is acceptable. For none of our anxious practices of working out, eating right, and going to the doctor will change our lifespan. That's not to say we shouldn't do those things, as we most definitely should, but our motivation must be good stewardship of our bodies. The motivation must not be worrisome and prideful assumptions that we actually have any control over our lives, including our marriage, relationships, or even our continued ability to convert oxygen into carbon dioxide. Accordingly, we can read the text like this: "And which of you by being anxious can precipitate your marriage day?" So let us peacefully, wholeheartedly, proactively, and steadfastly acquiesce to God's complete and loving control of the lives He has given us- a control that includes the "date and time" of our marriage, as well as whom we will marry.

"And why are you anxious about clothing? Consider the lilies of the field, how they grow: they neither toil nor spin" (v. 28). This is yet another verse where a mere cursory reading will simply not suffice to attain a proper understanding of its wisdom. For that, we must dive deeper. The Greek word translated as "consider" in this text is *"katamathete,"* which has a very strong meaning and appears only *once* in Scripture. It means to exactly and conclusively learn something through careful thought[86]. Thus, we understand that our command to "consider" the lilies has a much stronger meaning than the common English contemporary use of that word would imply. It's very important to note that the Lord referred to the flowers "of the field," that is, not the flowers cultivated by humans in gardens. So we must carefully look at how, with no human intervention whatsoever, the fields of the earth are bountifully full of flowers. These flowers grow with neither personal "toil nor spin". That is, they don't spend their days anxiously laboring to expand in stature; God just gives this growth freely. This leaves us with the question, "If God blesses the inanimate, instinct-less "lilies of the field" with increase, how will He not graciously pour out on His image-bearing children the same?!" This does not mean that we aren't to labor at all, as we discussed thoroughly in the "Work" chapter previously. In the context of our discussion here, this does not mean that we aren't to court anyone at all. Rather, this verse is a command to put away all *anxious* labor, all *anxious* courting, as it is useless and a sin. Heed the Lord's chiding of his worrisome servant, **"Martha, Martha, you are anxious and troubled about many things, but one thing is necessary"** (cf. Luke 10:41-42a). And of course, that one thing meant resting in and learning from Him, without anxiety. God will give us the spouse and the marriage in *His* time; we just need to receive and thank Him for those blessings, in complete peace.

"...yet I tell you, even Solomon in all his glory was not arrayed like one of these" (v. 29). To really gain a stronger understanding of Solomon's "glory," take 5 minutes and go read **1 Kings 10**. In the history of the world, there was nary a sinner as wealthy, wise, powerful, or in this immediate context, as "well dressed" as was Solomon. As you'll read in that chapter about him, even his *servants*' clothing was so magnificent that it impressed a *queen* (v. 5)! Armed with that knowledge, our Lord's reference to Solomon in our text, and not just the "normal" garb of that king, but Solomon "in all his glory," has further strength in our comprehension. What this means practically is that the best human beings could ever dress themselves is *nothing* compared to the beauty with which God dresses even mere flowers.

This is another reason why women are not commanded to dress up flamboyantly for beauty, but rather they are commanded: **"Do not let your adorning be external—the braiding of hair and the putting on of gold jewelry, or the clothing you wear— but let your adorning be the hidden person of the heart with the imperishable beauty of a gentle and quiet spirit, which in God's sight is very precious"** (1 Peter 3:3-4). So let us not tarry and fret trying to clothe ourselves with "gold and silver", which only tends to pride, in order to attract a spouse. Rather, let us "gently and quietly" allow God to clothe us with the true beauty of humility **(cf. 1 Peter 5:5, Colossians 3:12)**, His definition of beauty, and thus a beauty that the truly godly will find irresistible. For the God who arrays the insentient plants of the earth with allure beyond words is the same God who will undoubtedly array you and your spouse with the same, while also clothing your bodies, which house those "gentle and quiet spirits".

"But if God so clothes the grass of the field, which today is alive and tomorrow is thrown into the oven, will he not much more clothe you, O you of little faith?" (Matthew 6:30). The Greek word translated as the phrase "O you of little faith" is *"oligopistoi"*, which means a low quantity of *applications* of faith[87]. You see, it doesn't describe an absence of faith, or an absence of the godly knowledge that tends to faith; but rather, it describes those who *hear* the Lord's knowledge and promises, but don't truly *imbibe* them. This is yet another reason why I absolutely *love* the word pictures the Lord Jesus paints in this passage. We're told that all of the creation around us is a living testament to God's providence, in the animate *and* inanimate creations that we hear and see everyday. Yet, when we are evincing the disquietudes of anxiety, we are completely disregarding and ignoring what we are being told and taught through even "general revelation," not to mention the bigger sin of ignoring the promises of the "special revelation" we've received from God's Word. The simple flowers we walk by on the way from our front door to our car door testify to God's providential care for His creations; yet, how often do we espouse worry as soon as we get behind the wheel of that car? Brothers and sisters, let's learn from the "grass of the field," as we're commanded, and be as worry free as those little green blades.

"Therefore do not be anxious, saying, 'What shall we eat?' or 'What shall we drink?' or 'What shall we wear?'" (v. 31). "Therefore" means "having this knowledge, having this reminder of God's providential love for us..." Thus, we understand more deeply the importance of obeying these commands. We now see that when we are sinfully worrying about "what we shall eat," we are being just like the worldly whose **"god is their belly"** (Philippians 3:19b). Accordingly, when we willfully ignore the undeniable superintendence of our heavenly Father, we are placing the false "gods" of our marriages and future spouses above our worship and trust in the one true God who loves us. Indeed, this says much about the strength and application of our faith, given the relative superfluity of meeting the earthly needs and desires of our minds and hearts. So we see, if we can't even trust God to provide us with the most basic necessities and wants of our physical lives, that is a strong indictment against the true depth and breadth of our trust in God. Let this not be so! Let us obey these commands against worry; let us not be those "of little faith".

"For the Gentiles seek after all these things, and your heavenly Father knows that you need them all" (v. 32). Here the rebuke is continued in the comparison made. The "Gentiles" are the "sons of this world," the non-Christians, those who are still **"without hope and *without God* in the world"** (cf. Ephesians 12:2, NIV, italics mine). We were once just like them, **"But now in Christ Jesus you who once were far off have been brought near by the blood of Christ"** (Ephesians 2:13). And thus, we've lost the right to *chase* the things the worldly do, for we now have *eternal* hope in our *eternal* God. To better understand the strength of this verse, we must once again study what's been "lost in translation" to English. The Greek word translated as "seek after all" in our text is *"epizētousin,"* which is a strong, conjunctive word. It means to diligently and intensively crave and inquire for something[88]. There's an awesome way for us to more deeply comprehend the contrast made by the Lord here in our text, and that's by looking at other places where this Greek word is used! The writer of Hebrews uses it twice, but he uses it to tell us one of the main things *we as Christians* should be "seeking after". He wrote that those who **"died in faith,"** did so **"having acknowledged that they were strangers and exiles on the earth. For people who speak thus make it clear that *they are seeking* a homeland"** (vv. 11:13-14). And he wrote of us who are still alive in this world: **"For here we have no lasting city, but *we seek* the city that is to come"** (v. 13:14). The italics in those verses are mine and they were used to highlight the phrases translated from the *same* Greek word we just learned. So we see, while the "Gentiles" are *chasing* worldly things such as marriage, we must be *chasing* the Kingdom of Heaven. We need not, and must not, carry solicitudes about our marriages and spouses because our Abba **(cf. Romans 8:15, Galatians 4:6)** "knows we need them all". Indeed, He knows what we need even before we ask Him **(cf. Matthew 6:8)**. Knowing this, let's lay claim to the promise Paul made to our brethren in

Philippi: **"my God will supply every need of yours according to his riches in glory in Christ Jesus. To our God and Father be glory forever and ever. Amen"** (Philippians 4:19-20). That promise was made by Paul as a direct result of God's provision for him through gifts from the Philippians! And the lesson Paul learned from all of that is the same lesson we are learning from these texts and must espouse: **"I have learned in whatever situation I am to be content. I know how to be brought low, and I know how to abound. In any and every circumstance, I have learned the secret of facing plenty and hunger, abundance and need. I can do all things through him who strengthens me"** (Philippians 4:11b-13). Amen, brother! Single, married, or widowed, let our contentment be found in Christ and Him alone.

"But seek first the kingdom of God and his righteousness, and all these things will be added to you" (v. 33). As I studied this verse deeply, I realized just how much of God's wisdom I've been missing by merely giving it a superficial reading previously. This is an unbelievably amazing text. Verse 32, which we just studied, taught us that we are to seek the Kingdom of Heaven rather than earthly things, such as marriage. But here, we are told what to seek "first" (in Greek: *"prōton,"* which means of chief importance[89]) in our lives. We are told what to seek *above all else*. So, exactly what are we supposed to seek above the Kingdom of Heaven? The Kingdom of God!

Wait...what? You may be wondering what the difference is and the difference is huge. The phrase "Kingdom of Heaven," as it's used in Scripture, means the physical, tangible, organic, and earthly proliferation, diffusion, promulgation, and dissemination of the Gospel. To better understand this, take some time right now, go to **Matthew 13**, and read the parables told by the Lord there. From those texts, we gain a stronger comprehension of the

"Kingdom of Heaven". In my (weak) summation of those parables: the Gospel is spread throughout the world, and produces both true and false converts. Some of these "converts" die as "seeds," while others survive and "produce grain" (vv. 3-9). Some are "wheat" and some are "tares" (vv. 24-30). Some are "good fish" and some are "bad fish" (vv. 47-50). Indeed, many hear the Gospel and profess Christianity, *but* as the Lord Jesus said: **"unless one is born again he cannot see the *kingdom of God*"** (cf. John 3:3, italics mine). In this, we see the difference between the two kingdoms. The kingdom of Heaven is the Gospel that casts a worldwide "net" and gathers many men, but only those who are born from above get to "move up" and enter into the kingdom of God. It is this latter kingdom that *we*, who have been born again by the Holy Spirit of God, are told to put above all else. For it is *we* who, by God's sovereign grace, are the "grain", are the "wheat", are the "good fish". Thus, being recipients of this unfathomable mercy, we must seek our Father's kingdom above all else.

And how do we do this? How do we follow this command? It must first be noted that the Kingdom of God is an *internal* kingdom. That is, it exists in our regenerated souls, minds, and hearts, not in our physical bodies or the physical world. As Paul wrote: **"For the kingdom of God is not a matter of eating and drinking but of righteousness and peace and joy in the Holy Spirit"** (Romans 14:17). The Kingdom of God is not a matter of meeting physical needs, but of meeting the spiritual needs of the soul. Knowing this, we can now further understand what it means to seek first "His righteousness". We've already received the imputed, eternal righteousness of Christ through faith in Him **(cf. 2 Corinthians 5:21).** So now, we must seek first the *practical* righteousness of experiential sanctification by the Holy Spirit. By

His power, we must kill the "works of the flesh," which are **"sexual immorality, impurity, sensuality, idolatry, sorcery, enmity, strife, jealousy, fits of anger, rivalries, dissensions, divisions, envy, drunkenness, orgies, and things like these"** (Galatians 5:19b-21a). And instead, we must seek first to bear the "fruit of the Spirit", which are: **"love, joy, peace, patience, kindness, goodness, faithfulness, gentleness, self-control"** (Galatians 5:22b-23a). We must seek this righteous fruit above everything else in our lives, including all earthly desires and needs, including marriage. The desires of our heart must be for these things; we can't just seek them out of begrudgingly rote obedience.

As David wrote: **"Delight yourself in the LORD, and he will give you the desires of your heart"** (Psalm 37:4). There we see, when God and His righteousness are the chief desires of our heart, when we "delight ourselves in *Him*," we will be given the object of those desires. And on top of that, everything else "will be added" to us. That is, all of our earthly needs will automatically receive provisioning, including our marriages. We see a great example of this in the story of Solomon's request for wisdom. Take a minute and go read **2 Chronicles 1:7-13** right now.

There we see a perfect example for us to emulate. Solomon was given a "blank check" to receive anything he wanted from the Lord. And rather than asking for something selfish or vain, such as a godly spouse, he requested wisdom to lead God's people. This request came because **"Solomon loved the LORD, walking in the statutes of David his father"** (1 Kings 3:3a-b). It came from a heart that "delighted in the Lord". So these were, indeed, the "desires of his heart"; it was not some faux noble statement to try and impress God. Thus, in making such a selfless, righteous, sincere, service-oriented request, God not only honored it by giving him more wisdom than any man before or since, but He "added everything else to him," by more than meeting all of his physical needs as well. Compare this godly request to the selfish requests condemned by our brother James: **"You ask and do not receive, because you ask wrongly, to spend it on *your* passions"** (James 4:3, italics mine). So, rather than worrying about the physical needs and desires of *our* flesh, such as *our* marriage, let us peacefully "seek first the kingdom of *God* and His righteousness, and all these things (including marriage) will be added to us".

"Therefore do not be anxious about tomorrow, for tomorrow will be anxious for itself. Sufficient for the day is its own trouble" (v. 34). "Therefore" means, "knowing all of this". Drop the worry about tomorrow, which of course includes future events such as marriage. For "tomorrow will be anxious for itself," that is, it will bring its own cares and troubles, but also God's fresh blessings and sustenance. Truly, though each day will bring problems afresh, **"The LORD'S lovingkindnesses indeed never cease, For His compassions never fail.** *They are new every morning;* **Great is Your faithfulness"** (Lamentations 3:23, NASB, italics mine).

Each new day brings stormy seas and the grace that calms those waves. If all we could expect from tomorrow were strife, then we would have reason to worry. But we know that the same God who bears us up and carries us out of our valleys today, is the same God who will do it again tomorrow, if indeed it's His will that we see tomorrow. For we are not in any way guaranteed the physical breath of life in advance. That's why we are commanded: **"Do not boast about tomorrow, for you do not know what a day may bring"** (Proverbs 27:1, cf. James 4:14).

Knowing that we might not even be here tomorrow...how sinful, asinine, and utterly useless is anxious mental toil for a day that may never arrive? Again, this is not to say that we shouldn't be prudent and proactive in our planning for tomorrow, including preparing ourselves for marriage, but *it is* to say that none of this carefulness about our tomorrows should ever be, in any way, worrisome. Rather, our attitude should be more like this: "If God gives me tomorrow, I've planned for it and will trust Him. And if not, no worries, I will be home with Him". Indeed, since bearing the weight of even one day's "worries" on our own is beyond our strength, how much more is carrying two day's worth of the same? That amount of weight is enough to break anyone's back. Additionally, it's "double the sin," because it not only means we're not trusting God with our "today," but we're adding to that our distrust of Him for "tomorrow". So let these worries go, repent of them, and divorce them.

Only God is in charge of the future, including our marriage days, so let Him handle it all. As we're told, we have sufficient "trouble" to deal with and hand over to our Father today. The Greek word translated as "trouble" in our text is *"kakia,"* which is yet another strong, deep word. It means the underlying malice, the latent evil, and the inherent wickedness in this world[90]. These are the daily evils we encounter that tempt us to vexations of spirit. Thus, we know that today's "trouble" is more than enough for us. So let's live in "today and eternity," not "today and tomorrow". Let's trust God one daily dispensation of grace at a time, knowing that in His time, He will meet all of our needs and Godly desires...including marriage.

The Pauline Exhortation...

Toward the end of his letter to the church at Philippi, our brother Paul wrote one of the greatest denunciations of worry ever and revealed some of the greatest keys to killing this sin. This text is **Philippians 4:4,6-7.** Let's unpack it and be edified, transformed, and encouraged.

"**Rejoice in the Lord always; again I will say, Rejoice**" (v. 4). Picture this experience for a moment. You're locked in a jail cell that's freezing cold at night, blazing hot during the day, insect and rodent infested, and filthy. You're about to face the trial of and *for* your very life. This jail is in the worst place imaginable for a Christian, the capital city of an empire that hates and persecutes Christians. Yet, that place is exactly where Paul wrote this *command* to be joyous always. So how could he be feeling this unfathomable joy with a plight vastly worse than anything we are facing today? We're told to rejoice "in the Lord," but what exactly does that mean? The answer lies in the text. The Greek word translated as "rejoice" here is *"chairete,"* which in itself means "to be glad"[91]. However, to truly understand this text, we must dive deeper. *Chairete* is a cognate of the Greek word *"charis,"* which means grace, favor, kindness[92]. From this, we can easily deduce the essence of our command. We are commanded, regardless of earthly plight, to be joyous in God's unmerited extension of grace and favor toward us through the Lord Jesus Christ! No matter the circumstance, we must rejoice in God's love, which never ends and will never be removed **(cf. Romans 8:38-39)**. Married, single, or widowed...we must rejoice in God's free grace, paid for on the cross at Calvary **(cf. John 19:30)**. Accordingly, we can read the text like this: "Rejoice in the Lord, not your marital status, always; again I will say, Rejoice."

"*do not be anxious about anything,* **but in everything by prayer and supplication with thanksgiving let your requests be made known to God**" (v. 6, italics mine). The Greek word translated as "be anxious about" in this text is once again *"merimnate,"* which we studied in **Matthew 6:25** above, and literally means to be divided and pulled apart in opposite directions by distraction. This fact about worry is easy to see experientially. God is telling us, "Don't worry. I'm in control of when and who you will marry". The world and our flesh pull us in the opposite direction and say, "Worry about when that will happen and who it will be with". So we're torn. It is this bifurcation of our minds and hearts that we are commanded against. And therein lies another key to victory over anxiety. We must repent not only of the worry, but also of the divided attention and focus. Our verse here outlines exactly how we do that.

Rather than succumb to mental division, we must stay focused on the Lord by lifting *every* concern up to Him, "by prayer and supplication", and this of course includes our desires for marriage. And what exactly *is* supplication, and how does it differ from prayer? The Greek word translated as "supplication" in this text is *"deēsei,"* which means a heart-felt petition, arising out of a deep personal sense of need, lack, or want[93]. This is why Paul used both the Greek word for "prayer" (*"proseuché"*[94]) *and* the Greek word for "supplication" in his charge, as they are not the same thing. Prayer is *devotional*; supplication is *petitionary*. "Proseuché" can be addressed *only* to God, while "deēsei" can be addressed to *anyone*. Do you see how Paul sandwiched *our* requests in between worship and thanksgiving? This is not just an English translational word order; it's the same in the original Greek.

We are commanded to, in *everything*, first address God in devotional worship. And *then* we should lift up our requests, while at the same time thanking God for every blessing He has/is/will richly pour into our lives and souls, and praising Him for all of the concerns He has automatically addressed without our asking. This is just as our Lord Jesus Christ instructed us to pray. He commanded us: **"Pray then like this: 'Our Father in heaven, hallowed be your name. Your kingdom come, your will be done, on earth as it is in heaven.'"** And *then* we can lift up our needs: **"Give us this day our daily bread"** (cf. Matthew 6:9-11). This is the type of prayer God desires and deserves. This is the type of prayer God honors because it honors Him. Check out how our brother E.M. Bounds so poignantly put it: "Prayer honors God; it dishonors self. It is man's plea of weakness, ignorance, need-a plea that heaven cannot disregard. God delights to have us pray[95]." Accordingly, we can read our text like this: "Do not be anxious about when you will get married or who you will marry, but by prayer and supplication with thanksgiving let these requests be made known to God." And what is the promised result of this Godly prayer?

"And the peace of God, which surpasses all understanding, will guard your hearts and your minds in Christ Jesus" (v. 7). The Greek word translated as "peace" here is *"eiréné,"* which means a transcendent wholeness of mind[96]. I formally call this peace the "inimitable equanimity" of God. I colloquially call this peace "being zenned out like a sea turtle" (ha-ha). This peace "surpasses all understanding" because it's a supernatural peace, not a natural peace. It's a peace that can *only* be felt by God's children, washed in the blood of Christ, fully and eternally reconciled to God. This peace stems from a heart that understands the immutable truth that its salvation is eternally secure in Christ. This heart thus considers all earthly worries mere trivialities. It considers the vain, temporal vexations of day-to-day life more nuisance than anything else.

This wholeness of mind not only stems from the wholeheartedly imbibed knowledge of our relationship with God, it's also supernaturally given through His Spirit. As the Lord promised us: **"But the Helper, the Holy Spirit, whom the Father will send in my name, He will teach you all things and bring to your remembrance all that I have said to you. Peace I leave with you; my peace I give to you. Not as the world gives do I give to you. Let not your hearts be troubled, neither let them be afraid"** (John 14:26-27). "Not as the world gives," that is, not the superficial, temporal peace that may come from a large bank account, a marriage ring, or a clean bill of health from a doctor. Rather, it is the *real* peace that is the fruit of the Spirit **(cf. Galatians 5:22)**. Given this peace freely, we must not ever let our hearts "be troubled or afraid," for our hearts will be "guarded" by this peace.

How? The Greek word translated as "will guard" in our text is *"phrourēsei,"* which carries with it a military sense of guarding, that is, actively guarded as by a military sentinel posted at a gate, both offensively and defensively[97]. Indeed, we experientially understand the truth of this "guarding," for peace of heart itself helps protect us from sin. So much sin stems from an anxious heart, trying to attain calm through ungodly means, such as trying to forcefully expedite our marriage day. Peter described this perfectly when he wrote: **"His divine power has granted to us all things that pertain to life and godliness, through the knowledge of him who called us to his own glory and excellence, by which he has granted to us his precious and very great promises, so that through them you may become partakers of the divine nature, having escaped from the corruption that is in the world because of sinful desire"** (2 Peter 1:3-4). Applying this to our current subject, we know that God's divine power has granted to us *peace*, that through this *peace* we may "become partakes of the divine nature", escaping "the corruption that is in the world because of sinful desire". Pretty amazing, isn't it?

You see, God never commands us to do anything that He doesn't also *empower* us to do. He doesn't just say, "do this and that," and then sit back and cross His arms and watch us try to figure out how to do it ourselves. No way! Just as He is both **"just and the justifier"** (cf. Romans 3:26) of His people, He also gives us both the commands *and* the ability to obey those commands **(cf. Philippians 2:12-13)**. Indeed, there is no one like our God! So let's espouse this *true* peace, given to us freely by our Prince of Peace **(cf. Isaiah 9:6)**, a *real* equanimity that will *guard* our hearts and minds against sinful worries about our marital status. Just simply **"let the peace of Christ rule in your hearts, to which indeed you were called in one body. And be thankful "** (Colossians 3:15).

Patience from Peter...

"for 'God opposes the proud
but gives grace to the humble.'"
Humble yourselves, therefore,
under the mighty hand of God
so that at the proper time He may exalt you,
casting all your anxieties on Him,
because He cares for you."

(1 Peter 5:5c-7)

Imagine this. You're taking your 5-year-old son hiking for the first time. You pack his water, food, emergency medical supplies, bug spray, sunscreen, extra clothes, and emergency tent in your bag. You do this because all of that stuff would be extremely heavy for him to carry, and you want him to have a good time and be able to keep up with you rather than being slowed down by all that weight. But when you get to the base of the mountain, your son, in the natural hubris of a headstrong child, *insists* on carrying his own bag. He refuses to start the hike unless he gets to carry his bag. He says, "I don't need your help, I can carry this on my own. I don't trust you. I'm worried that you'll lose some of my supplies. I want to be able to eat as soon as I get hungry. What if we get separated? I'll need all of my stuff so I can be self-sufficient".

How would that make you feel? First off, you might be tempted to a little pride that you've raised a 5 year old that already uses 12 letter words (ha-ha). But then you'd realize the ridiculousness of his requests and arguments, and the absurdity of his ostensible "independence". You'd be righteously angry with him for being so disobedient and rebellious. You'd also feel grieved that your own son doesn't trust you; that he thinks he can get by without you and that his "supplies" are all he needs.

Get where I'm going here? If we as imperfect sinners would have this response to such a prideful, worrisome son, how do you think our perfect, holy God feels about *our* anxious toil? When we're worrying about *anything* in our lives, in this case about our future marriage, we're behaving just like that 5 year old. We're saying to God, "I don't need your help with my marriage, I can handle this on my own. I don't trust you, I'm worried that you'll forget to find me a spouse, or worse, find me the *wrong* spouse. I want to get married *right now*, not later. I need a spouse so my life will be complete and so I'll have everything I need".

Ouch.

So we see, our prideful worry is no small matter to God. We say much more with our actions and attitudes than we do with our words. Though we may give lip service to trusting in God for all things, if we're living in anxiety, all of those words mean nothing.

Throughout this chapter, we've studied the sinfulness of anxieties of spirit, particularly with regard to marriage and dating.

And now, we're learning how the paramount sin of pride greatly exacerbates the sin of worry. Anxiety and pride are intricately interconnected. Pride leads to worry, and vice versa.

The pride of thinking that we're in control of our lives leads us to worry about how to best use this ostensible "control" of our lives. The pride of knowing the truth that God is in control of our lives, but thinking we know better than Him what's best for us, leads to worry about whether His providence will satiate our selfish desires.

Careful preparation for life events, fueled by worry about the outcome, leads us to pride if those life events result in success. Anxious financial planning, which results in a large bank account, leads us to the pride of thinking we're responsible for this "increase," and thus results in the pride of placing our "security" in our earthly wealth.

Knowing all of this, the destruction of worry in our lives must take on a higher priority.

You're single right now for a reason. For God's purposes, He has placed you exactly where you are to His glory and for your good. He alone sits on the throne. He alone is sovereign over your life. Thus, when you live in anxiety about your marriage date and whom you will marry, you're taking God off His throne and placing yourself there. This attitude is one of incredible pride. And as David wrote, **"Though the LORD is on high, he looks upon the lowly, but the proud he knows from afar"** (Psalm 138:6). As Peter reiterates in our text, God *actively* opposes the proud. Disquietude over our marital status is yet another form of self-exaltation. And as the Lord Jesus Christ said, **"Whoever exalts himself will be humbled"** (Matthew 23:12). This means that if you're living in this "pride of worry," God may be actively opposing the success of the object of your worry. This is very serious. In our immediate context, this means that if you're pridefully worrying about when your marital state will change, you may be delaying the very blessing you so earnestly desire. So what is the answer to this haughty, anxious care? Peter gives us the answer.

In our desires for marriage to a Godly spouse, we must *humble* ourselves by making some admissions to God. We must admit to Him that we're *not* in control of when or whom we marry, but He is. We must admit that we *don't* know what's best for us, but He does. We must admit that under His mighty hand, a hand that is in omnipotent control of all creation, every second of our lives is determined. In these admissions to God, we must *truly* imbibe these truths and *fully* acquiesce to our Father's loving and perfect providence and timing. We must humble ourselves, or God will do it for us.

The result of this repentance, of this heart change, of this self-humbling, is a promise from God - a promise that, at the proper time, He will "exalt" us. That is the key to complete patience in this, and every area of our lives, knowing that the "proper" time and place will be when and where *God* decrees, when and where *God* makes it happen. Human marriage is a temporal institution, thus it's a worldly care. And as our Lord said, **"In the world you will have tribulation. But take heart; I have overcome the world"** (John 16:33b).

Accordingly, you must hand this care, and *all* of your cares, over to God precisely *because* "He cares for you". If He didn't care about you, He would let you make your own choices and decide your own timing for everything, undoubtedly destroying your life in the process. Think back to the 5-year-old child. If you let him do exactly what he wanted, he'd never get anywhere. He'd be stuck at the bottom of the mountain, the weight on his back much too heavy for him to make any vertical progress. Soon, he'd open up the bag and eat far too much food, far too quickly, making himself sick. He'd be as helpless as a baby in the womb and very soon he'd be crying out for you to come save him. Don't make this same mistake with God. Don't be pridefully worrisome; don't try to make things, such as your marriage, happen your own way on your own time, without truly trusting God. If you do, you'll end up just like that sick kid. Flat on your back, ill, looking up at the sky, screaming for God to come save you from the fallout of your own hard-headed mistakes. Rather, read the text like this and obey accordingly: "for 'God opposes the proud but gives grace to the humble.' Humble yourselves, therefore, under the mighty hand of God so that at the proper time He will exalt you with a spouse, casting all your marriage anxieties on Him, because He cares for you."

As **Isaiah** wrote:

"You keep him in perfect peace whose mind is stayed on you, because he trusts in you. Trust in the LORD forever, for the LORD GOD is an everlasting rock."

(v. 26:3)

EPILOGUE

> "The Spirit is God's guarantee that he will
> give us the inheritance he promised and
> that he has purchased us to be his own people.
> He did this so we would praise and glorify him."
> (Ephesians 1:14, NLT)

The Greek word translated as "guarantee" in that passage is *arrabon*, which literally means "an earnest"[98]. In its usage though, it means an engagement ring, the age-old symbol of promised and committed betrothal to marriage[99]. This is very important to consider. You must remember, whether or not it's God's will for you to have a human marriage, He *is* preparing you for an eternal marriage.

As we studied earlier, our brother John prophesied:

> "Let us be glad and rejoice, and let us give honor to him.
> For the time has come for the wedding feast of the Lamb,
> and his bride has prepared herself.

She has been given the finest of pure white linen to wear." For the fine linen represents the good deeds of God's holy people. And the angel said to me, "Write this: Blessed are those who are invited to the wedding feast of the Lamb." And he added, "These are true words that come from God."
(Revelation 19:7-9, NLT)

Once again, you must recall that *we* are those unfathomably blessed people who have been invited to that wedding, to the eternal marriage. Thus, remind yourself to make it your aim to steadfastly prepare for *that* marriage with a higher prioritization than your preparation for a worldly marriage. Do this because it has been promised, **"And I am sure of this, that he who began a good work in you will bring it to completion at the day of Jesus Christ"** (Philippians 1:6). So stand and live on that promise, as we've discussed how to practically accomplish all this throughout the book, and **"Work hard to show the results of your salvation, obeying God with deep reverence and fear. For God is working in you, giving you the desire and the power to do what pleases him"** (Philippians 2:12b-13, NLT).

Innervation...

"Then the LORD God said,
"It is not good that the man should be alone;
I will make him a helper fit for him."
(Genesis 2:18)

As we have studied in this book, singleness is a gift, an amazing gift! However, for most Christians, it should be seen as a temporal gift. In my study on this subject, and on kingdom singleness, I have discovered that for most Christians, marriage is absolutely best. For some Christians, such as Paul, God does give the gift of kingdom (lifelong) singleness, but those are few and far between.

Thus, all of the encouragement about your singleness contained in this book is not meant to make you seek this state as a lifelong goal, but rather to help you maximize your temporal singleness for the glory of God and the good of others!

In Matthew 19, the Lord is admonishing His disciples about the seriousness and sanctity of marriage, and the disciples' response was that it was better not to be married. The Lord's response to that was: **"Not everyone can receive this saying, but only those to whom it is given. For there are eunuchs who have been so from birth, and there are eunuchs who have been made eunuchs by men, and there are eunuchs who have made themselves eunuchs for the sake of the kingdom of heaven.** *Let the one who is able to receive this receive it"* (Matthew 19:11b-12, italics mine). Thus, it is easy to see that the gift of kingdom singleness is reserved for a select few and is definitely not normative.

For those who are kingdom singles, they usually know it because they don't have a desire to be married, nor do they battle loneliness. As one of my pastors says, there are two ways to know you are a kingdom single: complete freedom from sexual desire...and the lack of a need for intimate and deep human companionship[100]. If you have those two gifts, then praise the Lord. You might just be a kingdom single! And you should use that gift like Paul did! That's an amazing gift, but it's a different subject entirely.

For most single Christians, and especially for any Christian who already has a desire to be married, marriage absolutely should be pursued as a life goal. So espouse the truths discussed in this book, see singleness as the blessing that it is and maximize yours for the glory of God and the good of your brethren. But remember, if you want a Godly spouse, then pray with importunity for that gift.

Keep your focus entirely on the Lord and let Him take care of everything. Sisters, remember: "A woman's heart should be so lost in God that a man must seek Him in order to find her[101]." Brothers, seek a Proverbs 31 woman, and do not settle for those with merely superficial beauty.

Until then, live in joyful patience, the state of mind that is a fruit of the Spirit **(cf. Galatians 5:22-23)**. *"And let the peace of Christ rule in your hearts,* **to which indeed you were called in one body.** *And be thankful"* (Colossians 3:15, italics mine). Remember that you are not commanded to get married immediately. And realize that you ARE commanded to love, serve, and obey God and lovingly serve others, immediately and always... so get busy! Rest in the truth that at the perfect time, God will take away your gift of singleness and give you the gift of marriage...trading one blessing for another.

Until then, I beseech you to biblically maximize your singleness for God's glory and the good of others, always remembering your chief purpose, the Great Commission of your life:

> "Jesus came and told his disciples,
> 'I have been given all authority in heaven and on earth.
> Therefore, go and make disciples of all the nations,
> baptizing them in the name
> of the Father and the Son and the Holy Spirit.
> Teach these new disciples to obey
> all the commands I have given you.

**And be sure of this: I am with you always,
even to the end of the age.'"**

(Matthew 28:18-20)

Thus, I'm going to consummate this book just as Solomon did with the great holy book of Ecclesiastes. This is…

**"The end of the matter; all has been heard.
Fear God and keep his commandments,
for this is the whole duty of man."**

(Ecclesiastes 12:13)

ABOUT THE AUTHOR

Cody Botella loves Jesus, because Jesus loved him first. He was eternally saved at the age of 26, and his life has never been the same since. Cody has a God-given passion to serve and Biblically edify the Lord's single people. He is simply a vessel through whom God has graciously chosen to work. Cody makes his living as a PGA Golf Professional, and is a Tech Developer of many kinds. He lives a blessed single life in Laguna Beach, CA.

You can learn much more about Cody and follow his Social Media feeds at: **www.codybotella.com**.

ENDNOTES

[1] Fabarez, M. "Salvation is a big deal." Sermon series presented at Compass Bible Church, Aliso Viejo, CA.
[2] Keller, T. (2012). The freedom of self-forgetfulness: The path to true Christian joy. Chorley, England: 10Publishing.
[3] HELPS™ Word-Studies copyright(c) 1987, 2011 by Helps Ministries, Inc.
[4] Dolan, J. quoting Blizzard, C. (ca. 2010-2011). Personal communication.
[5] HELPS™ Word-Studies copyright(c) 1987, 2011 by Helps Ministries, Inc.
[6] HELPS™ Word-Studies copyright(c) 1987, 2011 by Helps Ministries, Inc.
[7] Watson, T. (2001). The art of divine contentment (2nd ed.). Soli Deo Gloria Publications.
[8] NAS Exhaustive Concordance of the Bible with Hebrew-Aramaic and Greek Dictionaries Copyright © 1981, 1998 by The Lockman Foundation.
[9] Can be heard on a YouTube video. The video had quoted John Piper's "Don't Waste Your Life." See: http://proverbs4-13.blogspot.com/2014/01/the-universe-parable.html Anonymous.
[10] HELPS™ Word-Studies copyright(c) 1987, 2011 by Helps Ministries, Inc.
[11] 116. (2011). Envy. On *Man up* [ALBUM]. Reach Records.
[12] THAYER'S GREEK LEXICON, Electronic Database. Copyright © 2002, 2003, 2006, 2011 by Biblesoft, Inc.
[13] HELPS™ Word-Studies copyright(c) 1987, 2011 by Helps Ministries, Inc.
[14] THAYER'S GREEK LEXICON, Electronic Database. Copyright © 2002, 2003, 2006, 2011 by Biblesoft, Inc.
[15] THAYER'S GREEK LEXICON, Electronic Database. Copyright © 2002, 2003, 2006, 2011 by Biblesoft, Inc.
[16] HELPS™ Word-Studies copyright(c) 1987, 2011 by Helps Ministries, Inc.
[17] HELPS™ Word-Studies copyright(c) 1987, 2011 by Helps Ministries, Inc.

[18] HELPS™ Word-Studies copyright(c) 1987, 2011 by Helps Ministries, Inc.
[19] HELPS™ Word-Studies copyright(c) 1987, 2011 by Helps Ministries, Inc.
[20] THAYER'S GREEK LEXICON, Electronic Database. Copyright © 2002, 2003, 2006, 2011 by Biblesoft, Inc.
[21] THAYER'S GREEK LEXICON, Electronic Database. Copyright © 2002, 2003, 2006, 2011 by Biblesoft, Inc.
[22] Donne, J. (1624). Meditation XVII. From *Devotions upon emergent occasions*.
[23] Barnes, A. Notes on the Bible. Courtesy of Internet Sacred Texts Archive.
[24] Henry, M. Concise commentary on the whole Bible.
[25] Keller, T. (October 30th, 2008). The Prodigal God. Riverhead; Reprint edition.
[26] Bridges, J. (April 22nd, 2008). Transforming grace. Kindle edition. Page 16, Location 84. NavPress; New Edition.
[27] Bridges, J. (April 22nd, 2008). Transforming grace. Kindle edition. Page 21, Location 137. NavPress; New Edition.
[28] http://wiki.answers.com/Q/How_many_diapers_does_a_baby_use_in_a_lifetime
[29] HELPS™ Word-Studies copyright(c) 1987, 2011 by Helps Ministries, Inc.
[30] HELPS™ Word-Studies copyright(c) 1987, 2011 by Helps Ministries, Inc.
[31] Christiansen, B.; Marsh, C. Foundry Bible Fellowship, Orange County. Personal Communication.
[32] HELPS™ Word-Studies copyright(c) 1987, 2011 by Helps Ministries, Inc.
[33] THAYER'S GREEK LEXICON, Electronic Database. Copyright © 2002, 2003, 2006, 2011 by Biblesoft, Inc.
[34] HELPS™ Word-Studies copyright(c) 1987, 2011 by Helps Ministries, Inc.
[35] Englishman's Greek Concordance.
[36] THAYER'S GREEK LEXICON, Electronic Database. Copyright © 2002, 2003, 2006, 2011 by Biblesoft, Inc.
[37] http://www.fallacyfiles.org/quotcont.html

[38] THAYER'S GREEK LEXICON, Electronic Database. Copyright © 2002, 2003, 2006, 2011 by Biblesoft, Inc.
[39] HELPS™ Word-Studies copyright(c) 1987, 2011 by Helps Ministries, Inc.
[40] HELPS™ Word-Studies copyright(c) 1987, 2011 by Helps Ministries, Inc.
[41] MacArthur, J. (August 21st, 2003). The MacArthur Bible handbook. Thomas Nelson, Inc.
[42] THAYER'S GREEK LEXICON, Electronic Database. Copyright © 2002, 2003, 2006, 2011 by Biblesoft, Inc.
[43] HELPS™ Word-Studies copyright(c) 1987, 2011 by Helps Ministries, Inc.
[44] Kavadoy, C. (ca. 2012-2013). Personal Communication.
[45] Muller, G.; Brooks, A. Answers to prayer from george muller's narratives. Kindle edition.
[46] Strong's Exhaustive Concordance.
[47] NAS Exhaustive Concordance of the Bible with Hebrew-Aramaic and Greek Dictionaries Copyright © 1981, 1998 by The Lockman Foundation
[48] Strong's Exhaustive Concordance.
[49] http://en.wikipedia.org/wiki/Ants
[50] THAYER'S GREEK LEXICON, Electronic Database. Copyright © 2002, 2003, 2006, 2011 by Biblesoft, Inc.
[51] THAYER'S GREEK LEXICON, Electronic Database. Copyright © 2002, 2003, 2006, 2011 by Biblesoft, Inc.
[52] Pascal, B. Pascal's pensées. Thought #425, edited by Trotter, 113.
[53] Strong's Exhaustive Concordance.
[54] http://en.wikipedia.org/wiki/Endorphins
[55] Brown-Driver-Briggs Hebrew and English Lexicon, Unabridged, Electronic Database. Copyright © 2002, 2003, 2006 by Biblesoft, Inc.
[56] Marsh, C. (ca. 2010-2011). Personal Communication.
[57] HELPS™ Word-Studies copyright(c) 1987, 2011 by Helps Ministries, Inc.
[58] HELPS™ Word-Studies copyright(c) 1987, 2011 by Helps Ministries, Inc.
[59] Strong's Exhaustive Concordance.

[60] Jacobs, J.; Nutt, A.; Wright, A. (1898). Folklore. Folklore Society of Great Britain. P. 128.
[61] Wagner, R. (1850). Lohengrin.
[62] Calvin, J. Institutes. Edited by John McNeill and translated by Ford Lewis Battles. I.XI.8
[63] HELPS™ Word-Studies copyright(c) 1987, 2011 by Helps Ministries, Inc.
[64] Fabarez, M. "ATAPAT." Sermon series presented at Compass Bible Church, Aliso Viejo, CA.
[65] Piper, J. (2003). Desiring God: Meditations of a Christian hedonist. Multnomah.
[66] Brown-Driver-Briggs Hebrew and English Lexicon, Unabridged, Electronic Database. Copyright © 2002, 2003, 2006 by Biblesoft, Inc.
[67] Fabarez, M. "Set free to live right." Sermon series presented at Compass Bible Church, Aliso Viejo, CA.
[68] 116. (2011). Temptation. On *Man up* [ALBUM]. Reach Records.
[69] Strong's Exhaustive Concordance.
[70] Lecrae. (2008). Got Paper. On *Rebel* [ALBUM]. Reach Records.
[71] http://en.wikipedia.org/wiki/Zeitgeist
[72] John Calvin's Commentaries. Text Courtesy of Christian Classics Etherial Library.
[73] Lecrae. (2008). Identity. On *Rebel* [ALBUM]. Reach Records.
[74] Lecrae. (2008). Intro. On *Rebel* [ALBUM]. Reach Records.
[75] Cash, J. (2007). Here was a Man. On *Cash: Ultimate Gospel* [ALBUM]. SONY Records.
[76] Switchfoot. (2003). Gone. On *The Beautiful Letdown* [ALBUM]. Red Ink Records.
[77] https://www.youtube.com/watch?v=IRT40Hpw07Q
[78] Cash, J. (2007). Here was a Man. On *Cash: Ultimate Gospel* [ALBUM]. SONY Records.
[79] Lecrae. (2008). Identity. On *Rebel* [ALBUM]. Reach Records.
[80] HELPS™ Word-Studies copyright(c) 1987, 2011 by Helps Ministries, Inc.

[81] HELPS™ Word-Studies copyright(c) 1987, 2011 by Helps Ministries, Inc.
[82] HELPS™ Word-Studies copyright(c) 1987, 2011 by Helps Ministries, Inc.
[83] HELPS™ Word-Studies copyright(c) 1987, 2011 by Helps Ministries, Inc.
[84] HELPS™ Word-Studies copyright(c) 1987, 2011 by Helps Ministries, Inc.
[85] NAS Exhaustive Concordance of the Bible with Hebrew-Aramaic and Greek Dictionaries Copyright © 1981, 1998 by The Lockman Foundation.
[86] HELPS™ Word-Studies copyright(c) 1987, 2011 by Helps Ministries, Inc.
[87] HELPS™ Word-Studies copyright(c) 1987, 2011 by Helps Ministries, Inc.
[88] THAYER'S GREEK LEXICON, Electronic Database. Copyright © 2002, 2003, 2006, 2011 by Biblesoft, Inc.
[89] Strong's Exhaustive Concordance.
[90] HELPS™ Word-Studies copyright(c) 1987, 2011 by Helps Ministries, Inc.
[91] NAS Exhaustive Concordance of the Bible with Hebrew-Aramaic and Greek Dictionaries Copyright © 1981, 1998 by The Lockman Foundation
[92] HELPS™ Word-Studies copyright(c) 1987, 2011 by Helps Ministries, Inc.
[93] HELPS™ Word-Studies copyright(c) 1987, 2011 by Helps Ministries, Inc.
[94] THAYER'S GREEK LEXICON, Electronic Database. Copyright © 2002, 2003, 2006, 2011 by Biblesoft, Inc.)
[95] Bounds, E. (1997). E.m. bounds on prayer. Whitaker House.
[96] THAYER'S GREEK LEXICON, Electronic Database. Copyright © 2002, 2003, 2006, 2011 by Biblesoft, Inc.
[97] HELPS™ Word-Studies copyright(c) 1987, 2011 by Helps Ministries, Inc.
[98] Strong's Exhaustive Concordance.

[99] MacArthur, J. (February 5th, 1978). "Divine promises guaranteed". Sermon presented at Grace Community Church. Sun Valley, CA.
[100] Lasutschinkow, Pastor P. (ca. 2011-2012). Personal Communication.
[101] Angelou, M. Christians. Poem.

www.ingramcontent.com/pod-product-compliance
Lightning Source LLC
Chambersburg PA
CBHW061629040426
42446CB00010B/1337